The Tinkering Mind

The Tinkering Mind

Agency, Cognition, and the Extended Mind

TILLMANN VIERKANT

OXFORD
UNIVERSITY PRESS

Great Clarendon Street, Oxford, OX2 6DP,
United Kingdom

Oxford University Press is a department of the University of Oxford.
It furthers the University's objective of excellence in research, scholarship,
and education by publishing worldwide. Oxford is a registered trade mark of
Oxford University Press in the UK and in certain other countries

© Tillmann Vierkant 2022

The moral rights of the author have been asserted

First Edition published in 2022

Impression: 1

All rights reserved. No part of this publication may be reproduced, stored in
a retrieval system, or transmitted, in any form or by any means, without the
prior permission in writing of Oxford University Press, or as expressly permitted
by law, by licence or under terms agreed with the appropriate reprographics
rights organization. Enquiries concerning reproduction outside the scope of the
above should be sent to the Rights Department, Oxford University Press, at the
address above

You must not circulate this work in any other form
and you must impose this same condition on any acquirer

Published in the United States of America by Oxford University Press
198 Madison Avenue, New York, NY 10016, United States of America

British Library Cataloguing in Publication Data
Data available

Library of Congress Control Number: 2022936457

ISBN 978-0-19-289426-7

DOI: 10.1093/oso/9780192894267.001.0001

Printed and bound in the UK by
Clays Ltd, Elcograf S.p.A.

Links to third party websites are provided by Oxford in good faith and
for information only. Oxford disclaims any responsibility for the materials
contained in any third party website referenced in this work.

Table of Contents

Acknowledgements   vii

PART I. THE AGENCY PROBLEM

1. Core Argument and Methodology   3
2. The Simple Argument   31
3. Objections to the Simple Argument   57
4. Extending and Shrinking Agents   78
5. Metacognition   100

PART II. SYSTEM TWO AND THE MORAL MIND

6. Willpower and Epistemic Agency   119
7. How Choices Can Be Actions   136
8. Diachronicity: Intentional or Rational?   154
9. At the Very End   171

Bibliography   181
Index   191

Acknowledgements

This book is the product of more than a decade of thought about mental actions. It is an attempt to show that there is a connection between work I have done on metacognition, willpower, mindreading, and topics relating to free will and choice. Ironically, in a book that features a chapter on the topic of choice, even now I feel unable to make a choice between the two options that I present to the reader within this book, but I hope that having the options on the table will help others as much as it did me to clarify their thinking on mental actions, epistemic agency, deliberation, and cognition.

The final piece of the jigsaw for this book was extended cognition and I am grateful to Andy Clark and everyone here at Edinburgh for making me think about Otto and his notebook and all the other wonderful intentional mind-directed actions that are staples of the extended cognition diet.

In particular, thanks to Dave Ward and Mark Sprevak who both read a complete draft of the book and whose feedback was invaluable. Thanks also to Suilin Lavelle, John Dorsch, Jonathan Hall, Rafael Coelho do Nascimento, and Paulius Rimkevicius, who all read at least parts of various drafts and discussed various issues with me.

The other major influence on my thinking is Pamela Hieronymi and I am very indebted to her for helping me to understand, at least partially, the notion of evaluative control and all the other wonderful ideas in her work, as well as for all her invaluable feedback. Here at Edinburgh, Matthew Chrisman was my guide through this literature, and I am very grateful for his line-by-line reading of one whole draft and his countless insightful comments. Sophie Keeling and Beri Marusic also deserve a mention for many useful ideas and for ensuring that my Moran understanding is hopefully not too far off the mark.

Away from Edinburgh, a big thank you also has to go to Maura Tumulty who read the whole thing and whose thoughts on first personal managerial control have been inspirational.

I started writing this book in earnest in 2015 in Berlin and Richard Moore and Anna Strasser at the Berlin School of Mind and Brain organized a wonderful symposium for me to discuss the ideas that became Chapters 2 and 3. Thanks also to Pepa Toribio, Josh Shepherd, Steve Butterfill, and John Michael for their wonderful input on the day.

Thinking about metacognition, metarepresentation and mindshaping were probably the earliest roots of this project and I have to thank Victoria McGeer, Joelle Proust, Josef Perner, and Peter Carruthers, all of whom have been major influences on my thinking here. I profited hugely from the many discussions with them.

Even further back go my links to Wolfgang Prinz and the Max Planck Institute for Psychological Research in Munich. I very much hope that Wolfgang will not think that this book belongs in the category of annoying philosophy books on topics that the cognitive sciences are concerned with.

Most recently, I would also like to thank everyone in the Neuro-Philosophy of Free Will project, but especially the organizers Uri Maoz and Liad Mudrik, for providing such a wonderful platform for stimulating discussions with individual members, as well as for organizing a number of spectacular conferences. At these conferences, I particularly benefited from interactions with Richard Holton who has been the most important influence on my thinking on the role of intentional mental action in willpower and choice.

Finally, thanks to everyone within my family and friends who has had to put up with me while I was trying to get this thing written. A special thanks here goes to Astrid Finke and Marcel Häussler who put me up in Portugal to finish the book and where I also found my book cover. Last but certainly not least a very big thank you to Jacq Cottrell who probably read this book more often than I have and to Jasper who helped with the Index.

This publication was made possible through the support of a joint grant from the John Templeton Foundation and the Fetzer Institute. The opinions expressed in this publication are those of the authors and do not necessarily reflect the views of the John Templeton Foundation or the Fetzer Institute.

PART I
THE AGENCY PROBLEM

This book is set at the intersection of philosophy and especially moral psychology and cognitive science. That is still a reasonably small subfield of the discipline, but philosophers like Arpaly (2002), Holton (2009a), Mele (2009), Levy (2012), and many more have by now created an excellent literature of empirically informed work in moral psychology. What is unusual about this book is not that it combines moral psychology and cognitive science, but its direction of travel. In the vast majority of work in this area, it is the empirical sciences that inform the moral psychology. This book journeys in the opposite direction. It begins with a puzzle about the nature of moral agents, but some of its central claims are in the philosophy of mind and cognitive science. Potentially at least, this might make one suspicious: Can work in moral psychology really shape the framework within which the empirical sciences operate?

When we take a closer look, it will turn out that this is less implausible than one might have thought. Agency is a folk psychological notion, full of pre-theoretical intuitions and centuries of theorizing in the humanities—and the notion of agency plays a very significant role in our cognitive sciences.

The puzzle at the heart of this book is one about the relationship between rationality and agency. There has been a venerable and long-standing debate about this relationship in philosophy going back at least as far as the medieval dispute between Dun Scotus and Thomas Aquinas. The latter thought that what is special about human agency is that it is intimately tied up with rationality, whereas Dun Scotus insisted that the will needs to be different from rationality (Scotus 2003).

In modern times, we can find this dichotomy between volitional and rational elements of human agency in the seminal work of Harry Frankfurt (1971) on the nature of moral agents, and it is against the background of

Frankfurt-influenced work in philosophy that this book aims to examine the relationship of agency and rationality in the philosophy and sciences of the mind. In order to do this we will in the next chapter introduce the core argument of the book that takes its inspiration from an attempt to make sense of Frankfurt's work on reflective deliberation.

1
Core Argument and Methodology

1. Prelude: The Core Argument

Deliberating is something we do, or so our pre-theoretical intuitions tell us. This book is about finding out what is behind this intuition. It sets out to investigate whether and in which way deliberating is like ordinary actions. What I mean here by ordinary actions are actions such as changing one's socks and lifting one's arm, but importantly as well complex physical actions which bring epistemic benefits, such as going to the library to find new evidence for a belief. Throughout the book I will call these epistemically beneficial intentional actions 'tinkerings', for reasons that will become clear a little later in this prelude. Ultimately, the book will argue that it is cogent to claim that deliberating is an intentional action like changing one's socks or going to the library, but only if one is willing to accept the radical position of extended cognition, which means accepting a position that contends that cognition literally extends into the environment.

Extended cognition has many friends, but it does remain a fringe position within philosophy of mind and the book will not claim that it is obvious that it is correct. But it will insist that not accepting extended cognition does force one to accept that all ordinary intentional actions, whether they are inside the head or not, cannot be a true part of deliberation—at least, not if deliberation itself is a form of cognition.

At this point it is important to say a little bit about what I mean by 'cognition'. The APA Dictionary of Psychology defines cognition as 'all forms of knowing and awareness, such as perceiving, conceiving, remembering, reasoning, judging, imagining, and problem solving'.[1]

One natural way to understand this definition is that cognition consists in the processes (e.g. judgings, conceivings, rememberings, etc.) that lead to the acquisition of new doxastic states (forms of knowing), like beliefs and intentions, and if deliberation is a form of cognition then this is also how

---

[1] https://dictionary.apa.org/cognition

we should think about deliberation.[2] When we talk about deliberation in ordinary language, we emphasize that this cognitive process of acquiring new doxastic states is something we do, rather than something that just happens to us. But although we do talk like this, perhaps we are wrong to do so. Perhaps the acquisition of new doxastic states really never is an action at all?

To understand this thought better, it will be useful to examine an initial but very deep worry about the very existence of rational agency. Probably the best person to turn to in this regard is Galen Strawson. In his much-cited article 'Mental Ballistics or the Involuntariness of Spontaneity', Strawson claims that there are no real mental actions, and that all the agent can do is shepherd their automatic flow of thought, while the thinking itself is always automatic. Strawson's position is radical and many philosophers disagree and contend that there are real mental actions. However, even among all these more sanguine approaches, there is a surprising amount of agreement on some of the things that Strawson has to say.

For example, in his introduction to the excellent collection on mental action, Matthew Soteriou writes that:

> one does not [...] decide to judge that p and one does not decide to decide to Φ. On this [...] point there is wide agreement. (Soteriou 2009, 4)

Soteriou contends that everybody can agree that judging that p is not like an ordinary intentional action like changing one's socks, because while an agent can decide to perform actions of the sock-changing nature at will, the same does not seem possible for judging that p.

We are now in a position to see the problem more clearly. If by deliberation or cognition we mean the process that leads to the acquisition of a new doxastic state, and if by that we mean things like judging that p, then as Soteriou says, everybody in the literature agrees that this is not something that we can do at will. On this reading, it appears that Strawson is right and deliberation and cognition are passive.

But this is clearly too fast. As already mentioned above, most philosophers disagree with Strawson's claim that there are no mental actions,

---

[2] It should also be clear that this argument does concern all forms of cognition not just deliberation. I focus on deliberation here because the claims advanced in the book seem most striking and intuitively counterintuitive to me.

despite the fact that there is widespread agreement that judging that p is not an action that we can perform at will.

The book will argue that there are two plausible ways that can justify the intuition that deliberation and cognition are nevertheless agentive.

One of these options admits that deliberation and cognition might not be like changing one's socks, but that it consists of a different form of agency. The other option holds on to the idea that deliberation contains actions of the sock-changing type, but this has two consequences. First, it means that our definition of deliberation/cognition—that they consist in the direct acquisition of doxastic states like judgings that p—was false. Now, one might think that this first consequence seems like a small cost. After all, this was my own definition, so knocking it down might not seem particularly impressive. But things are not quite that simple: if we break the definitional link between deliberation/cognition and the acquisition of new doxastic states, then we are also forced to accept the second consequence which is that the theory of extended cognition turns out to be correct (or so I will claim).

Let's take both options in turn, beginning with the latter option. Why do I contend that if it is true that deliberation/cognition can in part be constituted by intentional actions that we have to accept extended cognition?

Andy Clark and Dave Chalmers (1998) argue very convincingly in their seminal paper 'The Extended Mind' (1998) that we should accept the principle that cognition literally loops into the environment in those cases where the environment plays a role that we would not hesitate to call cognitive had it taken place within the skull. They call this the 'parity principle'. Yair Levy has recently (2019) pointed out that we can apply the parity principle to the case of mental actions. If we think that doing algebra in the head is clearly cognitive then according to the parity principle, we should also call the same action cognitive if it is done on paper. Claims to the contrary appear to be no more than a brain bias.[3]

This is a powerful argument and I will argue that there is only one way to escape it. Namely, to contend that calculating on paper is a complex action and that only a part of it is truly cognitive, and that this cognitive part of the action does not extend. The obvious candidate for the part of the action that might not extend is the forming of judgments. These judgments can be

---

[3] We will discuss Levy's argument in detail in Chapter 4, but to avoid misunderstandings it should be pointed out that Levy applies the parity principle to epistemic actions and aims to stay neutral on cognition.

separated from the writing of symbols on the paper. These judgments, one might argue, clearly do not happen outside the head. However, if we use that argument then we get hit by an inverse parity principle. According to inverse parity we should resist calling something cognitive inside the head if we would call it not cognitive if it happened outside the head. If we want to claim that the intentional actions that are part of calculating on paper are not cognitive because they are different from the judging events then according to this principle all components of calculating inside the head that are not judgment formation itself also should not be called cognitive. This applies to all the internal intentional actions where we can imagine doing the functional equivalent action outside the head, like bringing an argument before our inner eye (we could use our eyes and written text) or rehearsing an argument in inner speech (we could also use real speech). Actions like this cannot be cognitive anymore even if they happen inside the skull.

Ultimately, this is not surprising, because we have now arrived back at our original definition of cognition, which contends that it consists in things like judgings and we already know that this means that intentional actions are not themselves cognitive.

One short aside before we move on to the second alternative. One might be tempted to break the definitional link between deliberation and cognition. Perhaps it is right that cognition consists in things like judgings, but the same is not true about deliberation. While this is clearly a possibility, it implies that deliberation is not cognitive and that the agency that we have in deliberation is not one over judgings that *p*. If we want to maintain that we do have this agency, then we have to look at an alternative understanding of agency in deliberation/cognition.

The idea that *judging that p* might not be an intentional action but could be agentive nevertheless is an idea that features prominently in the work of Pamela Hieronymi (although not only in her work—there are a number of people who, like Hieronymi, hold that the agency that we have over our beliefs cannot be thought of as a form of intentional action, such as Moran 2001, Boyle 2011, Toribio 2011, Mc Hugh 2011). Her account is very helpful in bringing out what exactly is at stake in the forced choice that is the main claim of this book (i.e. accept extended cognition, or accept that (cognitive) deliberation does not contain intentional actions). Even better her discussion of the issue brings out two ways in which one could understand Harry Frankfurt's seminal account of rational agency and these two ways are the two options of our choice.

Hieronymi does not think of these two options as two equal alternatives. She thinks that the idea that changing beliefs is like changing socks is seductive but false and that we need to think of the agency in changing beliefs in a different way.

So why does she think this? According to Frankfurt, what is at the heart of human rational agency are higher order attitudes. Having attitudes about our first order attitudes is what makes us different from, in Frankfurt's terms, mere wantons that only have desires about the world and not their own mentality, because it allows us to control our own mentality. One way to understand control here is along the lines of the kind of control that we have over effects in the world by means of our actions. It would be natural to think that we control, for example, our desire to smoke in the same way that we control the reaching for a cigarette. We first form an intention about our desired goal state (i.e. have a different desire, or holding a cigarette and then perform an action to bring that goal about).

But Hieronymi argues that it would be a mistake to think in this way, especially in the case of beliefs and intentions. Hieronymi is happy to admit that we can control attitudes using intentional actions, she calls this 'managerial control', but at the same time, she argues that it is not the normal way in which we exercise control over our propositional attitudes.

Instead, according to Hieronymi, we should think of the normal and fundamental control of propositional attitudes through deliberation more like an expression of the workings of the rational mind. When we become aware that a belief of ours is false, then the belief automatically changes with this realization. We do not have to do anything extra after the realization, as we would have to in the case of ordinary intentional actions. Realizing that one ought to change one's socks does not put new socks on one's feet, but in the case of a belief, understanding the need for change and changing are one. Hieronymi refers to this special direct form of control over beliefs as 'evaluative control'. For her evaluative control is the 'urform' of rational agency and as such, is at the very core of human rational agency and intimately linked to autonomy and free will. All intentional actions require the forming of intentions and as that is normally done by means of evaluative control, all forms of agency are ultimately parasitic on evaluative control.

Importantly, while Hieronymi's idea of a special form of agency in belief formation is contentious, the thought that inspires it is not. It is not controversial that one defining feature of beliefs is that they follow the evidence. There is no space here for a discussion of the belief concept, but Neil Levy gets the key thought across nicely:

> Beliefs are inferentially promiscuous and beliefs are responsive to evidence. Beliefs are inferentially promiscuous inasmuch as the belief that p can interact (appropriately) with any other propositional attitude (Stich 1978). For instance, my belief that it is raining will interact appropriately with my desire to stay dry, as well as my belief that roads can be dangerous when wet, and any other of my attitudes concerning water and wetness. Whereas inferential promiscuity is a matter of how beliefs cause behavior and update other mental states, responsiveness to evidence is a matter of how the belief itself can be expected to update, given appropriate evidence.
>
> (Levy 2015, p. 805)

The thought Levy expresses here is very much the same as the one that inspires Hieronymi. Under normal circumstances,[4] beliefs update as soon as it becomes clear to the agent that they are not supported by the evidence. Surely, Hieronymi is also right in pointing out that this updating happens directly with the realization that the belief is not supported by the evidence. There is no need for an extra step of tinkering with the mind that follows after the realization. I assume that despite the extensive literature on the nature of mental action, the only controversial issue in this specific context is whether this updating of beliefs is ever a form of agency or not.

If that is correct, then for this specific point about what the sensitivity to evidence consists in, there seem to be only two options: either one thinks in line with Hieronymi that evidence sensitivity itself is a form of agency; or one agrees with Strawson and argues that evidence sensitivity is an automatic process. It is worth emphasizing here that this is an important difference. For Hieronymi, it is essential that belief updating is not a passive mental phenomenon like a headache. Even in cases where the belief is tacit, for it to be a belief, Hieronymi requires it to be under evaluative control. As she writes:

> My beliefs do not sit in my mind as last week's lecture sits on my hard drive, recording what I once thought. . . . . My beliefs are not like the 'out of

---

[4] We will discuss exceptional circumstances in Chapter 3.

office reply' feature that I set up for my e-mail account: they are not something I create and then allow to affect things on my behalf.

(2009, 176)[5]

But while this difference between Strawson and Hieronymi is crucial for their accounts, in our context it is enough to point out that it exists, rather than trying to adjudicate. Because for our specific interest in the role of intentional actions in cognition, it does not matter whether the non-intentional part of attitude formation can be thought of as a form of agency, or whether it should be understood as fully automatic. However, as our overall topic in this book is agential accounts of cognition, we can—for now—forget about Strawson and focus on Hieronymi's agentive account of evaluative control.

Given this, I agree with Hieronymi that one very plausible interpretation of Frankfurt's intuition[6] is to contend that controlling one's thought could be thought of as evaluative control, but I also want to maintain that this reading leads us straight to one of the two options of our core choice. If evaluative control really is what explains the Frankfurtian intuition—that taking a stance on one's mentality is what makes us deliberative agents—then the role of intentional actions in this is very limited. Indeed, on this reading, intentional actions are not an integral part of our rational agency at all.

Given what has been said so far, one might think that I would ultimately recommend understanding rational agency in the way Hieronymi suggests, but this is not quite right.

Rather, I want to suggest that there are two different equally justified but incompatible ways of understanding rational agency. So far, I have only offered reasons to accept the one, namely Hieronymi's evaluative control and potential consequences (accepting extended cognition) for the other. However, as intimated already, we discussed Hieronymi's position by looking at what she has to say about Frankfurt for a reason: namely, that there is an alternative reading of Frankfurt's intuition that control of our mentality is what makes us rational agents. On this understanding, the control in question is the control afforded to us by intentional actions.

Hieronymi is clearly right in saying that managerial control is not what taking a stance on one's mentality means on her evaluative control reading,

---

[5] Thanks to Matthew Chrisman for the example and for pointing me to the quote.
[6] Even though it is one that Frankfurt himself would probably not endorse.

but it might nevertheless be the case that on an alternative reading, it makes sense to say that human epistemic agency is nothing else than mind-directed intentional action.

Let's have a short look at why that might make sense despite Hieronymi's valid points about the relationship of managerial and evaluative control. When Hieronymi talks about managerial actions, she talks about intentional actions that have the goal of managing an attitude. However, this type of intentional mind-directed actions is just a small subset of all the intentional actions that play an important role in human cognition, and even though the actions in this subgroup are important, it is implausible to understand them as a fundamental characteristic of human cognition. However, the same might not be true of the bigger group.

I call this wider group of intentional mind-directed actions collectively 'tinkerings', because at some point Hieronymi states that in direct belief acquisition there is no room for tinkering (it is not like changing socks, because once the understanding is there, the belief changes and no tinkering is required—unlike in the changing socks case). I agree with her, but still think that the many different forms of tinkering have not received sufficient attention in the literature.

For example, and perhaps most importantly, there are tinkerings where the agent manipulates material symbols without necessarily being aware of the fact that these tinkerings will bring about a change in a psychological attitude. In such cases there is no mind-directed goal, and these actions are therefore not properly managerial in Hieronymi's sense. Clark and Bermudez both argue that these tinkerings might well be what human cognition is all about, because tinkerings in this sense might be what enables linguistic thought, which very plausibly is fundamental for human rational agency.

Furthermore, there are even less cognitively demanding tinkerings: tinkerings which are simply intentional actions that bring about a cognitive benefit in cases where the agent has no goals that relate to attitudes or symbols. One example of this is the visual rotating of Tetris pieces on a screen using a controller, instead of employing mental rotation in the head; a case Clark and Chalmers take from Kirsh and Maglio as an example of extended cognition, because it clearly is the more efficient strategy to find the necessary orientation of the Tetris pieces. Obviously, such intentional actions also have benefits for creatures which have no understanding of symbols, but as Clark and Chalmers demonstrate, this does not imply that they could not be used as an argument for extended cognition, which seems to suggest at least that such intentional actions can be understood as cognitive. In this case, given their relative simplicity, it might well make sense to understand them as a form of cognitive bedrock of human cognition.

Together, these three different forms of tinkering suggest that intentional mind-directed action might well be an integral part of human cognition and thereby provide us with a different non-Frankfurtian but nevertheless plausible reading of Frankfurt's idea that human rational agency is at heart about taking a stance on one's mentality. On this alternative reading, taking a stance is very prosaically understood as being able to affect one's mind by means of intentional actions, which despite its prosaic nature, goes a long way to explain many distinctive features of human cognition.

Just to be absolutely clear: I am not saying either option is better and it is perfectly possible to say that these are simply different ways in which to understand epistemic agency. It seems also plausible to say that both of these forms of epistemic agency co-exist. But it is not possible to think that both of them are what we refer to as deliberation and cognition. They are different things and if evaluative control is deliberation/cognition then deliberation/cognition cannot be an intentional action. If on the other hand tinkering can be a constitutive part of deliberation/cognition then extended cognition has to be correct and we can therefore not say that cognition is limited to evaluative control.

Why should one care about what is going on in this argument? One good reason obviously is that it is important to be clear about what we mean when we say that taking a stance on our mentality is what makes us rational agents. I will demonstrate in this book that there are two very different interpretations of this idea and that they are not compatible. Furthermore, understanding this also leads to practical consequences. The most important one is that if one is attracted by the tinkering picture of the mind, then that means that in many areas across philosophy and cognitive science from system two processing to self-control one is forced to accept that extended cognition is correct, and from that as the book will show it is easy to construct arguments that there is no reason to treat environment-involving tinkerings any differently to the more traditional forms of executive function and willpower.

It is important here to remind the reader how radical this result is. Nobody wants to deny that interacting with the environment is critical for the cognitive process of humans and it is tempting to think that this is all that extended cognition claims. But that is most emphatically not the essential claim of the theory. The critical claim is that, for example, in doing arithmetic on paper the calculating literally happens partially outside the head. It is not that writing numbers down is merely helpful for cognitive processes inside the head, because, for example, they reduce load on memory, but the writing down is a constitutive process of cognition itself. Such an account of cognition does not sit easily with the idea that there also could be a form of evaluative control that is somehow prior and separable from the cognitive process that allows for extension. On the extended cognition picture the loops between brain and the environment are constitutive parts of cognition and they are not separable into an evaluative[7] truly cognitive and a merely managerial part.

Embracing extended cognition is very radical, but avoiding it—at least, according to the argument I put forward here—will also require an acceptance that cognitive control and willpower are, like all intentional elements of the deliberative process, mere shepherdings of true deliberative or cognitive agency. In Chapter 2 I will use this for an argument that proves the seemingly absurd conclusion that cognitive control or system two processing are not really cognitive, but this is the consequence of understanding cognition along the lines of evaluative control.

Coming down on either side of the main argument of the book is also a decision on what is special about human cognition. On Hieronymi's picture evaluative agency is foundational. It is what grounds human agency and she uses it to explain notions like free will and moral responsibility. But on the alternative picture it is tinkering that explains the difference between human and animal cognition (Chapter 5). And if that is true then that is difficult to reconcile with the foundational nature of evaluative control.

Finally, one might worry that the book is doing too little because it does not offer a clear opinion on which of the two options one should embrace. I have to accept that I do not. But hopefully, it has become clear that the options that this book is offering are not just about a discussion of details between a few philosophers. I claim that everybody who works in philosophy or the cognitive sciences with notions like deliberation and cognition has to be clear what they mean by those terms and as far as this book is concerned there are only two broad options on the table. Either tinkering is

---

[7] I think that many of the intuitions behind evaluative control are about the active grasp of meaning. If this is correct, then the notion might well be related to the notion of original intentionality, which is often seen as the mark of the cognitive and also about the mind's ability to grasp meaning. The inability to explain original intentionality in extended terms is seen as a strong argument against extended cognition by extension sceptics like Adams and Aizawa (2008, 2009).

truly cognitive or it is not and both options have very much non-trivial consequences.

With the outline of my main argument sketched out, let us now turn to a more detailed map of how the argument in this book is going to proceed, and address some possible worries about the methodology used. Once that is done, we will then turn to one very drastic example of how to apply the main argument to cognitive science to get us to the main part of the book. This will be the claim in Chapter 2 that system two processing in dual process theory cannot be cognitive.

2. Chapter Outline

The book is divided into eight chapters. The rest of this chapter will justify the methodology employed. It will discuss why it is appropriate to use tools from armchair philosophy to investigate a framework designed for empirical work. It will discuss potential pitfalls of such an enterprise, but even more importantly, it will try to provide a first argument of why such a strategy could be fruitful. In particular, it will elaborate on the already mentioned claim that cognitive science frameworks, like two systems accounts, are deeply rooted in philosophical conceptions of how to understand agency and rationality and the relationship between the two. Using the example of the dual system theorist Keith Stanovich, the chapter investigates how his story is indebted to the Frankfurtian hierarchical account of human agency and how, because of this indebtedness, it is also subject to a worry that Pamela Hieronymi raises about an interpretation of Frankfurt's hierarchical account that understands mental agency in her words as a form of 'tinkering with the mind'. Understanding what this phrase means and why the associated worry is pertinent will bring us to the end of the introductory chapter, while by the end of the whole book it will become clear in which way human minds might nevertheless be tinkering minds after all.

Chapter 2 will investigate two systems theory using tools from the doxastic agency debate in epistemology and moral psychology. Doxastic agency deals with the issue of whether judgments, decisions, beliefs, and intentions just happen to us in a passive way, or whether we do stand in an agentive relation to them. There is a lot of literature on this topic (Strawson 2003; Shah and Vellemann 2005; Smith 2005; Chrisman 2008; Hieronymi 2009), but so far this issue has not been discussed against the background of two systems theory, even though there has been some work recently on doxastic agency in a philosophy of cognitive science context (Wu 2013; Shepherd 2015; Fairweather and Montemayor 2017; Lockie 2018). This book will build on this work.

Critically, the book will make use of a distinction in the literature between two kinds of mental agency. On the one hand, it will look at intentional mental agency. Intentional mental acts are supposed to be very much like physical intentional actions, such as lifting one's arm. On the other hand, the book will also look at one reading of what has been called doxastic or evaluative or cognitive or even rational agency. Very roughly, proponents of this notion of doxastic agency have put forward the idea that only doxastic agency can bring about new content-bearing states directly, while intentional mental agency can do so only in an indirect, and as many argue, inferior way (see e.g. Moran 2001 or Hieronymi 2009; see McGeer 2007 or Vierkant 2013 for a different view). The reason for this, again very roughly, is that in doxastic agency the subject reveals itself in exercising its rationality, while in intentional mental agency, the agent treats their mind as an object to manipulate (Moran 2001). This is crucial for this book, because of the very close link between rationality and this form of agency that these authors assume.

Using this distinction will bring into sharp relief a problem for dual systems theories, because it seems that a central assumption of the doxastic agency debate (namely that the formation of doxastic attitudes is not ever something we can do voluntarily), together with an equally central assumption of two systems theory (namely that all system two processing is controlled), leads to a very counterintuitive simple argument about doxastic agency in a two systems framework: namely, that system two processing never directly leads to the acquisition of a doxastic attitude.

Chapter 3 will discuss objections and clarifications. Is the simple argument dependent on a specific understanding of belief? Could we not think of beliefs in system two along the lines of mental states like acceptance that clearly can be acquired voluntarily? Does motivated reason not demonstrate that we can acquire belief voluntarily? And, most importantly, are judgments not simply a part of the skilful intentional mental action of deliberation? It will transpire that all these objections are unsuccessful, but they will help nevertheless to make the case behind the simple argument clearer, and thereby make it seem less radical than it might have seemed initially. Finally, the chapter considers the question of whether the argument depends on a specific definition of cognition. This turns out to be an interesting objection and one that can only be resolved fully in Chapter 4.

Chapter 4 will bring the lessons from the simple argument in contact with an argument recently put forward by Yair Levy (2019) that there is no relevant difference between mental and physical actions, so that mental actions can literally extend. Applying our distinction between cognitive agency and intentional mental actions, it can be shown that this argument works, but only for intentional mental actions. This can turn Levy's conclusion that there are intentional cognitive mental actions because there are intentional physical actions on its head and show that there are no intentional cognitive actions either inside or outside the skull, and that cognitive agency in the evaluative sense does not extend.

It is here that the chapter considers the objection raised in the third chapter, namely whether or not there are intentional cognitive mental actions simply depends on the definition of cognition. This turns out to be a crucial turning point for the progress of the argument. This is because if extended cognition is correct, it allows for a new answer to this question: if we accept extended cognition, then it is entirely possible to define cognition in such a way that there are intentional cognitive mental actions, but if one does that, then one also has to buy Levy's argument and to accept that physical intentional actions can also be cognitive actions. If, on the other hand, one is not willing to accept extended cognition, we are back at our initial definition of cognitive and in that case, the central message of the simple argument remains that intentional actions inside the head are just as little cognitive as physical actions.

Chapter 5 starts with the idea that perhaps the investigation so far had overlooked one systematic difference between intentional physical and intentional mental actions. Most intentions that guide physical actions are directed at some goal in the extra mental world, but most prototypical intentional mental actions are directed at doxastic attitudes. As the investigation will demonstrate, they are not what directly leads to the acquisition of new attitudes, but their primary purpose is the shepherding of this process. So perhaps mental actions inside the head can be individuated by the specific goal that only they have? In order to answer this question, the chapter has to perform some conceptual legwork. It looks closer at the notion of metarepresentation and whether thinking about thinking always involves targeting doxastic attitudes.

On the basis of these conceptual clarifications, the chapter then argues that there is a number of different ways in which intentional actions can shepherd cognition. These actions are incredibly important, especially for human cognition, but most of them are not directed at the manipulation of a doxastic attitude. So here we have an answer in which way tinkering with the mind might actually be what makes human agency special, despite Hieronymi's justified worry about tinkering and the nature of cognitive agency.

Chapter 6 begins the second part of the book. This chapter aims to understand Richard Holton's work on willpower through the lens of my argument in the first part of the book. Holton is the perfect interlocutor, because his whole account starts from a worry about the agency problem of compatibilism. This problem is, as it were, the inverse problem to the one that we started our discussion with. While our agency problem is concerned with the idea that at heart human rational agency cannot be intentional agency, this problem is concerned with the reverse issue that non-intentional rational agency does not seem agentive enough.[8]

Holton has developed an intuitively and empirically plausible account of willpower that charts a course between the Skylla and Charybdis of these two problems and which aims to show how the exercise of willpower under temptation can consist in intentional action.

The chapter does not aim to establish Holton's account as superior to competing accounts of willpower, but it does want to build on Holton's insight that every plausible account of willpower needs a satisfying solution to the agency problem.

However, Holton wants to argue that these intentional actions are also rational actions, and that they are different from self-control strategies that involve intentional actions that manipulate the environment (so-called 'tying to the mast' strategies), rather than the psychology of the agent directly. Applying the lessons from this investigation to this account, the chapter argues that willpower and environment-involving self-control strategies are not qualitatively different when it comes to their involvement in rational agency. This, as it turns out, is a very desirable result as a lot of recent empirical work (Duckworth et al. 2016; Nielsen et al. 2019) seems to demonstrate that strategies that rely on pure psychological inhibition are far less effective than environment-involving strategies. It is therefore important to show that these strategies are not somehow inferior simply because they are not connected to the agent in the same way as inhibition.

Chapter 7 goes on to look at Holton's account of choice. Again, Holton's account is a great starting point for the arguments examined in this book,

---

[8] Which is quite similar to the worry by Strawson already alluded to in the Prelude and discussed later in this chapter.

because he understands choices as intentional actions and argues that this means that they cannot simply be reduced to rational practical judgment. At the same time, as choices are supposed to be crucial in moral agency, they can also not turn out to be completely random, because randomness does not show anything about the morality of an agent. In order to solve this puzzle of choice, Holton turns to system one hunches, which explain why choices might feel random when actually they are not. However, it is not clear exactly how hunches can play the role Holton assigns to them. To address this question, the chapter uses work from Chapter 5 to argue that hunches should be thought of as metacognitive epistemic feelings that initiate intentional mental actions to bias seemingly random choices.

Chapter 8 returns directly to one of the key questions of Chapter 1. Here, we will look at Neil Levy's (2014) work on the nature of the moral agency. Levy's main claim is that the acquisition of conscious beliefs is special because the way these beliefs are acquired leads to the unification of the moral agent. According to Levy only conscious beliefs are able to unify the agent over time. We will agree with Levy that diachronicity is a key feature of the moral agent, but we will see that it is unclear exactly how conscious beliefs contribute to it. The reason for this is again our main issue that it is not clear how important intentional mental actions are supposed to be.

Finally, Chapter 9 rounds up the arguments presented in the book.

3. Methodology: Philosophy and Cognitive Science

In his polemic article *Philosophie nervt* (Prinz 2008) the influential German cognitive scientist Wolfgang Prinz argues that philosophy and science should go their separate ways, because philosophy is more of a hindrance for the cognitive sciences than a useful complementary approach to the scientific enterprise of understanding the mind. Prinz states very clearly that his paper is a polemic, and it therefore does not necessarily try to paint a fair picture of all contemporary philosophy of mind, but the polemic does make some interesting and for this book very relevant observations. As they take a sceptical stance on the essence of what this book is about, namely philosophers making claims in the cognitive sciences, it will be interesting to have a closer look at them.

Prinz has three main reasons for his view. He claims that philosophy is interested in a view of the mind that has long been abandoned by scientists;

that philosophers are unhelpfully quibbling about explicit concept definitions; and that philosophers often do not take empirical scientists seriously enough. The last worry seems more a worry about philosophers than about philosophy, so while interesting in itself, it does not seem crucial in the methodology section of this book.

In reply to Prinz's first worry, we can state that it is clearly a caricature to say that philosophy only engages with prescientific notions of the mind. Philosophy as a discipline is clearly varied, and contains everything from very traditional views to very radical contemporary views like eliminativism, predictive coding or the embodiment revolution, which have often gone further in their rejection of traditional folk psychological ideas about the mind than have many scientists. This brings us to Prinz's third point.

4. The Metaphor Mistake

The worry not yet discussed is Prinz's claim that philosophers unfairly accuse scientists of being sloppy with their concepts. Prinz accepts that scientists are not always very exact in their use of terms, but he sees a virtue in this and accuses the philosophers of fundamentally misunderstanding scientific practice. Science often does not have clear explicit definitions at the beginning of the process, but slowly works out the extension of a term through years of painstaking experimental practice. If scientists were to work out in detail the definitions they use before their experimental work has begun, that would hinder rather than help their work. For this reason, scientists tend to use a form of heuristic lab talk like 'the brain decides', but they are really all the time clear that this is not more than a heuristic. Scientists are not so naïve that they really believe this literally, and they can feel insulted by philosophers who seem to accuse them of such naivety.

This charge can also be levelled at philosophers who aim to clarify the meaning of folk psychological terms in scientific practice. They might simply misunderstand what scientists are doing when they use folk psychological terms. This worry also really does seem to apply very much to this book. The book aims to show that conceptual armchair work in moral psychology can help us understand central concepts in the cognitive sciences more clearly. More specifically, it wants to achieve this by investigating a conceptual argument that shows how we should understand the notions of doxastic and intentional mental agency, and claims that this better understanding will make for better science. But currently this discussion of doxastic agency is not even in direct contact with the cognitive sciences, but an old chestnut of archetypical armchair epistemology.[9]

Perhaps the central proposition of this book is an example of the attitude that Prinz has in mind? Is this book an instance of an unwarranted criticism of concepts used by empirical scientists, because it insists on a highly detailed but ultimately fruitless discussion of concepts rather than focussing on careful experimental research?

In order to investigate and ultimately reject this serious worry about the methodology employed here, it will be useful to look at a specific piece of work by one of the eminent scientists in the field of two systems theory to see why the charge does not stick. In Keith Stanovich's book *The Robots Rebellion* (2005), Stanovich makes a very similar point to Prinz. When introducing the characteristics of system two, Stanovich notes that:

> Philosophers are constantly on the watch for psychologists sliding into the homunculus problem and into other conceptual errors because of the metaphors they use when describing analytic processing.
> (Stanovich 2005, 46)

Like Prinz, Stanovich thinks that it is because of the need to communicate efficiently about experimental results that psychologists use the language of executive function and cognitive control, even though they are quite aware that there is no homunculus and that the mechanisms behind executive control are distributed in the brain.

As this book is very much about a worry that is not unrelated to the dreaded homunculus problem, it is of the utmost importance to make sure that it does not fall into the trap of mistaking metaphors adopted for communicative ease for deeply held metaphysical convictions. Philosophers sometimes accuse psychologists of making category mistakes when they mix the language of science with folk psychology, as in the infamous 'the brain decides'.

Given the importance of the issue, this book will have to do its utmost to avoid the converse mistake that both Prinz and Stanovich talk about, which one could name the metaphor mistake, namely the worry that philosophers often mistake lab talk for metaphysical commitments. Looking at Stanovich's plot for his book will allow us to see that it is not because he

---

[9] Incidentally, this charge could also be levelled against Mele (2007) or Levy (2012), perhaps even Bayne (2004).

commits the homunculus fallacy that an engagement with philosophical conceptual armchair work can be useful for the framework he aims to develop, but because his positive account of rationality and human autonomy is deeply interlinked with a hugely important and unresolved debate on the nature of human agency in philosophy. It is because of these deep links that the empirical work cannot escape the consequences of making assumptions within that debate.

5. Rationality and Avoiding the Homunculus in Stanovich's Two Systems Accounts

Stanovich starts *The Robot's Rebellion* with a discussion of a seemingly very worrying consequence of Darwin's work. Where before humans were convinced that they were rational autonomous individuals, perhaps even designed by an intelligent and benevolent god, all that Darwin has to offer is the blind logic of evolution. In fact, the robot in the title of Stanovich's book refers to us humans. In the Darwinian picture, humans seem to be nothing more than robots designed by their genes with the sole purpose of helping them to survive. The rest of the book investigates how we can accept the truth of the Darwinian picture, but without giving up on human autonomy. So, while Stanovich's project is one that tries to dispel myths of human rationality and autonomy that are clearly not compatible with modern scientific knowledge, he is clearly not an eliminativist. He does not want to show that we should give up on concepts like autonomy and rationality. Instead, he wants to paint a picture of the human condition that makes our pre-theoretical self-understanding as autonomous agents compatible with modern science.

Stanovich argues that this can be achieved because the rather bleak picture of humanity he paints in the first chapter of his book is not the whole story, because humans do have some unique tools that allow them to rebel against the tyranny of their genes. There is on the one hand what Stanovich refers to as the robot's secret weapon, also known as instrumental rationality (Stanovich 2005, 85). Humans do not have to follow the rationality that is embedded in their genes, but can trade off goals that their genes might favour, like reproduction, against goals like longevity, which might be less important for the genes but very important for the human being itself.

However, as Stanovich notes, instrumental rationality is not enough for autonomy, because there is another trap lurking here; humans might escape the tyranny of their genes only to be ruled by another replicator that also does not necessarily care about the wellbeing of the individual, namely memes. Part of what makes human rationality so special is the fact that ideas can be effortlessly transmitted from individual to individual. These ideas can be very powerful. They can help humans to build rockets to fly to the moon, but they can also convince them to end their own existence by means of a suicide belt. Memes like genes do not care about the happiness of the individual: their whole raison d'etre is to be replicated in as many hosts as possible. Escaping the clutches of such memes seems even harder than escaping the control of our genes, because in a Darwinian world the only tools that are at our disposal to evaluate the truth and usefulness of memes (apart from the mind in the service of the genes) are meme-complexes themselves.

It is at this point that it is very tempting to commit the homunculus fallacy and to postulate a little agent in the head who evaluates which ideas to adopt and which to reject. But tempting as this solution might seem at first sight, it obviously solves nothing, partly because it is simply wrong, but perhaps even more importantly, because it does not really make any sense. If we struggle to give a naturalistic account of cognition in the brain it does not help to simply pack the problem in a box inside the brain, because the obvious next question would be: How could we give a naturalistic account of the evaluations of the homunculus? Given that in a Darwinian world we only seem to have genes or memes at our disposal to achieve this task, the homunculus has not really helped us at all. In the end, if we want to take the Darwinian strictures seriously, our rationality can only be driven by either genes or memes: there is nothing else.

Instead, Stanovich argues that human rationality is more than just instrumental rationality. Instrumental rationality allows the person to pitch her goals against the goals of the genes, but this in itself does not allow her to question the goals themselves. However, according to him, this is not the end of the story, because humans are capable of reflective meme evaluation. Importantly, this evaluation cannot happen from an independent perspective (that would be smuggling in the homunculus) but has to happen by a process which leaves some assumptions (memeplexes) in place in order to test others. Thus, according to Stanovich, what is special about human rationality is not that there is an independent soul in the background that can evaluate the rest of the mind objectively, but the capacity of human rationality to use its machinery to evaluate itself. As the evaluating is always done by a part of the system, there will always be blind spots in the evaluating, but while it is not perfect, this process of constant testing of the system by itself permits humans to not be passive receptacles of ideas that use them as hosts, but to acquire what Stanovich terms 'thick rationality'.

The idea of understanding human autonomy in terms of the ability to self-evaluate our minds has a venerable tradition in philosophy. Stanovich is very aware of this and references the work of eminent philosophers such as Harry Frankfurt and Charles Taylor to support his account.[10] Frankfurt is probably the most famous proponent of what has been termed 'hierarchical compatibilism'. According to Frankfurt, freedom of the will resides in the ability to form second order volitions.[11] In contrast to what Frankfurt calls a 'wanton', namely a creature that possesses only first order desires, an agent with second order volitions can evaluate her own desires. Where an animal is simply hungry, a human agent can take a position on her first order desire. If she for example felt that eating meat were immoral, then she might evaluate her desire to eat the bacon negatively.

It is this Frankfurtian idea that the ability to have a standpoint towards one's mentality is at the heart of human autonomy that Stanovich's account of thick rationality builds on. His idea that human autonomy is about being able to evaluate one's own mentality is heavily influenced by probably the most influential philosophical account of autonomy in the twentieth century.

In discussing the metaphor mistake, the complaint made by empirical scientists has been that philosophers strayed into scientists' territory and were hyper-critical about heuristic lab talk. But as the last section demonstrated, this is clearly a caricature. As Stanovich's work perfectly illustrates, the links between philosophy and psychology are often much closer than that. When Stanovich lays out his concept of thick rationality, it is not just heuristic lab talk, but a sophisticated conceptual argument about how to think about the nature of human rationality. It is also not just at the fringe of his project, something of an aside that one could easily dismiss, but central to his account. The nature of rationality is a critical feature of Stanovich's entire project. He is clearly aware of this, and he is also aware of the fact that

---

[10] Stanovich uses Taylor and Frankfurt as proponents of the same point. This is slightly problematic as Taylor is explicitly very worried about Frankfurt's second order model, because, according to Taylor, it is still far too rooted in the logic of preference. Frankfurt seems to be the better candidate for the point Stanovich wants to make, so the focus in what follows will be on Frankfurt.

[11] i.e. desires that the agent wants to be effective.

in this arena there has been a longstanding philosophical tradition grappling with very similar questions. Rationality and agency are at the heart of what dual processing accounts are all about, but both concepts are inextricably linked with the philosophical tradition. Unfortunately, this also means that Stanovich encounters the same or at least very similar problems to those that have plagued this philosophical tradition: although Frankfurt's account has been enormously influential, unsurprisingly, it has not been without its critics, as discussed in the next section.

However, there needs to be one last remark before we can leave the methodology section behind. One might think that in arguing for a role of an armchair debate in philosophy to help understand work in the cognitive sciences better, I am taking a stand on the independence of the analytic philosophical method (Kornblith 2017).[12] To be clear, I intend to do no such thing. While I am not defending this here, I am convinced that ultimately philosophical and empirical work on the mind are deeply interdependent and that there are not many interesting questions that philosophers can answer completely independently of an examination of the empirical work. But I hope the last section has shown that much of psychology is not free of folk psychological notions and as these notions are complex and often not used consistently in everyday life, pointing out and analysing the puzzles that are contained in them is an important job if we want to get a clearer grip on how empirical data and our pre-theoretical concepts relate. Doing this for the relationship between intentional agency and rationality is the job of this book.

6. The Bone of Contention: Reflective Control

Gary Watson pointed out very early on (1975) that not all second order desires seem to express the person in the way Frankfurt envisaged. The anorexic has very pronounced negative evaluations about her hunger, but in contrast to for example a vegetarian, these volitions seem pathological, rather than an expression of autonomy.

Here, Stanovich agrees with Frankfurt's critics that it does not seem obvious that it will always be the case that the higher order desire should trump the first order desire. Sometimes it will be the case that the first order

---

[12] Thanks to Paulius Rincekivius for pressing me here.

desire expresses the agent better than the second order desire, as in Stanovich's example of an agent who comes to understand that her first order enjoyment of celebrating Christmas might well outweigh her atheist negative evaluation of that desire. For Stanovich, autonomy resides in the ability to represent one's desires and to constantly question them from the different perspectives that are at the agent's disposal, without committing to one perspective as the one that ultimately expresses the agent. There is never one independent perspective, but the agent can nevertheless strive for cognitive integration by switching between perspectives and by learning in the process.

But Watson's criticism is not the only worry about the Frankfurtian model. Pamela Hieronymi (2009) points out another problem with reflective self-evaluation à la Frankfurt that takes us directly to the central issue of this investigation. The core of the problem is a seemingly strong point of reflective self-evaluation: namely, that it allows one to think about the mind one would want to have. In Frankfurt's (1971) own famous example, the unwilling drug addict might well have an overwhelming desire to take the drug, but he is capable of evaluating this desire as bad and as not being in line with his conception of the person he would like to be.

This is very attractive, because it allows us to think of reflective control as if it were an ordinary action. When we complete ordinary actions, we have intentions about how some object or state of affairs ought to be, and we then try to bring the world into line with our intentions. This picture is powerful, because we have an intuitive grip on the kind of control that intentional action gives us. If we can control our mind in the same way that we can control parts of the world when we act intentionally, then the control of the mind that the autonomous agent is supposed to have is no longer puzzling. It is exactly the same kind of control that we ordinarily exercise when we act intentionally.

Unfortunately, as will be discussed in detail in Chapter 2, the powerful picture is also deeply problematic, because one might suspect that it derives some of its intuitive plausibility from being dangerously close to the homunculus. It suggests a picture according to which humans change their propositional attitudes in the same way they change their socks. We first form the judgments that it would be justified to change, for example a belief, and having formed the judgment, we begin the tinkering with our attitude. But this is a problematic picture because in the case of the attitude change, unlike in the case of the socks, we cannot clearly separate the judgment from the action. As Hieronymi writes:

> The revision of the belief is not subsequent to the making of the judgment; it is accomplished in arriving at that judgment. Once the judgment has been formed there is nothing left to command nor anything with which to tinker. (Hieronymi 2009, 160f)

In other words, Hieronymi argues that once the agent has realized that their attitude is unjustified, it is thereby automatically changed. There is no room here for a further intentional action that brings about the change. Importantly, this is not some radical idea developed by Hieronymi: the idea that beliefs follow the evidence and are changed automatically once the evidence changes is a standard assumption in philosophy.

Hieronymi does not want to claim that Frankfurt's reflective control is supposed to work like ordinary intentional control, but that it is easy to misread it in this way.[13] More importantly, however, she also claims that all other ways in which the notion of reflective agency could be understood do require a reading of reflective control where control is spelled out in a non-intentional way.

Unfortunately, this claim is also not without problems, because while it seems right that beliefs adjusting to evidence is not an intentional action, it is quite unclear in which sense it is agentive at all. Amongst the people who agree with Hieronymi that the production of a new doxastic attitude is never a voluntary action are not only people who want to argue that instead there is a different form of mental agency. In his very influential and radical paper 'Mental ballistics or the involuntariness of spontaneity' (2003), Galen Strawson argues that arguments like the ones put forward by Hieronymi against intentional mental actions simply mean that cognitive processes are passive. Hence, where Hieronymi wants to argue that cognitive agency is importantly different from intentional agency, according to Strawson, cognitive processes simply are not agentive at all: they just happen to us. To give a flavour of his arguments, here is an extended quote of the central passage in his paper:

> All the cognitive work that thought involves, all the computation in the largest and most human sense, all the essential content-work of reasoning and judgement, all the motion or progress of judgement and thought

---

[13] In fact, exactly how one really should read Frankfurtian reflective control, and even whether it is control, at all is hotly debated see e.g. Sripada (2017). For us, only the caricature matters here to get across the point.

considered (so to say) in its contentual essence-the actual confrontations and engagements between contents, the collaborations and competitions between them, the transitions between them is not only not a matter of action but also non-conscious or sub-experiential. It is not itself a phenomenon of consciousness, however much it is catalysed by conscious primings. Rather, the content outcomes are delivered into consciousness so as to be available in their turn for use by the catalytic machinery that is under intentional control. One knows that P is true and wonders whether [P-*Q], holding this content in consciousness. Into consciousness comes 'No; possibly [P A -Q]'; immediately followed, perhaps, by 'But R, and [[P A R] -> Q], so Q'. (Strawson 2003, 233ff)

Strawson goes on to discuss to examples of thoughts that might look like counterexamples to hammer home his point:

I'm now going to think that grass is green, and my thinking that grass is green is going to be a premeditated action: grass is green. There. And now I'm going to think something—I don't yet know what—and my thinking it is going to be a premeditated action: swifts live their lives on the wing.
(Strawson 2003, 233ff)

But while both these thoughts might look like counter examples, Strawson argues that they actually support his point. Here he is again:

In the first case, that of thinking grass is green, it may seem that there is an especially concentrated, fully fledged action of comprehension-involving entertaining of a content. But is this really so? Is there really any such thing as an action of comprehension-involving entertaining of a content? What one finds, I think, if one reflects, does at one stage involve some sort of action, but this is just a matter of a silent mental imaging of words (as sounds or visual marks, say): the actual comprehending thinking of the content is something that just happens thereafter or perhaps concurrently. [...] the event of entertaining itself is not an action, any more than falling is once one has jumped off a wall. In the case of swifts live their lives on the wing there is again a certain sort of action: an action of setting oneself to produce some content or other. But what happens then is a content just comes. Which particular content it is is not intentionally controlled; it is not a matter of action. It cannot be a matter of action unless the content is already there, available for consideration and adoption for intentional production. But if it is already there to be considered and adopted it must already have 'just come' at some previous time in order to be so available. (Strawson 2003, 233ff)

Let us try to paraphrase the key argument of this passage: unlike in the case of ordinary intentional action, the intention guiding a potential intentional mental action cannot contain the goal state. If one wants to hit a bull's eye on the dart board the intention will contain some representation of the goal state, but in the case of mental actions, this seems impossible. If one's goal is to solve a puzzle, one cannot have the solution as part of the content of the intention, because in that case the puzzle would already be solved. This is a powerful argument and very hard to argue against directly. In his introduction to the excellent collection *Mental Actions* (2009), Matthew Soteriou states that on this point there is wide agreement. As Soteriou states, even philosophers like Peacocke or O'Shaughnessy[14] who are much more sanguine about the importance of intentional mental actions for cognition than Strawson, agree with this point (Soteriou 2009, 4).

One important complication needs to be pointed out here though. While it is true that we cannot form the intention to think a certain content without having thought the thought already, we can form the intention to think about a content that is not completely specific but also not completely unspecific as in Strawson's 'swifts live on the wing' example. Al Mele has a wonderful example in his contribution to the *Mental Actions* collection (2009). Mele here asks us to imagine the case where we are trying to think of seven animals beginning with the letter g. As Mele rightly points out, it seems like this is something that we can do intentionally and so when we come up with gnu, gnat, goose, and so on, we are thinking intentionally of animals beginning with g and it clearly is not the case here that having the intention and the actual specific thoughts are just the same thing. However, as Mele freely admits, obviously it is not specified and cannot be specified by our intention whether we will think of for example gnat or giraffe. Otherwise, we would encounter Strawson's problem again. So, while an intentional action can trigger not only random thoughts but also thoughts about very specific topics the actual specific content of the thought will always be acquired non-intentionally.

Perhaps surprisingly, despite his worries about intentional mental actions, Strawson accepts that his scepticism about the role of intentional

---

[14] Both Peacocke and O'Shaugnessy employ a strategy roughly similar to the one employed by Shepherd (which is discussed in Chapter 3 under deliberation and skill).

action in producing new mental content does not rule out that there is a sense in which producing content can be called spontaneous in a Kantian sense, but that this sense is very unlike ordinary usage. In ordinary usage when we use the word spontaneous, we mean that the agent acts intentionally without any external stimulation or pressures that necessitate the action. In the Kantian tradition, according to Strawson, spontaneous means something more like rational necessitation and has little to do with action in the ordinary sense. Thus, in a way it does not seem that there is very much of a substantial difference between Strawson and the defenders of the form of doxastic agency that Hieronymi defends. Rather, it seems more a difference in temperament: they all seem to agree that the nature of cognitive processes is very unlike intentional actions, but for Strawson that difference is enough to deny that there is agency at all, whereas Hieronymi argues that the Kantian spontaneity that Strawson accepts might exist is indeed a form of agency—the most important and basic form of mental agency, in fact.[15]

It is time to sum up: it has become clear that not only is the work in the dual processing theory rooted in the philosophical debate on the nature of rational agency, but more importantly, there is a deep unresolved conflict at the heart of that debate: What is the role of intentional mental action for our cognitive processes and our rationality? Reflective control does not provide us with an easy answer to this problem. Either reflective control is understood on the model of ordinary intentional action, in which case it does risk becoming homuncular, or the control we are referring to here is one that is quite unlike intentional control. However, going down this second route does risk losing a recognizable notion of agency altogether.

7. The Aim of the Book: The Role of Tinkering

The task of this book is to see whether we find this puzzle at the heart of philosophical work about the nature of mental agency in the cognitive

---

[15] One reason why one might prefer Hieronymi's agency account to Strawson's automatic one is that the kind of agency that we are supposed to exercise in evaluative control might well be what e.g. Cantwell Smith takes to be the characteristic feature of human judgment that distinguishes it from the mere reckoning power of artificial intelligence. See e.g. Cantwell Smith (2019). Obviously, this special power of judgment also gives evaluative accounts an advantage over accounts that reduce agentive cognition to tinkering. Artificial intelligence (AI) should be able to thinker with itself so it is far harder to see what the deep difference between AI and humans would be with regard to tinkering. The price tag for this advantage is that evaluative control is a notoriously slippery concept.

science literature, and to see whether it is possible to clarify thinking in that literature using the tools that have been developed in the philosophical debate. In particular, the book will show that the idea of something like reflective control faces the same problem in cognitive science as it does in the philosophical literature. If we don't want to commit a homunculus fallacy, then intentional mental action necessarily becomes in Hieronymi's apt phrase 'tinkering' (2009, 160).

If that is so, then the obvious next question is what the relationship between tinkering and cognition could be? Is it the case that the cognitive sciences can learn from philosophy that intentional mental actions are at best indirectly related to cognition, or will we find that in this literature it makes sense to call intentional mental actions cognitive, despite the problems identified with that move in the traditional philosophical debate? Perhaps it is even the case that intentional mental actions are the only agentive part of rational processes. Cognition, which according to our earlier working (and in this case faulty) definition refers to nothing more than the acquisition of new doxastic states, might never be agentive at all, unless it has intentional components.

This might seem like a very tempting option. Robert Lockie in his fascinating book *Free Will and Epistemology* (2018) for example argues that it is a mistake to think that the intentional mental actions that Strawson describes as mere shepherding are not truly epistemic. Lockie's work is particularly interesting because he thinks that executive function and system two processing can demonstrate how essential intentional mental actions are for epistemic agency.

However, as we will see by the end of Chapter 3, arguing that tinkering really is truly cognitive demands a different definition of cognition and more importantly, has very significant consequences for our wider thinking about a broad range of cognitive phenomena.

This is important because we should aim to avoid making this simply a definitional issue. If it were the case that all sides could agree on what the contribution of tinkering is in the cognitive process, then that would make the result of the investigation rather disappointing. Luckily, however, as the book will demonstrate, this is not the case. Instead, what will become clear is that once we separate intentional mental actions from direct doxastic attitude acquisition (or cognitive agency depending on temperament) in the way that Strawson suggests, it is much easier to refocus on the important roles that tinkering really does play. Most significantly it will show that intentional tinkering inside the head is no different from environment-involving tinkering. This means that the book will demonstrate that if one wants to argue that tinkerings can be truly epistemic, one has to accept the truth of extended cognition.

The purpose of this book is not (as one might suspect because of its embrace of the involuntarist arguments) to show that tinkering is less important than one might have thought, but that the reasons one might have for thinking that tinkering is a constitutive part of cognition are very different from the ones that one would traditionally expect.

Tinkering is not important because it enables reflective control.[16] Hieronymi's arguments against reflective control are strong arguments! But at the same time, tinkering has much more wide-ranging epistemic influences than is normally acknowledged in the literature on epistemic agency.

Especially once we understand that many of these tinkering actions do not even have to be directed at the manipulation of mental attitudes, it becomes clear that tinkering truly is one of the defining characteristics of the human mind. Given this, it might well be that the better way of understanding cognition accepts that extended cognition is true, which then allows us to say that the intentional actions that prepare the acquisition of doxastic states are genuinely cognitive, despite the fact that it remains true that one cannot intentionally directly acquire a belief.

As the second half of the book will show, understanding tinkering as cognitive in this way will also change our understanding of central moral psychology concepts like willpower, choice and the moral agent. But before we can get to these applications, we will first turn to our main application of the puzzle to a popular paradigm in the cognitive sciences. The next chapter takes a look at a very strange argument that can be constructed by combining dual process theory with doxastic involuntarism, one of the central ideas behind Hieronymi's criticism of standard accounts of rational agency. As we will see, when first presented the argument seems to be very radical and could easily be understood as hostile towards the two systems approach. However, this is not at all the purpose of the argument. Rather, it aims to help us better understand cognitive control talk and to show that the easiest way to avoid the conclusion of the simple argument is surprisingly radical. It means accepting that cognition literally extends into the physical environment.

---

[16] Which I suspect is in the end where Lockie (2018) ends up, because he argues that executive functions show that epistemic agency can be voluntary.

2
The Simple Argument

1. Introduction

It seems obvious that human cognition differs in important respects from the cognition of other animals. Humans are able to perform complex rule-based syntactical cognitive operations that are beyond any other animal we know of. Though this still seems to hold true, in recent decades we have also learnt that we are rather less different in the way we understand the world from our animal cousins than we might have thought. A large proportion of what humans do to get along is done in the same way as it is done elsewhere in the animal kingdom.

Dual processing accounts are one very popular attempt to bring these two facts together. They suggest that humans might have two different ways of solving cognitive problems. One is evolutionarily old (system one), which we share with the rest of the animal kingdom, and one is evolutionarily young (system two), and is specifically human. The younger system two is supposed to be the home of a completely new and uniquely human way of making decisions and forming judgments.[1] Often this system has been called the 'rational system', while system one has been termed 'experiential' (see e.g. Epstein and Pacini 1999). There have been criticisms of this, because it is not obvious that system two strategies are always more rational than system one strategies, but until now, no one seems to doubt that system two at the very least provides us with a different and new form of judgments and decisions.

However, this is exactly the claim that this chapter aims to defend—a denial that there can be system two judgments. The claim is not that system two judgements are rare, or that they are not as special as one might have thought, but rather to deny flat out that system two judgments can exist.

---

[1] As dual systems theory evolves, this claim has been weakened by some. Evans (2013), for example, argues that animals do have 'higher-order and controlled forms of cognition' (Evans 2013: 132), but he still stresses that this system is vastly more developed in humans and probably uses modules that are uniquely human, such as the ability to meta-represent.

This might seem like a very bold claim, but the book will show that it is simply the logical consequence of the truth of two extremely plausible premises. A closer investigation will also reveal that the argument properly understood is far less controversial then it might seem initially, and it will help us to get closer to a plausible understanding of what system two might be for.

First of all, to get this strange argument off the ground it is necessary to take a look at the premises necessary for the argument. The two premises in question are, first, the assumption that system two processes are intentional and, second, the assumption that doxastic involuntarism is broadly correct.

Both of these do not seem to be terribly strong assumptions. In the literature, system two processing is standardly characterized as effortful, voluntary, and intentional (Evans 2008; Kahnemann 2011; Masicampo and Baumeister 2008). As we will see in the discussion of the premises later in this chapter, authors in this literature have quite varied positions on what exactly characterizes the processes in system two, and as two systems accounts are very fashionable, there are new accounts being created all the time, so obviously premises relating to system two might well not be true of all possible two systems accounts. Nevertheless, for the vast majority of accounts, the premise that two systems processes are intentional does hold true and as the book will argue, this might well be the most plausible way to understand system two.

The second premise of the simple argument is to assume that doxastic involuntarism is correct. Doxastic involuntarism holds that acquiring doxastic attitudes, such as beliefs,[2] is not up to us in the same way that ordinary physical intentional actions are: I can decide to lift my arm, but I cannot decide what to believe. Now, obviously, there have been famous doxastic voluntarists in the past (e.g., Descartes), but a clear majority of contemporary philosophers seem to be doxastic involuntarists of some description (e.g., Williams 1973; Plantinga 1993; Alston 2005; Chrisman 2008), so this assumption also does not seem too bold.

---

[2] Some have argued that the same reasons that make involuntarism about beliefs plausible also hold for intentions (e.g., Hieronymi 2006). This is convincing if we understand intention-forming processes as decisions or practical judgments about what the best thing to do is, all things considered. In this book, I assume this to be the correct account. If intentions are not directly formed by practical judgments, and if they should not count as doxastic attitudes in this sense, then obviously they are not within the scope of the argument of this book (see Shepherd 2018 for an argument that intentions are not like judgments in this respect).

With these premises in place, we can now run the following very straightforward argument:

All system two processing is intentional.
Doxastic attitude formation processes are never intentional.

From assumption one and two, we can conclude that doxastic attitude formation processes are never system two processes. The argument is clearly valid and if the premises are true, then so is the quite surprising conclusion: we would be forced to accept that system two, which we ordinarily take to be a special human cognitive tool that allows a new way of judging and deciding, really is a system in which no doxastic attitude formation processes ever happen at all.

2. Is the Argument Really Valid?

One way to escape the simple argument is to say that the argument only looks valid on the surface, but that the notions of process in premise one and two are really not the same. In Chapter 1, I already discussed how this move might go. One could say that the notion of process in premise two is one where the process in question is something like judging that p, and as we said there, and as we will explore in a bit more detail in the next section, no one really denies that judging that p is never intentional. One could even complain in this context that using the term process is a stretch here. One could say that judging that p is better described as an event. This is a fair point to make. However, as judging that p does describe a transition from a state without a doxastic state to a point where the doxastic state is acquired, the term process does not seem inadequate either. This is especially true if we think of judging as something that is a form of agency. Agency is supposed to make a difference in the world, and this transition that agency brings about is described as the relevant process here.

On the other hand, it is absolutely fair to point out that the notion of process in premise one is quite different. The intentional processing in system two is about processes like inhibition, rehearsal, shifting attention, and so on, and all these things can clearly be intentional. Processing in system two is like a race. It is a drawn-out process unfolding in time to find the solution to a problem, whereas the doxastic attitude acquisition processes in premise two are more like crossing the finish line at the end of a race. Sure, there is a connection between the two. One is the result of the other, but the notions of process in question are very different.[3]

This is one easy and legitimate way to avoid the conclusion of the simple argument. However, as with all simple solutions, it comes with a price tag. The obvious one is that if we go for this option, then we have to accept that judging that p cannot be a system two process, because judging that p is our paradigm case for the notion of process employed in premise two. As was already discussed in Chapter 1, it also means that if we want to claim that the processes in premise one can be cognitive processes, then we will also have to accept extended cognition. Readers who are not deterred by either of these consequences may wish to skip the rest of this chapter and the next, because the purpose of these two chapters is to discuss the force of the simple argument with anyone who is not yet sold on extended cognition and/or who does not want to give up on the notion that judgings are system two processes.

Another neat way to escape the simple argument[4] would be to understand intentional in premise one in the Brentano sense, i.e. as aboutness or representational. This use might well be justified, because system two processing is propositional and not associative like the processing in system one. If we understand intentional in this sense, then clearly intentional means different things in premise one and premise two. But while this is a neat move, it clearly does not explain the idea that system two processing is controlled, or that it involves working memory which allows for inhibition and updating. To explain these characteristics of system two, we need the other meaning of intentional, which is similar to voluntary, and which is the same meaning as in premise two.

A third terminological clarification concerns the term judgment: I take it as uncontroversial that judgments often lead to the acquisition of a belief. In fact, it seems uncontroversial that this is what they normally do. However, there is a debate about whether this is always the case. Prominently, Peacocke (1998) suggests that someone may for example judge that an undergraduate degree from a different country is equivalent to his own, but his hiring decisions show that he does not really believe it. But is this really a convincing example? The example suggests that the agent presumably has contradictory beliefs, but it still seems to be the case that the judgment generates at least a fleeting belief that interacts at the time in the

---

[3] Thanks to an OUP reader for pressing me on this point.
[4] Suggested to me by Mark Sprevak.

right way with at least a part of the belief network. So, the agent in one sense does believe that the undergraduate degree from the different country is equivalent and this would be reflected in part of his behaviour. He would, for example, say that he believes this to be the case if asked, while on the other hand it is obviously true that he also has a dispositional belief that is inconsistent with his assertions. (See also Hieronymi 2006, 2009, and Boyle 2011 for similar worries about Peacocke's argument). There is more that could be said here, and we will return to this issue in Chapter 3, but for now it is enough to be clear that in the terminology employed here in this book, judging always leads to the acquisition of a new belief. If somebody claims that they judge that *p*, but clearly even while engaging in the speech act does not believe *p*, then that person does not understand properly what it means to judge. I also consider that it should be uncontroversial that judgments are the only plausible candidate for agentive direct belief acquisition.

We have now established the validity of the argument, but is it also sound? In order to establish that we will have a look at the premises. We will begin by having a closer look at doxastic involuntarism and its links to evaluative control, and in the light of this, re-examine our first premise. In so doing, we will establish why the distinction between evaluative and managerial control really can be helpful for a better understanding of what is going on in one of the most successful paradigms of cognitive science.

3. Doxastic Involuntarism

Suppose somebody offered you a million dollars to believe that the earth is flat. If you, like most people, are quite motivated by the idea of earning a million dollars just like that, then you would be also very motivated to acquire the relevant belief. But interestingly, this does not seem to help you. It seems impossible to simply decide what you want to believe, even if you are very motivated to acquire the belief in question. This has been described as the 'no rewards' principle (Chrisman 2008).[5] Simply acquiring

---

[5] The no rewards principle seems very plausible, but not everybody thinks that it provides conclusive evidence for doxastic involuntarism. Miriam McCormick (2014) for example contends that the no rewards argument does not work because there are other things that we can do, such as commit murder, that we would not do no matter how much money we were offered. However, this does not seem to be a very convincing argument. The difference between the two cases is that it seems easy to imagine how I would go about committing the murder, despite the

a doxastic attitude does not seem to be under voluntary control, even if the agent is highly motivated to acquire it. The no rewards principle gives us a very powerful way of understanding why so many philosophers hold that premise two is true. The acquisition of doxastic attitudes is simply not something that is up to the agent in the way that lifting one's arm is. Rather, what we come to believe is sensitive to the evidence that we believe that we have for the truth of a proposition. If we have enough evidence, we acquire the belief and if we do not, then we do not acquire it.

One very famous example of the no rewards principle in the history of ideas is the discussion of Pascal's wager. Pascal famously argues that it is rational to believe in God, because it is the least risky option in terms of overall happiness. This is because if God doesn't exist and one still believes in him, it is not obvious that one would be any less happy during one's lifetime than if one had not. On the other hand, if God does exist and one does not believe in him and then goes to hell, it would have significant happiness implications.

Pascal therefore suggests that it is rational to try to believe in God. However, Pascal also realized that trying to follow this recommendation is problematic, because even if it is true that it would be rational to acquire the belief that God exists because of overall happiness considerations, this simply does not help one to acquire the belief: if one is not convinced that there is evidence for the existence of God, then one will not be able to acquire the belief because of the no rewards principle.

The strategy to deal with this problem that Pascal suggests is crucial for a clearer understanding of the second premise of our target argument. Pascal accepted that the sceptic might find it difficult to acquire the belief in God just like that, but argued that she was also not helpless. She could decide to mingle only with believers, to go to mass regularly, and to pray a few rosaries every day. Experience shows, according to Pascal, that partaking in the practice will soon lead to a new perspective and that in turn will very likely lead to the acquisition of the desired belief.

This is very important for the issue under consideration here, because it might seem as if Pascal's reply contains a serious objection to our second premise: at first glance, it appears that Pascal's example demonstrates that it is quite possible to acquire beliefs intentionally. Praying rosaries and

---

fact that it might well be psychologically impossible to actually carry it out, whereas in the case of the false belief, it is impossible to imagine how one would be able to do it (apart from using managerial actions as discussed later in the chapter).

mingling with fellow believers are clearly intentional actions that the agent can perform at will. If, as Pascal asserts, those actions will lead to the acquisition of the desired belief in God, then that seems to suggest that the belief can be acquired by means of these intentional actions.

However, if we take a second look, things are not quite as clear as they might seem. First of all, it should be noted that it is not entirely clear in which way the partaking in the practice will lead to the acquisition of the belief. Either it could be that the practice provides the agent with new evidence, and the agent then evaluates on the basis of that new evidence that God does actually exist, or it could be the case that the partaking in the practice bypasses the agent's rational processes altogether and simply manipulates the mind of the agent, using some form of conditioning to acquire the belief.

In the former case, the agent still acquires the belief because she finds the evidence convincing, but this does not seem like a voluntary action. In this case, while it is true that the voluntary action led to the agent being in a different doxastic environment, the actual acquisition of the attitude does take place because the agent evaluates the new evidence rationally, and again, this evaluation does not seem up to the agent.

To see that belief acquisition is not up to the agent, we just have to consider the following scenario: suppose that after she took in the new evidence for God's existence in her new doxastic environment, we offered the agent good reasons to acquire the belief (rather than the content of it) that God doesn't exist, because, for example, hell is actually a fun place to be, and all she would have to do to get there according to our setup is not to believe in him. But without changing her newly acquired evaluation that the evidence points toward the existence of God, the agent now could not acquire the more rewarding sceptical belief—at least not according to the no rewards principle. She could not do it in this case because the belief follows what the agent perceives to be rational evidence, and it is not possible for the agent to control this process intentionally. All the agent can do is trigger the non-voluntary process of belief acquisition by intentionally preparing the ground.

Pamela Hieronymi (2009) has employed a very helpful distinction here. She calls intentional preparation processes 'managerial control' and non-voluntary belief acquisition processes 'evaluative control'.[6] Importantly,

---

[6] Others use the distinction between non-intentionally judging that p and intentionally bringing it about that one judges that p (e.g. Chrisman 2008; Mele 2009).

as she notes, every act of managerial control always contains two evaluative episodes. The agent has to form the intention to control managerially, and then the agent needs to evaluate again, once the management has brought about suitable changes in the environment. While managerial control does play a causal role in belief acquisition, it is not constitutive. In all acts of managerial control, the process that constitutes belief acquisition is an evaluative one. Premise two in the case of managerial control survives the objection: while it is true that intentional actions do play an important role in belief acquisition, this role is merely causal and the constitutive process in acquiring the belief is always a non-intentional evaluative one.

But what about our second case in which Pascal simply conditions himself to believe in God? Hieronymi has a term for this scenario as well. She calls this form of control of the mind 'manipulative control', because here the agent bypasses normal belief acquisition processes and directly implants the belief within the system. This looks like a trickier case for premise two.

In this scenario, it does indeed seem to be the case that the belief is brought about in an intentional way. However, we should worry here about whether we truly are still talking about a real doxastic state. If one assumes, as most philosophers would, that beliefs are inferentially promiscuous and part of a network of beliefs, then it is not clear whether these states really are beliefs. When they are implanted, they will not have interacted with the network of other beliefs yet. However, once the state does come into contact with this network of beliefs, it will be evaluated by the network to establish whether it is consistent with the other beliefs or not. If it does fit, then it becomes a belief, but it becomes a belief because of this evaluation, which again is not intentional.

On the other hand, if a mental state does not fit, it will be rejected by the network. In such a case, the agent might still be convinced that the content of the attitude in question is true, but the agent will be alienated from this attitude in a very important way, because she will not be able to integrate it with her other beliefs. Such an attitude is probably better described as a phobia or a delusion, rather than a fully functioning belief.[7]

To sum up the Pascal discussion: managerial or manipulative control over our beliefs is clearly possible, but this does not mean that we can ever acquire a doxastic attitude intentionally. In both cases, the intentional action clearly

---

[7] Some authors think of delusions as beliefs, but they also argue that there needs to be at least some integration with the network, even if the network might well be fragmented.

plays a causal role, but it is not the right causal role. In both cases, a belief in the full sense of the word can only be achieved if the intentional action is followed by a non-intentional evaluative process.

4. Doxastic Deliberation

Armed with the distinction between different forms of control, it is now possible to tackle an important objection to the argument presented. The objection runs: deliberation is an intentional action and judgments are a part, normally the conclusion, of deliberative processes. As such, judgements are a part of the intentional action of deliberation that leads to the acquisition of a doxastic attitude.

Deliberation is also importantly different from the kind of managerial actions described in the Pascal case. In the Pascal case, the intentional action has the goal of bringing about a belief as an attitude independent of the truth of its content, but in deliberation, the aim is to acquire a true belief.

One prominent example of an argument for the existence of intentional doxastic deliberation comes from Shah and Velleman (2005). They argue that intentional doxastic deliberation exists because judging clearly is an act, because it is about affirming, and there 'cannot be any problem about the possibility of deliberating whether to perform the mental act of affirming that p' (Shah and Velleman 2005: 503). The problem, as they see it, is how we get from the act of affirming to an attitude itself. They write that that is 'of course ineffable' (503). Let's look a bit closer at what is going on here.

First, Shah and Velleman claim that affirming can be an intentional action,[8] but they then go on to distinguish between two different understandings of affirming. On the one hand, affirming can mean an inner speech act and that clearly is under voluntary control. An agent can easily affirm in this sense either p or $-p$ in the same way that they could either raise or not raise their arm. That is obviously still true if the agent is aware that what they assert is not true. They are aware of this, but they can simply choose to affirm either what they believe to be correct or what they do not believe to be correct. On the other hand, affirming can also mean performing the inner speech act with conviction. Here affirming is about acquiring a

---

[8] In line with the general consensus, an intentional action for Shah and Vellemann is an action one can perform arbitrarily or 'at will', as Williams puts it (1973).

belief which is done by affirming its content in the speech act and whether or not one affirms with conviction is clearly not under one's voluntary control.

Shah and Velleman rightly say that it would be very odd to describe a judgment as an inner speech act of the first kind, because judgments aim at truth. However, Shah and Velleman contend that things are different in cases where the affirming happens with the aim of acquiring a belief. According to them, this form of affirmation is what acts of judgment consist in.

It should be noted here that Velleman and Shah do not think of judgments as definitionally leading to the acquisition of a belief as we have so far assumed in this book. Rather, for them it is an act of affirming with the right intention that ordinarily leads to the acquisition of the standing attitude, but how that happens is 'ineffable'.

Once this difference in the meaning of the term 'judgment' is clear, it also becomes clear that this objection turns out to be merely terminological. If one understands judging as we have done so far as always leading to the acquisition of a belief, then it is clearly not the intentional inner speech act of the agent that the judgment consists in, because we can affirm a proposition with the aim to acquire a belief without this aim being achieved.[9] On the notion of judgment developed here, the process that leads to the acquiring of the attitude that Shah and Velleman describe as ineffable is part and parcel of the judgment. On this latter notion, it seems clear that judging is not something that we can do intentionally.

However, if we mean by judging (as Shah and Velleman seem to) that we affirm something in the hope that it might lead to a true belief, then that is clearly something that we can do intentionally. If we use the terminology employed in this book this understanding of judging does not appear to differ greatly from a managerial action.

Having the aim of settling the question of whether p does not directly contribute to whether one will find one's inner speech act convincing or not, because it does not provide any evidence for or against p. What the speech act can do is to bring the proposition before the inner eye, so that it can be evaluated, but it is not in itself part of the evaluation. Like all managerial actions, the speech act has a catalysing function and does not directly contribute to the evaluation of whether p is actually the case.

---

[9] Obviously this is merely definitional, but intuitively at least to me if one affirms a proposition without believing it then one did not judge it to be true, even if one affirmed it in order to acquire the belief.

However, what is undeniable here is that the affirming in this case is done with a specific motive in mind, i.e., it is done to acquire a true belief. One could argue that because certain intentional actions are defined in such a way that they only can be that type of action (e.g. a judgment) if they are performed with the right epistemic motive, they also fall under the no rewards principle. Given that I introduced doxastic involuntarism with the no rewards principle, if these kind of affirming actions do fall under it, this looks like it might be a problem for our second premise.

5. Intentional and Still No Reward?

The idea that the right motivation might make the no rewards principle applicable to some intentional actions is nicely illustrated in a similar argument by Keith Frankish. Frankish argues in his 2007 paper that judgments are like promises. They are intentional actions, but the no rewards principle nevertheless applies. As discussed before, I use intentional and voluntary as synonyms in this book, but Frankish suggests that there might be intentional actions that are not voluntary, because only voluntary actions are the ones where the no rewards principle does not apply, because they can be done for any reason the agent chooses. But some intentional actions according to this argument are not voluntary and can therefore be subject to the no rewards principle.

To illustrate this point Frankish uses the example of promising. One cannot promise something unless one intends to keep it. Only if one performs the intentional action of promising for the right reasons is it really a promise. Even if it would be very useful to make a promise, if one did not intend to keep it, it would not really be a promise.

In the same way, one might think that perhaps the no rewards principle does not rule out that doxastic attitude acquisition processes could be intentional. What the no rewards principle shows is that we cannot acquire beliefs for any other reasons than the ones that generate a sufficient amount of evidence for the belief. One cannot, for example, believe that Edinburgh is in China, even if someone offered to pay a lot of money if that belief was acquired. But what about intentional actions that we undertake in order to find new evidence? Suppose you don't know where Edinburgh is and whether there might not be one in China. If you now go to Wikipedia to find out, you are not doing this to acquire a specific belief, as in the Pascal case, but to acquire the correct belief, whatever that may be. Going to

Wikipedia is clearly an intentional action, but the no rewards principle still applies, because you can only do it in the service of doxastic deliberation if you think it is suitable for your epistemic purpose.

There is something odd going on in arguments like this one, however. The claim that the no rewards principle applies in these cases only works in a very specific sense. It is clearly not the case that I can only go to Wikipedia in order to achieve an epistemic goal—I can also do it if someone gives me money for it. It is not the executing of the intentional action that falls under the no rewards principle, but the intention to perform the action for the right reasons. Yet obviously, forming that intention is not normally an intentional action.

More importantly, we have to ask ourselves why it is that we want to call actions like going to Wikipedia (or rehearsing an argument, etc.) epistemic. Presumably, it is because they help to bring about a new doxastic attitude. But that seems a problem for the claim that the no rewards principle applies here, because for the doxastic effect, one does not need the right motivation. One is going to get the information and acquire the belief from Wikipedia, regardless of whether one performs the action for money or for epistemic purposes. That the right motivation cannot be what makes an intentional action a doxastic action also becomes clear by thinking back at the difference between managerial and manipulative control. If intentional actions that are performed with the intention to acquire a true belief would be doxastic, then going to a neuroscientist to have a true belief implanted in one's brain would also count as a doxastic action, as long as one went to the neuroscientist with the right epistemic intention. But that is patently absurd. It is absurd because in the manipulative scenario, in contrast to the managerial one, the truly doxastic element (the evaluation of the plausibility of the proposition) is absent.

Finally, could one not say that at least in ordinary deliberation there is a difference to managerial actions as described in the Pascal case, because they are not really concerned with the acquisition of an attitude at all, but merely with the content. There is a really important point about the nature of tinkering here that requires careful discussion, which is why the whole of Chapter 5 is dedicated to it, but here are two quick answers. Crucially, while the specific nature of intentional tinkerings with the mind is fascinating, it is obvious that all forms of tinkerings are just that: they are catalytic intentional actions and their precise nature does not impact on the question of whether and in which ways the no rewards principle applies to them. Second, it is at the very least not obvious that such actions do not have an attitude-directed dimension like the Pascal case. As Shah and Velleman point out, judging that p is different from mere wondering whether p. The latter does not have necessarily any specific goal, while the former is done precisely because one deliberately wants to acquire a belief.

With this final objection addressed, we can conclude that premise two looks solid. There are intentional actions that play an important role in the causal aetiology of doxastic state acquisition, but they are all managerial or catalytic and the evaluations that do lead directly to the acquisition of new attitudes are never intentional.

6. A Few Words on Evaluative Control

This is a book about intentional mental actions and their relationship to cognition and rationality. It is not a book about evaluative agency. The main reason for this is that this book is based on the suspicion that the role of intentional mental action often is described misleadingly, because it is not distinguished sufficiently clearly from evaluative agency, and this means that many interesting things that can be said about intentional mental actions are obscured, simply because the distinction is not clear enough.

The other reason why this book is not about evaluative agency is that, in contrast to intentional mental agency, there is a large literature on the phenomenon Hieronymi calls evaluative agency—although it does go by different names, for example Boyle (2011) and Jenkins (2018) refer to it as doxastic agency, and Chrisman (2018) calls it cognitive agency. Nonetheless, the problem to which these forms of agency are the answer is the same. Evaluative-doxastic-cognitive agency is an answer to Williams's (1973) famous quip that we cannot form beliefs at will. At least not if the belief-forming process is not like the managerial 'bringing it about' discussed in the Pascal case, but more direct as seems intuitively necessary for ordinary belief-forming processes.

There is a very wide and subtle debate about what exactly this non-intentional form of agency exactly consists in (see Chrisman (2018); Toribio (2011); McHugh (2011); Boyle (2011); Moran (2001); Jenkins (2018);[10] O'Shaughnessy (1980); Peacocke (2009); and Soteriou (2009), to

---

[10] Jenkins is partly an exception here, because he does argue that judging, while not an intentional action in itself, is simply token identical to the endpoint of deliberation—and deliberation is clearly intentional. I discuss this point in the rest of the chapter and in more detail in section 7 of Chapter 3.

name but a few). As we have also already heard, some, like Strawson, don't think that this is really a form of agency at all and that belief-acquisition processes simply happen in a passive way. The important thing for our purposes is that we can stay fully neutral on this debate.

One might wonder at this point why evaluative control has such a prominent status within the investigation if it is not defended. The reason is simple: while I do not defend evaluative control, as was discussed in Chapter 1, I assume that it is the only possible account of cognition that is agentive and does not commit to extended cognition. The only other and intuitively most natural alternative i.e. reflective control is highly problematic. The simple argument is an illustration of that very point. With that reminder of the structure of the overall argument, let us now turn to premise one of the simple argument and see whether all system two processing really is intentional.

7. What Is System Two?

Before we can answer the question whether all system two processing is intentional, a few words are in order about what system two actually is: system two is one of two systems in so-called dual process theories (e.g., Carruthers 2009; Evans 2008; Stanovich 2011). These theories have over the last decade become ever more popular and it is no hyperbole to say that they have been extremely influential. Their influence is not even confined to the bounds of academia, even though it is huge here too, but they have also become very widely known outside the academic context, not least due to the popular science bestseller by Daniel Kahnemann, 'Thinking fast and slow' (Kahnemann 2011).

The two systems are supposed to describe two different modes in which humans do their cognitive processing. They are often introduced with a list of dichotomies. Carruthers, for example, has a table that introduces system one as associative, heuristic, parallel, automatic, unconscious, with low demands on cognitive capacity, relatively fast, contextualized, evolutionarily old, and conserved across species, while system two is described as analytic, rule based, serial, controlled, conscious, with high demands on cognitive capacity, relatively slow, decontextualized, evolutionarily new, unique to humans (Carruthers 2009: 109). Frankish (2004) adds to his system two list amongst others language involving and apt to be actively formed and controlled, while Stanovich (2005) has a list with over two dozen dichotomies, very much along similar lines.

System one is the system that most animals use all of the time, and humans use most of the time. It is very efficient in dealing with a hostile environment, where processing speed will make the difference between survival and being eaten. However, the efficiency of system one comes at a cost. System one is not very good at dealing with novel or abstract problems and is very inflexible. But humans seem unique within the animal kingdom in being very proficient in dealing with such problems. According to two systems theory, this is because humans have a second system that specializes in dealing flexibly with novel situations, in contrast to other animals.

The distinction has been fruitfully employed in a wide variety of contexts. It is at the heart of the burgeoning heuristics and biases literature (e.g. Kahnemann 2011; Stanovich and West 2000). The system one/system two distinction is also widely used in the literature on social cognition: Apperly and Butterfill (2009), for example, have developed a very influential dual systems account of belief ascription. In designing the account, they in turn refer to work in mathematical cognition that also supports the idea that there are two systems. These are just a few examples of influential uses of dual systems accounts. A further example is provided by two of the most prominent proponents of dual systems accounts which exemplify the breadth of interest in the idea; Evans and Stanovich (2013), write in a review article:

> [dual system accounts] have their origins in the 1970s and 1980s (Evans, 1989; Wason & Evans, 1975) and have become the focus of much interest in contemporary research on these topics (Barbey & Sloman, 2007; Evans, 2007, 2008; Evans & Over, 1996; Kahneman, 2011; Kahneman & Frederick, 2002; S.A. Sloman, 1996; Stanovich, 1999, 2011; Stanovich & West, 2000). Over a similar period, dual-process theories have proved popular in the psychology of learning (e.g., Dienes & Perner, 1999; Reber, 1993; Sun, Slusarz, & Terry, 2005) and especially in social cognition, which has the greatest proliferation of dual-processing labels and theories (see Chaiken & Trope, 1999; Epstein, 1994; Kruglanski & Orehek, 2007; Smith & DeCoster, 2000).

Finally, in the context of a book on the role of intentional action for cognitive processes, one more application of dual systems has to be mentioned: the literature on self-control. In a fascinating series of delayed gratification experiments, Roy Baumeister and his colleagues provide evidence for their claim that self-control works like the flexing of a mental muscle: it takes effort, and this leads to exhaustion. To support their argument, they were able to show that having to flex the muscle in one task would lead to decreased performance in another unrelated task that also requires effort. They call this phenomenon ego depletion and argue that it is a system two characteristic (Baumeister et al. 1998).[11]

Nonetheless, despite—or perhaps because of—their immense popularity, dual process theories are not without their critics and some have pointed out that different dual systems theorists seem to mean very different things when using dual systems terminology. Indeed, it has been argued that it might well be possible to explain the data using just one system, and that mental phenomena often come graded rather than in dichotomies (Gigerenzer 1996; Keren and Schul 2009). Even many proponents of dual systems accounts do not deny that the flurry of different accounts has led to ambiguities, and that it is necessary to sort out exactly what the core message of dual systems accounts is.

Given that the simple argument is supposed to be about current mainstream dual systems accounts and not about an outdated strawman, it seems worthwhile to have a closer look at where the debate within dual processing accounts is now.

In their article 'Dual Process Theories of Higher Cognition: Advancing the Debate', Evans and Stanovich (2013), two of the key proponents of dual process theories, strike a cautionary tone.[12] They list a number of developments that dual process accounts have made in response to the criticisms raised. Their first worry acknowledges that the talk of system one might be misleading, because it is not obvious that system one really consists of just one specific system. On what they describe as the received view,[13] system one processes have been characterized as more or less like reflexes: but that is clearly a caricature, because the defining feature of type one was always that it was not type two. Type two processing is closest to the traditional, folk psychological mind, but as cognitive science has taught us, our minds are so

---

[11] The mental muscle view has been very popular and is a clear example of the use of two systems theory in an important domain of the field, but it is also highly contentious. For a critical evaluation of the theory (see e.g., Kurzban et al. 2013, for a recent meta-study in support of the effect see Dang 2018).

[12] We are discussing Evans and Stanovich here because they are amongst the most important defenders of dual processing accounts. However, the worry that the dichotomies do not align has been pointed out not only by friends of dual processing but also by sceptics. (e.g., Melnikoff and Bargh (2018), Coelho de Nascimento (in preparation)).

[13] The received view according to Evans and Stanovich assumes 'that one kind of thought process must be conscious, controlled, reflective, and rule-based, whereas another is nonconscious, automatic, impulsive, and associative' (2013: 227).

much more than that. One reason why dual process accounts are so intuitive is that they allow us to retain a large part of the intuitive conception in system two while at the same time doing justice to the by now undeniable fact that the mind is clearly much more than the conscious mind. Thus, the essential element of type one processing was always its autonomy from the things that were considered essential for type two processing, i.e. that they do not require working memory or controlled attention (Evans and Stanovich 2013: 236). On the other hand, the processes that fulfil this definition do form a very heterogeneous group. They contain innate reflexes, but they also contain overlearned processes that once were system two but have become automatized, implying that it might well be problematic to describe system one processes as the modular system.

System one in contemporary dual process theory is a long way away from the mere reflex picture of the received view. This is good news for the simple argument, because it makes it sound a lot less absurd than it would seem on the received view. It is clearly impossible that all our judgments are reflex-like, but if system one is simply the system that is not system two, but which might contain nevertheless all kinds of powerful cognitive machinery, then the conclusion seems at least a lot less absurd.[14]

This is even more true for many dual systems proponents who also think that system two makes use of a number of new and special modules, most notably the mindreading system. So not only are the processes in system one more complex and flexible than was initially assumed, it has also become clearer and clearer that the idea that all of system two is entirely free from the influences of modular processes is also a caricature. As Evans writes:

> Attributing modular cognition to system one is not compatible with a two minds theory in which modules play a critical foundation for the new mind. To be sure, there are ancient modules within, for example, our perceptual systems but these provide inputs for both old and new mind learning. Also, there are some modules, more recently evolved, which seem distinctively human and essential to the new mind. For example, without the aid of linguistic representations and the meta-representational power provided by theory of mind, it is difficult to see how the flexible and higher-order forms of cognition associated with human beings could operate.
>
> (Evans 2010)

---

[14] See also e.g. the work by De Neys and Pennycook (2019) which shows that logical principles can be processed in system one.

Given this interdependence between the systems, Evans and Stanovich recommend no longer using two systems terminology, but instead to use the phrase 'dual processing'. Again, in our context, softening up the extremely black-and-white picture can only be an advantage for the plausibility of the simple argument.

Continuing in the same vein, Evans and Stanovich also argue that over the years it has become less and less clear whether the attributes that are usually listed as characteristic for the individual processing types in the received view (see the Carruthers list above) really always fall together. Particularly important in this context is that it no longer seems obvious that system two is always controlled and intentional, while system one processes are automatic. Obviously, while it is good news that systems one and two are less black and white than the received view used to assume, it would be bad news for premise one of the simple argument if it turns out that systems one and two are no longer distinguished by the dichotomy automatic vs. controlled.

Unfortunately, Evans and Stanovich do not say much about this worry, but quote Wegner (2002) and Bargh (2005) as the relevant authors. Both of these authors are famous for claiming that processes that look very system two, like conscious will (Wegner) or picking and acting on goals (Bargh), are in actual fact driven by automatic system one processes. Perhaps the argument here is the same as the one that Evans (2010) advances when he sets out to demonstrate that dual systems theory is fully compatible with the idea that consciousness plays far less of a role in the control of behaviour than commonly assumed. Here, Evans does discuss Wegner's work in a bit more detail. Wegner (esp. 2002) is obviously famous for claiming that conscious will is an illusion. He argues that experimental evidence shows that the experience of conscious will is not what causes us to behave, but rather that the unconscious intention which does cause behaviour also causes a conscious thought which is experienced as the will, but which remains causally inert.

Evans agrees but contends that this is entirely compatible with dual process theory. He rightly emphasizes that Wegner does not show that there is no difference between automatic and voluntary cognition. Evans very much thinks that voluntary cognition obviously exists and points to the ability of subjects to follow instructions and executive functions as clear proof of this. But what Wegner shows is that these kinds of voluntary cognitions are not in turn controlled by conscious intentions. The existence of voluntary cognition does not entail that 'there is a conscious person in charge of our behaviour' (Evans 2010: 173). Or, in other words, there is no homunculus. Instead, 'the reflective mind posts a feeling of willing into phenomenal consciousness as a result of carrying out an intentional act, which is often but not necessarily an indication of the actual intention' (Evans 2010: 173).

Understood in this way, Evans's point does not seem to be a challenge to premise one of the simple argument but rather a helpful clarification of something already discussed at length in Chapter 1. Two systems accounts do try to explain a form of cognitive processing that is specific to humans, at least to a large degree, but such accounts are at pains to avoid any dualistic or homuncular fallacies.

It is time to sum up: dual process theories have been enormously successful over the last two decades. They have been used across the cognitive sciences in a wide variety of fields. Traditionally, they were organized into a list of dichotomies that were supposed to show the different processing styles in the two systems. At the same time, however, and very importantly, there are very many different and often not fully compatible accounts. Furthermore, especially in the last ten years, there has been a great deal of criticism of dual processing accounts. In part, this criticism might well be attributable to the fact that the critics did not always appreciate the heterogeneity of accounts on offer, and in part, the accounts themselves were in need of clarification.

But, despite all the criticisms and despite the fact that the jury is still out on whether dual processing accounts are ultimately more plausible than their competitors, it is very hard to deny that they have been, and indeed still are, enormously popular and influential.

As Evans and Stanovich conclude:

> In short, we do not support dual-processing approaches on the basis of whim and fashion. We do so both because the evidence is compelling and because a very clear theoretical basis for the two-process distinction has now emerged. Such theories can account for a wide range of phenomena in the reasoning, judgment, and decision-making literatures that have been the subject of several recent books. (Evans and Stanovich 2013: 237)

It is certainly undeniable that despite all the criticism, dual process theories remain enormously successful. What also has become clear is that despite the fact that the dual processing landscape has become very different, there is no reason to think that the simple argument cannot apply any more. If anything, the newer versions of dual process theories which reject the caricature of system one processing as merely reflexive make the simple argument less fantastical than it otherwise might seem. Also, their emphasis on being compatible with the Wegner-inspired literature which suggests that consciousness plays less of a role in human cognition than we might have thought makes the conclusion of the simple argument less damaging to such contemporary versions of two systems theory. However, thus far we have not looked at the status of premise one directly, and so that is where we will now turn.

8. Is System Two Processing Always Intentional?

Having had a short look at the dual systems literature in general, it is now time to hone in on the first premise of our target argument. Is it really true that all system two processing is intentional? As just discussed, one issue with this question might be that it is not clear exactly what is meant by system two processing, because there are so many different accounts. Hence, one answer to the question will unfortunately have to be that it is not possible to ascertain that on all dual systems accounts all system two processing will turn out to be intentional. Thus, there is an easy way to escape the conclusion of the simple argument, by simply denying premise one.

The story does not end here, however. There are a large number of dual systems accounts that explicitly state that system two processing is always active (e.g. Carruthers 2009, 2015; Frankish 2004). At the same time, what Stanovich and Evans call the received view clearly also describes system two processing in terms of volitional, intentional, effortful control. Finally, even all the accounts that are less explicit about the connection between intentional action and system two processing use a terminology that suggests that perhaps volition plays a much bigger role in their accounts implicitly, and it might well be that once the terminology is fully spelled out that system two processing is always intentional after all (as I will argue in the next section, this might well be the case for Evans and Stanovich). For all these accounts, the simple argument will remain in force.

To understand better whether the simple argument is valid, it is necessary to have a look at these claims in a little more detail: what can certainly be said is that the terms controlled, intentional, voluntary, and effortful are standardly used in the dichotomies that are supposed to describe the system two mode of processing (see e.g., Evans 2008). Looking at the literature, it becomes clear that for a large number of accounts, intentional control is also not just one feature amongst many, but at the very heart of what system two processing is all about.

One clear example of system two processing being intentional control are the two systems accounts in the self-control literature. When Masicampo and Baumeister (2008),[15] for example, distinguish the two systems, they write:

> one reasoning process makes quick and automatic judgments based on associative and intuitive feedback, and the other process is more effortful and relies on the application of normative rules of reasoning.
> (Masicampo and Baumeister 2008)

The notion of effort is central to how the self-control literature understands system two processes. This is particularly salient in the idea of ego depletion and the metaphor of the mental muscle. System two processing is like using a muscle, and because of the effort in straining the muscle, a finite glucose-based resource becomes exhausted. The idea of effort is also central to the philosophical use of mental muscle accounts, such as those by, for example, Holton (2009a).

Another excellent example of the importance of effort for dual processing accounts is the work of Daniel Kahnemann. When introducing the dual system hypothesis, Kahnemann (2011) writes:

> System one: operates automatically and quickly, with little or no effort and no sense of voluntary control.
>
> System two: allocates attention to the effortful mental activities that demand it, including complex computations. The operations of system two are often associated with the subjective experience of agency, choice and concentration.   (Kahnemann 2011: 21)

In the next chapter, after his introduction, Kahnemann introduces the workings of system two in more detail. The title of this chapter already hints at what is to come: it is called 'Attention and Effort' (see Kahnemann 2011: 31).

---

[15] As mentioned before, the ego depletion literature is heavily involved in the replication crisis, but whether or not the position remains viable, the point here remains. This literature is a prominent example of dual processing approaches that do focus on the notion of effort.

According to Kahnemann, what makes system two processes system two processes is that they are 'effortful'. Obviously, according to Kahnemann and others in the self-control literature, effort and intentional action are very tightly connected. Making an effort is something that agents do when they act intentionally, when they try to achieve something. Here it is quite clear that effort and hence intentional control is not just one of many perhaps dispensable items for Kahnemann, but at the very heart of the idea of what system two is all about.

But we need to be careful here: while Kahnemann does stress effort as one key characteristic of system two, he also makes it very clear that he describes subjective *experiences* here. If we describe system two processes at the functional level that underpins the personal level experience, then he wants to talk instead about i.e. increased arousal, dilated pupils, or focused attention (Kahnemann 2011: 415). Furthermore, it is also unclear whether we always need to understand the ubiquitous talk about effort in the literature as a personal-level phenomenon at all. Kahnemann tests for effort in his experiments simply by making subjects perform a cognitively demanding task while performing the target task at the same time. If the distraction affects the performance of the target task, then the task is said to involve cognitive effort.[16]

Given the muddle surrounding terms like effort and control in the literature, it is perhaps not surprising that Evans and Stanovich (2013) do not use the label 'effortful' at all and use the term 'controlled' sparingly. Instead, they define system two processing as requiring working memory resources,[17] but as Evans (2008) notes, the working memory notion in play here is one where working memory is not only about short-term memory capacity but also about executive and inhibitory functions that working memory is supposed to have (Evans 2008: 259). However, these executive and inhibitory functions are exactly the ones that are usually associated with intentional control and effort. This is also what Robert Lockie (2018) suggests when he writes that we should 'identify Type 2 processing with executive functioning' (p. 99) which, according to him, is clearly voluntary.[18]

---

[16] Interestingly, cognitive effort in these experiments is much higher for novices than for experts. This is because experts have automatized their behaviour, in contrast to novices, who do use intentional control.

[17] Thanks to John Michael for pressing me here.

[18] Lockie has an excellent summary of different executive functions and why they are voluntary. Lockie would probably agree with the simple argument but because of his sympathies for a form of doxastic voluntarism deny that direct doxastic attitude acquisition processes are everything that there is to cognition (Lockie, 2018: chapter 4).

To give just one more example that the links between executive functions and working memory are usually thought of as intentional actions, let's have a short look at how researchers describe the executive function of updating. Here is Miyake and colleagues:

> the essence of updating lies in the requirement to actively manipulate relevant information in working memory, rather than passively store information. (Miyake et al. 2000: 57)

But it is not only these researchers who clearly share the suspicion that working memory is strongly related to executive function, and that executive function is about active manipulation of content. In a similar vein, Rydell et al. provide a list:

> Updating, then, may tap into several important features underlying reduced performance [...] online computation, renewing information [...] incrementally during problem solving, determining if incoming information is needed [...], deciding what information should be retained, and focusing on the goal of solving the problem. (Rydell et al. 2014: 379)

In other words, updating in working memory consists in executive functions like deciding, focusing, and renewing, which are prototypical intentional mental actions. Obviously, this is just one example, but as far as I can see, this linking of working memory with executive function, which in turn is described in terms that sound very much like intentional actions, is far from untypical.

Furthermore, Evans and Stanovich offer us the characteristics of type two processing that they consider indispensable: decoupling and hypothetical thinking. They define the feature that makes humans unique as 'cognitive decoupling': the ability to distinguish supposition from belief and to aid rational choices by running thought experiments (Evans and Stanovich 2013). Yet suppositions are presumably made in inner speech and running through thought experiments are clearly intentional mental actions. So, in effect, Evans and Stanovich themselves seem to see the ability to perform intentional mental actions as the crucial reason for the importance of working memory: it seems as if premise one is very relevant for their accounts.[19]

---

[19] For an in-depth discussion of Evans and Stanovich that shows that their account of working memory is not separable from a personal level understanding of intentional executive control, see Coelho do Nascimento (in preparation).

Finally, some of the very prominent philosophers in the dual processing world explicitly endorse the idea that system two is action based. This is very obvious, for example, in Peter Carruthers' work, but also in the work of Keith Frankish. Carruthers writes:

> What is distinctive of the theory of System two reasoning presented here is that it is *action based*. According to this account, it is mentally rehearsed actions that initiate and sustain System two reasoning, thereby recruiting and utilizing the mechanisms that also subserve System one reasoning, as well as activating normative beliefs about proper reasoning, together with the stored schemata for skilled action sequences, and so forth.
>
> (Carruthers 2009: 122)

With this in mind, it might not come as a surprise that Carruthers is also very sympathetic to the claim advanced by the simple argument. In fact, in a number of publications Carruthers himself argues that belief formation is not something that happens in system two. But while Carruthers is clearly a natural ally for the conclusion of the simple argument, there is an important difference between Carruthers' position and the idea contained in the simple argument.

For Carruthers, the fact that our beliefs are formed unconsciously is an accident of architecture. In fact, in a paper he discusses the architecture of a system where intention formation would be conscious (Carruthers 2007). According to him, it would have been eminently possible for the architecture to have been different.[20] What the simple argument says, however, is that there is nothing contingent about the fact that beliefs are not voluntarily formed, but that this is simply a matter of logic once we accept that system two is constitutively action based and that doxastic involuntarism holds.

Frankish also endorses the idea that many of our beliefs are formed unconsciously. According to him, this belief formation is part of the functional profile of beliefs and can therefore not be changed by changing the architecture just slightly. Instead, Frankish holds that there is a specific

---

[20] According to Carruthers, a mental state becomes conscious when it is made available to the mindreading faculty, which allows thought not only about the content of the state but also about the occurrence of the state itself. Carruthers argues that percepts can be made available to the mindreading system, but belief formation processes contingently cannot (Carruthers 2007).

type of beliefs in the conscious mind which are formed voluntarily. We will come back to these conscious beliefs, which are very different from ordinary beliefs, in Chapter 3. For now, it is enough to note that according to Frankish, ordinary beliefs are also not formed in system two.

So where are we at the end of this section? It has become clear that premise one is not necessarily true for all two systems accounts, because the world of dual processing accounts is simply too heterogenous. However, it is nevertheless worth exploring the simple argument in more detail, because it is relevant for a very large number of accounts. On the one hand, there is the received view, i.e. the very many views that use the traditional lists of dichotomies to characterize the differences in processing of the two systems. While this view has come under sustained pressure, not only from wholesale critics of the dual processing project but also from some of its most vocal defenders like Evans and Stanovich, such views are still incredibly influential. A hard and fast move like the simple argument that makes it clear that voluntary control in system two and doxastic attitude processes can never be the same thing should be helpful here to avoid confusion.

On the other hand, looking at the work of authors like Evans and Stanovich it has become clear that their invocation of working memory does not prove that the simple argument is not relevant for them, because the way they use working memory relies heavily on executive functions and these in turn tend to be spelled out as intentional mental actions.

Finally, there are philosophers like Carruthers and Frankish who already agree with the conclusion that ordinary beliefs are never formed in system two, but who argue that this is for architectural contingent reasons. Here the simple argument can demonstrate that the real reason is actually the simple fact that a system that is constitutively formed of intentional actions cannot logically be a system that allows for the formation of doxastic attitudes, if doxastic involuntarism is accepted.[21]

With the simple argument established and its premises explained, in the next chapter I examine a number of clarifications and objections, before wrapping up the discussion of the incompatibility of doxastic agency in processes like judging that p and intentional agency. Once that is achieved,

---

[21] It should be added here that Frankish (2004) is a doxastic voluntarist, at least in relation to beliefs in what he calls the super-mind. We will look at Frankish's position in more detail in Chapter 3.

we can then turn to the critical step introduced in Chapter 4: why rejecting the idea that agentive cognition should be understood along the lines of Hieronymi's evaluative control will lead us straight to a necessity to embrace extended cognition, if we want to hold on to the possibility of agentive cognition at all.

3
Objections to the Simple Argument

1. What Are Beliefs?

The simple argument is at its most powerful when applied to a very traditional idealized concept of belief. In the ideal world of this tradition, one important feature of the belief concept, in contrast to other states, is that beliefs are inferentially promiscuous (see e.g., famously Evans 1982). Beliefs are always integrated in belief networks, and these networks are sensitive to evidence. For example, acquiring the belief that it is not raining will create a whole host of other beliefs that are dependent on it, like the belief that it is not necessary to take an umbrella when leaving the house, or that it might be a good day to hang out the washing. This picture also includes the idea that it is difficult to understand how one could hold contradictory beliefs at the same time: it seems hard to understand how one could believe that it is raining and that it is not raining at the same time. This picture also tends to characterize beliefs as digital. Either one has enough evidence to believe a certain proposition, or one does not.

Unfortunately, not all usages of the term beliefs map neatly on these ideas. According to many representationalists, a belief is simply a functional state of an organism that represents some state of affairs in the world (see e.g. Schwitzgebel's entry on belief in the *Stanford Encyclopaedia of Philosophy*). With a belief notion like this, some of the cherished elements of the traditional belief definition are much weakened, if not completely absent. Both Bayne and Pacherie (2005) and Schwitzgebel (2011), for example, rightly note that most of our beliefs are not fully inferentially promiscuous. On the basis of this, Bayne and Pacherie argue that even states such as monothematic delusions should be counted as beliefs, even though they are clearly not integrated with a large part of the network (Bayne and Pacherie use the example of patients who suffer from Capras delusion, which leads patients to believe that a loved one has been replaced by an impostor, but who nevertheless do not normally call the police, even though that would seem the rational thing to do if the loved one really were an impostor).

However, this is not to say that there are no connections between such accounts of the extension of the belief concept and the traditional picture. For example, Bayne and Pacherie argue that these delusions should still count as beliefs because while they are clearly not integrated with some parts of the network, they are clearly integrated with others (the patient avoids contact with the spouse, gets agitated in her presence, etc.). Thus, even in these cases, what makes the delusional state qualify as a belief is the fact that there is some integration in a network of beliefs.

That full inferential promiscuity is only an ideal is important here, because one critical argument of Hieronymi in Chapter 1 was that beliefs automatically follow the evidence, as it were. Her argument is that there is no room for tinkering (i.e. for intentional attitude directed actions) in belief acquisition because in the normal case, once the agent understands that she has evidence that makes her belief implausible she automatically changes that belief. She does not have to do anything extra to bring about the desired attitude change.

However, if delusions are beliefs, this seems not always the case. Worse still, it is not only delusions that seem to behave in an unruly way. The more general phenomenon of belief perseverance shows that resistance to evidence not only happens in full-blown delusions. Even someone like Richard Moran (2001: 85), who argues in his seminal monograph *Authority and Estrangement* that acquiring beliefs is all about weighing evidence in deliberation, accepts that not all beliefs are formed this way. Indeed, Moran discusses a nice example of the phenomenon of beliefs that seems resistant to evidence. On the therapist's couch, a patient might accept that from his behaviour it must be concluded that he believes that his mother has wronged him, despite the fact that the same patient would hold that there is no real evidence for this belief. In such a case, Moran says the agent is aware of this belief in what he calls the 'theoretical stance'. The agent accepts that there is theoretical psychological evidence for the presence of the belief in his psychology despite the fact that there is no good evidence for the content of the belief in question. Moran does not think that the existence of these beliefs is a problem for the general picture of belief acquisition in an account like Hieronymi's,[1] because he argues that most of our beliefs are not like that, but are acquired in what he calls the 'deliberative stance', in which beliefs are acquired by means of weighing the evidence.

---

[1] Perhaps unsurprisingly as Hieronymi develops her account in a Moranian framework.

Whether or not phenomena like belief perseverance are rare, they clearly show that it is not the case that people only have beliefs for which they have evidence. In her book *Believing Against the evidence: Agency and the Ethics of Belief*, Miriam McCormick (2014) has a whole collection of beliefs that do not seem to be evidence based. She argues that we can have beliefs even if the evidence is neutral, that we have inescapable framework beliefs, beliefs about loved ones, and religious beliefs—all of which do not always follow the evidence.

The problem for the simple argument with all these types of beliefs is that it is far less obvious that we cannot acquire them intentionally. Let us take the case of acquiring beliefs when the evidence is neutral. In such cases, it seems quite possible to decide to believe one of the options for practical purposes. For example: suppose that all you know is that if you do nothing a bomb will explode and kill you, but you do not know whether the red wire or the green wire is the one that will disable the bomb if you cut it. If the agent in this case suspends belief and because of that is unable to form an intention (because she might e.g. be paralysed by her fear that her action might kill her), she will be dead in 100% of all cases, whereas if she simply decides to hold either the belief that the red wire is the one that will save her or the belief that the green wire is the one that will save her, then her chances of survival are 50%. Luckily, it seems that humans are entirely capable of forming these beliefs despite the absence of evidence.

How should we interpret such cases? Let us recall the discussion of the previous chapter. When we are faced with a problem where the evidence is neutral, but we might have very good practical reasons to acquire the belief, it is nevertheless not possible to acquire the belief directly because of the no rewards principle. The formation of beliefs seems to require evidence and if there is no evidence, then the belief cannot be formed, even if the practical reasons are very good. We encountered a case like this in the Pascal scenario: we can take steps to manage our evaluative system, for example we can try to condition ourselves into acquiring the belief, although this is often impractical. And, while it is true that we can change our beliefs in this way over time, it is close to impossible to do it quickly, and often we do not have the luxury of being able to wait. In the bomb case it is no good that it is possible to condition oneself to believe that it is the red wire and so reduce my risk of death from 100% to 50%. It is not good enough, because in all likelihood the conditioning process will be slow and the bomb might well go off before one has had time to acquire the belief.

60 THE TINKERING MIND

Nonetheless, we are not helpless in such situations, because instead of managerially acquiring a belief, we can simply accept that it is better to act as if one believed that one of the two wires is the right one. This is indeed something that one can even do voluntarily, but in such cases, one does not acquire the belief, but a different type of mental state which is referred to as 'acceptance'. Acceptances are strange beasts, which are not very far away from beliefs, but they are voluntarily controlled, and they deserve further discussion in section 2, below.

2. Acceptance

The mental act of acceptance is special, because it has characteristics that make it seem belief-like, while at the same time being something that we can do intentionally. Unfortunately, the term has at least two different meanings, as pointed out by Jonathan Cohen in his seminal article *Belief and Acceptance* on the issue (Cohen 1989). Acceptance can be understood to be rather similar to a supposition, i.e. it can refer to the intentional holding of a proposition in mind as if it were true, even if one is not convinced that it really is.[2] Doing so allows the agent to use the accepted proposition in further mental operations—for example, the agent can work out the logical implications of a proposition being true. This is clearly what would happen in our bomb scenario. The agent knows that it is much better to hold one of the two beliefs rather than suspending judgment. Hence, she simply decides to behave the way she would if she really did hold one of the two beliefs, despite the fact that it is perfectly obvious to her that she does not really believe that it is more likely that the red wire will disarm the bomb rather than the green one.

Cohen himself favours a different and stronger notion of acceptance, in which acceptance requires that the agent adopts a policy to treat the accepted proposition as true. On this understanding, the agent commits herself to treating the accepted proposition as true in her thinking and behaviour. Obviously, to distinguish this sense of acceptance from belief, it

---

[2] Note that the intentional holding in mind of the proposition is not the same thing as the metacognitive judgment that this is the appropriate thing to do. As discussed in the section on managerial control, the latter is evaluative and not intentional. If one were to understand acceptance as the metacognitive judgment, it would cease to be intentional.

is important to note that just because the agent treats the proposition as true, this does still not mean that the agent really believes that it is true.

It is very important to keep these two different senses of acceptance separate when thinking about acceptance and managerial actions. Acceptance as another word for supposition is a very powerful tool of the managerial armoury, but it is very clearly just that: an intentional action that allows one to perform other mental operations. In the second sense, on the other hand, acceptance appears to be much closer to a belief than to an intentional action.[3] If an agent has the policy to treat a proposition as true and if policy rules their behaviour, then this kind of acceptance performs a fair number of the jobs that a belief is supposed to perform. Nevertheless, it does not fall under the no rewards principle, as agents are able to accept a proposition for practical considerations that are independent of its truth-value. Thus, it seems that acceptance so understood might be a cognitive attitude over which we have full intentional control.

To understand this in more depth, it is necessary to take a closer look at what happens when one forms the policy to treat a proposition as true. In such cases, the agent first performs a managerial action. This action will take the form of something like an inner speech act: 'let's treat proposition p as if it was true from now on'. Ideally, doing so will lead to the agent treating the proposition p as true from now on, but why does this happen? Presumably, it happens because the agent forms a metacognitive belief that having this policy is the best thing to do under the circumstances, and obviously this metacognitive judgment is not under the voluntary control of the agent, but follows the evidence and thereby the no rewards principle.

In this sense, acceptance is indeed an attitude. Acceptance is a managerial intention to treat the target proposition as true. The confusion arises if we think that because an agent can intentionally treat a proposition as true that the intention to do so also can be formed intentionally. However, to draw this conclusion would be simply wrong: forming the intention is an evaluative act, not an intentional act. It is interesting because it is a metacognitive evaluative act, but that does not make it intentional. The no rewards principle holds.

Therefore, it is not possible to form the intention to accept a proposition intentionally, and it is also not possible to make it the case that an

---

[3] In fact, Keith Frankish thinks that acceptance in this sense is a form of belief in system two, which he calls 'the supermind' (Frankish 2004). We will discuss Frankish position on this in the next section.

acceptance will lead to a belief intentionally. Hence, as long as the unintentionally formed intention to treat a proposition as true is intact, it can lead to intentional actions that ensure that the proposition is treated as true. However, this will only work as long as this intention is ensuring the continued exercise of effort, because no dispositional belief in the truth of the proposition exists. It is possible that a dispositional belief will be formed, but if that happens, it will not be an intentional act. Therefore, the no rewards principle holds also in this case.

To put it another way: acceptances are fascinating but they are not beliefs. To use McCormick's own example of a parent who does not want to believe that her son is a drug dealer: there is a difference between thinking (a) he might well be a drug dealer, but it is impossible to be sure and it is better to behave as if he were not, and (b) he might well be a drug dealer, but I will believe that he is not. The first strategy seems eminently sensible while the second seems distinctly odd.

3. Two Types of Belief?

Another possible route to question the claim that all beliefs are formed involuntarily is to argue that there might be different types of beliefs. This is exactly what Keith Frankish proposes (Frankish 2007b). His suggestion is of particular interest in the context of this book, because Frankish takes the simple argument head on. As one of the main proponents of dual processing accounts, Frankish argues that system two beliefs can be formed in a voluntary manner. Frankish accepts that doxastic involuntarism is true for system one beliefs, but claims that system two has its own type of beliefs and that those are voluntary. In this way, Frankish can easily accept that all system two processing is voluntary, and he can accept that doxastic involuntarism is true for system one beliefs. However, the simple argument still doesn't follow, because at the same time, he contends that system two beliefs can be formed voluntarily.

What are these system two beliefs that according to Frankish can be formed voluntarily? Frankish argues that system two beliefs are in their nature quite similar to acceptances. However, he acknowledges that not all acceptances can be beliefs, because it is easily possible to accept a proposition without believing it. The difference between what Frankish calls non-doxastic acceptances, which are just acceptances, and doxastic acceptances, which he regards as equivalent to system two beliefs, is that non-doxastic acceptances are never used as premises in arguments where the purpose of the argument is finding out the truth.[4] In his example, an agent might have agreed with his therapist to have a policy to treat himself as a confident and capable person in all contexts, despite not believing it. According to Frankish, the agent would not believe that he is capable and confident, because in contexts where truth is the overriding criterion, there might be for example high penalties for getting it wrong; in such cases, the agent would not use his acceptance as a premise in his deliberation.

Frankish's distinction is elegant and subtle, but there is a simple reason why it does not provide a threat for the simple argument. Frankish thinks of system two beliefs as a subclass of acceptances and as we already have seen in the last section, acceptances understood as policies do not undermine the simple argument, because they are simply meta-cognitive beliefs, and the acquisition of these metacognitive beliefs is clearly non-voluntary. Frankish seems to mix together acceptances as intentional actions, which are inner speech acts, with acceptances as policies. The former are indeed voluntary, but they can never be beliefs. The latter are metacognitive beliefs and as such do fall under the no rewards principle. Doxastic involuntarism still holds for system two!

4. Motivated Reasoning

The last section dealt with the objection that there might be situations where the evidence is neutral where we can still form beliefs, and that in these situations we can do so voluntarily. As the section showed, in these situations we do not form beliefs but acceptances and even Cohen's stronger notion of acceptance as policy did not give us a way to bypass the no rewards principle, because these policies clearly are metacognitive beliefs formed in the usual involuntary way.

However, neutral evidence was only one of the cases that seemed worrying for the kind of account of belief that the simple argument

---

[4] Frankish rejects the wider traditional distinction between beliefs and acceptances that acceptances are context sensitive, while beliefs are not, because believing acceptances in certain contexts means that one does not believe what one otherwise believes in these contexts. If this were true, then beliefs would also have to be context sensitive. For example, the lawyer who accepts that her client is innocent in a professional context might not believe it in a private context, but if it were a belief, it would have to be constant relative to context. In this case, however, the belief clearly is not constant, because for professional purposes she does accept the innocence of the client.

operates on: there is also the problem that humans seem to be perfectly capable of holding two inconsistent beliefs at the same time. In fact, the phenomenon of motivated reasoning is a very well-studied area in the empirical literature. If belief formation is always aiming at truth, how can it be possible that there are many cases where agents hold p and not p at the same time?

This is a serious worry, as there clearly are many cases like this. For example, the Moran case discussed earlier, in which the agent asserts that he has no reasons to believe that his mother has wronged him, but he accepts that he must believe that she did, because his behaviour clearly indicates that he does hold the belief. Importantly in this case, there are a number of ways in which one could understand the belief that the agent only knows of in the psychological stance. It could be the case that this belief is a gut feeling that rightly identifies that his mother has wronged him, and he simply is not able to give reasons for why that is.

Alternatively, the belief could have been formed for reasons that are not aiming at truth. For example, it might be the case that he needs this belief in order to blame her for his own failings. Only this second case looks like a problem for evidentialist accounts of belief. This is because in the first case, the belief formed by the gut feeling clearly is aiming, perhaps even succeeding, in getting facts about the world right. The conflicting beliefs arise because the agent cannot easily reconcile the two different tools he has at his disposal to make sense of the world.

The second case is more worrying for evidentialist accounts of belief because it seems to suggest that we sometimes form beliefs for practical reasons that are not aimed at truth. However, such self-deceptive beliefs seem clearly parasitic on normal belief formation: they can serve their practical purpose only by piggybacking on the rest of the belief network which does aim at truth. Keith Frankish (2007b: 128) is not convinced by this objection and argues that it is possible that a demon might directly insert a belief into our system which might well escape detection for a long period. Therefore, truth-related considerations cannot be necessary for belief acquisition. That Frankish resorts to a reference to a demon already gives an indication of how difficult it is to find potential cases, but if the demon case were to succeed, then this would still be good enough to show that truth-related considerations are not a necessary condition for belief acquisition. However, the example is not really convincing. As discussed in Chapter 2, for such implanted states to plausibly count as beliefs of the system there needs to be at least some integration with the network (however fragmented) and this integration would obviously involve truth-related considerations.

5. Do Unruly Beliefs Pose a Threat for the Simple Argument?

The previous sections demonstrated that beliefs can look quite different from the idealized traditional version. But despite the fact that not all beliefs might be fully integrated in a coherent belief network, and despite the fact that there are many interesting belief-like states that can be voluntarily acquired, doxastic involuntarism and with it premise two stood firm.

At the same time, it clearly cannot be denied that there are many controversies around the nature of beliefs and the way they are acquired both in philosophy and the cognitive sciences. Luckily, thus far we have been far more conservative than we need to be for our argument. Doxastic involuntarism is, as we have seen, plausible for all beliefs, including even the most difficult cases. Yet for the substance of the argument to work, a much weaker premise is sufficient. This is because the kind of beliefs discussed in the previous section are very clearly not the ones that dual processing theorists have in mind when they discuss how beliefs are formed in system two. System two beliefs are clearly not of the sort discussed when trying to find beliefs that might not be truth apt. They are not like delusions or biases, and system two also does not use demons.

Given that, for the simple argument premise two* would do the job:

> Doxastic attitude formation processes in rational deliberation are never intentional.

Dual processing theorists believe that system two beliefs are the result of deliberation, so in order to avoid the simple argument, it does not really matter if it turns out that some unconscious beliefs are not evidence sensitive. The beliefs that are relevant for our purposes are not ones that we can discover by observing our own psychology in the same way we would observe somebody else's psychology (by checking under the hood, in Moran's apt phrase), but are beliefs that are the result of our rational deliberation. Because of this, they are the explicit manifestation of our rational mind. It might be helpful here to stress again that Moran does believe that we have a form of agency in acquiring belief this way, but he makes it very clear that this rational agency is very different from ordinary agency, which he describes as 'like reaching for a glass' (Moran 2001: 114).[5] The main point of contention behind the simple argument is that it is often not made clear enough that beliefs acquired in deliberation are never directly voluntarily acquired, and for that point it is simply not relevant exactly what the nature of beliefs in the unconscious is, because nobody would want to argue that these unruly system one beliefs are acquired in an intentional way.[6]

6. Spinozean Accounts of Belief Acquisition

One seemingly elegant and simple solution to accommodate the simple argument into a dual processing framework comes from the work of Eric Mandelbaum (2014). According to his account, it is true that belief acquisition processes are never voluntary, because we automatically believe whatever we entertain. Mandelbaum argues that this Spinozean account of belief acquisition is better supported by the empirical evidence than what he refers to as 'the Cartesian alternative', according to which we first entertain propositions before our inner eye without endorsing them as true and then actively accept or reject them. Mandelbaum for example cites evidence that seems to demonstrate that in a memory experiment subjects under cognitive load will encode sentences as true despite being told that they are false, but conversely, will not encode sentences they are told are true as false ones.[7] Asymmetries like this lead Mandelbaum to argue that the cognitive system automatically believes all propositions it entertains. Obviously, these beliefs might well be very fleeting and might be rejected by the system within seconds, but the default of the system is to believe rather than to test. To make this seemingly very radical proposal plausible, Mandelbaum compares belief acquisition with perception. In the perception case it seems not at all implausible that under normal circumstances we simply believe what we perceive and need to effortfully reject false beliefs formed on the basis of perceptual error. All that Mandelbaum argues is that this is true not only for perception but also for the acquisition of all other beliefs.

---

[5] As discussed in Chapter 2, section 5.
[6] It is obviously possible to reject the Moran picture and to understand the indirect bringing about as part of the belief acquisition processes, but this in turn does have dramatic metaphysical consequences—as we will see in Chapters 4 and 5.
[7] Gilbert, D., D. Krull, and M. Malone (1990).

According to Mandelbaum, what we do have voluntary control over is the rejection process. Mandelbaum himself is sceptical about dual processing accounts,[8] but one could easily imagine a dual processing variation of his account. This account could hold that belief acquisition processes happen in system one and active rejection in system two. The simple argument would work for such accounts, but for very unexpected reasons. On such a view, there are no belief acquisition processes in system two, because system two is about the effortful voluntary rejection of automatically acquired system one beliefs that turn out to be false.

Unfortunately, however, this approach does not really solve the puzzle provided by the simple argument, because Mandelbaum's account is not compatible with doxastic involuntarism in the case of rejection. While Mandelbaum argues that 'rejecting is an effortful mental action',[9] he is silent about how rejection processes evaluate whether or not it is appropriate to reject a proposition. And obviously, it is exactly at this point that the doxastic involuntarist will insist that this evaluation cannot be a voluntary action. Thus, Mandelbaum's Spinozean account reduces the potential realm of active belief acquisition to the acquisition of beliefs by negation of passively acquired beliefs, but he does not address the issue of how to think about the role of intentional actions in rejection. On this picture, the role of intentional agency for active cognition remains unclear. Despite their elegance and initial promise for our question, Spinozean accounts do not provide a solution to the puzzle of the simple argument.

7. Deliberation and Skill

The most promising route to show that deliberation is an intentional action makes use of the thought that deliberation might be something like a skilled action, see for example, Wayne Wu (2013). Wu makes this point by first thinking about the structure of intentional actions in general. He argues that an action can be agentially controlled and automatic at the same time, because it can be controlled with regard to some features, but automatic

---

[8] Even though he remarks that on a superficial level his account looks not dissimilar to Frankish.

[9] He also says that rejection is a sub-personal process and that understanding is a mental act, and that mental acts can occur unconsciously. Unfortunately, he does not elaborate here, but his terminology clearly does not map very well on the one used here. Fortunately, this does not interfere with the general point discussed in the text (Mandelbaum 2007b: 61).

with regard to others. For example, when running an agent might intentionally run at a speed of under 5 minutes per kilometre, but the exact movements of the legs will be automatic. On Wu's account, an agent's behaviour is only passive when it is automatic under all descriptions.

Wu then applies this thought to the mental action of deliberation. It is undeniable that deliberation contains many elements that are straightforwardly intentionally controlled. One can direct one's attention, rehearse an argument in inner speech, and so on. The agent engages in these intentionally controlled activities because deliberation often leads to the solution of a specific problem, such as whether p is the case. At the end of such a deliberation, the agent will hopefully reach a judgment whether or not p. Wu accepts that the actual judgment is automatic and not under intentional control, but he argues that the judgment is part of the intentional action of deliberating about the question whether or not p and that as such, the judgment is not passive but under agentive control.

Is this a problem for premise two of our target argument? Not at all—in fact, it simply helps us to understand the premise better. The premise does not state that deliberation cannot be an intentional action, but insists that *the process that directly leads to the acquisition of a doxastic attitude is never intentional.*

The claim that deliberation can be understood as an intentional action only becomes problematic for premise two if we make it considerably stronger. We can find this stronger claim, for example in the work of Joshua Shepherd (2015). Shepherd also has an argument that discusses the intentionality of mental actions using an analogy to skilled bodily actions, arguing that decisions are intentional actions in an analogous way to skilled bodily actions. Shepherd writes:

> Analogously [to a skilled bodily action], an intention formation is produced when attention-mediated (perceptual or cognitive) feedback causes an adjustment in how the intention to decide what to do guides the sequencing of various mental operations, or in the generation of the mental operation of intention formation that fills in the details of the original intention's plan. (Shepherd 2015: 347)

Shepherd explicitly wants to take a stronger line than Wu, because he feels that Wu's acceptance that judgments and decisions are automatic means that he holds a non-actional view, which he wants to oppose. Shepherd only discusses intentions and not judgments. Nonetheless, as we will see, the argument is instructive, because an analogous argument can be constructed for judgments.[10]

But first, let us unpack the claim in the quote: according to Shepherd, the mental agent has the intention to decide, and because of that, intentionally begins an episode of deliberative activity. In so doing, she might rehearse the argument, direct her attention to relevant evidence, and so on. Because of these intentional actions, she will receive attention-mediated perceptual or cognitive feedback. She will have the relevant features of the problem before her inner mental eye, and this feedback will change the way in which the intention guides the sequencing of mental operations.

The intentional activity of deliberating might cause an adjustment to the original intention to decide and make the agent attentionally attuned to the right moment to engage in the intentional action of terminating deliberation and thereby form an intention at a particular moment. The right moment here is the moment when the agent, because of her attentional attunement, recognizes an appropriate indication to terminate deliberation and form the intention. According to Shepherd, therefore, deliberation is a skilled intentional mental activity, the exercise of which leads to a situation where the agent intentionally starts and subsequently terminates deliberation, because it is appropriate to do so.

Shepherd discusses this for the case of intentions, but the characterization of deliberation lends itself very much to describe a case where the agent deliberates in order to come to a judgment. Just as in the intention case, the agent engages in the skilled activity of deliberation because of the intention to come to a judgment. Just as in the intention case, deliberation will lead to an attentional attunement that will allow the agent to terminate deliberation intentionally when there is an appropriate indication that now is the moment to form a judgment.

---

[10] Shepherd himself would not want to do this. In his 2018 paper, he repeats the argument discussed here for the possibility of voluntary intention acquisition, but argues that this move would not work for belief acquisition, because the functional profile of beliefs is different to intentions. He argues that while beliefs aim at truth, intentions aim at successful action and are therefore all about initiating and sustaining actions. If intentions are understood as essentially about initiating and sustaining actions then that seems plausible, but it seems to me that the more plausible understanding of intention that seems to be implicit in Shepherd's 2015 paper discussed above understands intentions as practical evaluative judgments about what would be the best thing to do. If we understand them in this way, then intentions do fall under the no rewards principle. However, in Chapter 7 I discuss the notion of choice as an intentional action as introduced by Holton. Choices in Holton's sense have a shepherding function that is quite similar to Shepherd's account of intention formation here.

Much of this description sounds very plausible. It seems correct to say that deliberation does lead to an attentional attunement, and it seems also phenomenologically correct to say that we can start and terminate deliberation at will. But what follows from that?

To explore this further, let's consider the question of whether it really is true that the agent intentionally terminates deliberation and that this action is what causes a specific judgment? If we want to answer in the affirmative here, it seems we need to imagine a scenario where the intentional action of stopping to deliberate will lead to a judgment that either *p* or not *p* and that it is up to the agent which way that judgment goes. Let's call this the first scenario. This scenario does sound implausible though, because it seems in this case that we would need to violate the no rewards principle in order to make it possible for the agent to decide at will which way the judgment goes.

It seems much more likely that something like this second scenario is what happens: the agent comes to a decision that makes it appropriate to terminate deliberation now, and because of that, intentionally refrains from further engaging in the intentional activities that are part of deliberation. This second scenario respects the phenomenological intuition that we can terminate deliberation at will, but insists that the decision-making is the last rational stage of deliberation, even though it comes before the last intentional stage of deliberation, namely, the inhibition of further intentional deliberation activities. According to this scenario, a decision does not end deliberation, because the deliberation is ended by means of an intentional action that the agent engages in because of the non-voluntary decision to end deliberation now.

This intentional inhibition of further deliberation is a perfect example of managerial control. It is an intentional shepherding action that controls the context in which to use evaluative resources. As with all managerial actions, it is dependent on a prior non-voluntary evaluation: namely, the decision to stop deliberating now. The second scenario can also explain why we ordinarily talk about decisions concluding deliberations, because in terms of the *cognitive* work that is exactly what they do. For this reason, the second scenario can explain the phenomenology but at the same time, it can remain true to the no rewards principle.

This is a very powerful argument in favour of the second scenario, because the first scenario has a real problem here. The obvious worry for the first scenario comes with the word 'appropriate'. How does the agent know when it is appropriate? This is clearly an evaluative process, and it is clearly not up to the agent to decide whether or not it is appropriate to terminate deliberation. As before, the recognition follows the evidence and the no reward principle holds. The agent cannot decide that it is not appropriate, if the evidence leads her the other way.

One might say that this is not true, because the agent will have to be attentionally attuned to the situation and attentional processes clearly are intentional.[11] But even if it were true that intentionally attending to a stimulus is a necessary condition in order to recognize it as appropriate, it is still the case that this recognition is evaluative. It is still the case that the attentional attunement is nothing more than an intentional mental shepherding[12] process that prepares the ground so that the recognition can take place. The recognition that leads to the decision that it is appropriate to terminate deliberation is evaluative and follows the no rewards principle.[13]

This allows us now to deal with Shepherd's concluding argument. He writes:

> If they [non voluntarists about decisions] can countenance deliberative activity as (sometimes) a matter of intentional action, then they need a special reason to deny that events of intention formation deserve the same treatment. (Shepherd 2015: 349)

This distinction between managerial and evaluative control gives us exactly the reason for the special treatment of intention formation. Deliberative activity is clearly a hybrid of managerial and evaluative activity. Because of this, it is obviously true that deliberation does contain some intentional action, but the non-voluntarist will insist that all the steps that consist of a judgment or a decision are evaluative and therefore non-intentional.

---

[11] The first thing to be noted here is that it is not quite as obvious as Shepherd makes out that attention is always intentionally controlled. Top-down attention control is indeed clearly an intentional action, but it is a lot less obvious that bottom-up attention-grabbing effects are. Le Pelley et al. (2015) have conducted e.g., an excellent study showing that attention capture can even be directly in conflict with behavioural goals.

[12] To use Galen Strawson's (2003) apt term for this.

[13] Here it does not matter whether the recognition of appropriateness happens to be a recognition of having sufficient evidence for the proposition in question, or whether it is simply the recognition that it would not be practical to deliberate any further. In the latter case, it is true that there is no new evidence for the proposition, and yet something changes in the epistemic position of the agent. However, what brings about this change is still an evaluative and not an intentional act, and follows the no rewards principle. Thanks to Josh Shepherd for pressing this point.

To sum up: the no rewards principle is very intuitive and makes doxastic involuntarism convincing. Acquiring doxastic attitudes simply is not something over which we have control in the same way that we control moving our limbs. Obviously, it is true that intentional actions do often make important causal contributions to prepare the acquisition of doxastic attitudes (i.e. managerial or manipulative control), but the actual acquiring is done non-intentionally. This is also true in deliberation, which clearly does contain many important intentional elements, but where it also is true that actual belief acquisition follows the no rewards principle and is non-voluntary. This remains true even if intentional and non-intentional elements are intricately meshed, because we might think of deliberation as a skilled activity.[14]

8. The Lessons from the Simple Argument?

As we have seen in the previous two chapters, there are very good reasons to think that doxastic attitude formation processes are never intentional, while system two processing is always intentional. This gives us the surprising result that judgments and decisions (if intentions are understood as doxastic attitudes) logically cannot be system two processes.

However, even though it seems clear that intentional system two processes cannot be doxastic attitude acquisition processes, it is important to remind ourselves how powerful the indirect ways in which intentional processes do contribute to belief acquisition are in order to be clear about the scope of the claim of the argument. Managerial actions in Hieronymi's helpful terminology are clearly enormously powerful: management allows the agent to direct their attention to a specific problem; it allows them to inhibit responses or to rehearse an argument mentally; or finally, to accept a proposition as true and to use it in further argument.

In fact, the many mental actions that fall under the heading managerial are very much the ones that two systems proponents often use when they describe typical system two processes. This might lead to the suspicion that

---

[14] This book is in no way critical of the idea that deliberation could be like a skill. In fact, the book very much sympathizes with recent work about skills that emphasizes how intertwined cognitive and automatic elements are in skilled actions (Fridland 2014; Christensen et al. 2016). All that follows from the argument in this book is that we need to undertake a careful rethinking of what we mean when we use the dichotomy automatic and cognitive—because if doxastic involuntarism is correct, then cognitive and intentional do not and cannot go together.

perhaps there is simply a misunderstanding here. Perhaps two systems thinkers never meant that judgments are intentional, but simply that system two is characterized by the presence of managerial processes. Perhaps the simple argument really is making a mountain out of a molehill? It sounds as if it says something radical about system two processing, but perhaps all that people in the two systems literature ever wanted to claim was that intentional system two processes are crucially important for the formation of certain beliefs. Perhaps nobody ever wanted to claim that the last step in a belief formation process is under intentional control. Intentionality talk might well just refer to the onset and maintenance of a psychological process, and not to its outcome.

Mandelbaum has a neat clarification on what might be meant by the term 'automatic' when it is used in contrast with 'controlled' in the literature. He argues that an automatic process can be understood either as a ballistic process, i.e. one that cannot be interrupted once started, or as mandatory, i.e. the process is always triggered if the relevant stimulus is present. Mandelbaum describes processes that are not mandatory as 'effortful' (see Mandelbaum 2015). It seems very plausible to think that perhaps proponents of dual processing are only talking about the difference between ballistic and mandatory processes on the one hand and controlled processes on the other.

After all, even though most dual process theories state that the processes of system two operate intentionally, they also explicitly make the claim that system two is governed by the rules of logic. This clearly implies limitations to the intentionality of outcomes of doxastic attitude acquisition processes, but it does allow for the intentional onset and maintenance of these processes.

The best response to this point seems to be what Galen Strawson says at the beginning of his article 'Mental Ballistics or the Involuntariness of Spontaneity' (2003), which is as influential as it is controversial, because in it Strawson claims that thinking never is an action. Right at the beginning of this article, he writes about the claim that thinking is never active, which many people clearly find very counterintuitive to say the least:

> Perhaps the point is obvious and no one disagrees with it, but it may be worth an airing.   (Strawson 2003: 227ff)

In the same way, I would very much agree that it does seem obvious that a process that is in line with the rules of logic cannot at the same time be a process where the outcome is under the intentional control of the agent. However, while it may be right to claim that this should be obvious, there are a number of consequences of abiding by the strictures of the simple argument that at least have not been obviously accepted in the literature, so it might be worth airing them here.

The first consequence of the simple argument is that the dual processing literature is in need of urgent clarification: if everybody thinks that it is obviously right that intentional processes are not belief acquisition processes, this means either that there are non-intentionally controlled processes in system two or that doxastic attitude acquisition processes are not system two processes. The current literature is not clear on this, but it is really quite important that some clarity is established on this point in future.

At this juncture, it is important to remind the reader about a few moves that are not available to the dual process theorist. First, it is not good enough to point to working memory as a form of control that does not seem to require the language of intentional action. As discussed at length in Chapter 2, the notions of working memory and executive function are heavily interwoven, and both very much rely on intentional mental actions such as attention shifts and inhibition. The control involved here is about processes being not ballistic and not mandatory, which is a very good re-description of processes under intentional control.

So far, there is no account in the literature that delivers a clear account of system two processes that explicitly eschews personal level notions like inhibition or top-down attention shifts. Moreover, it is not obvious that this is where dual process theorists would want to go, because there are many thinkers in the tradition who might well be comfortable with the idea that belief formation processes are not ever system two (famously in the work of Carruthers 2011, but probably also in the work of Mercier and Sperber 2017, or Levy 2014).

A second point that seems to be important is highly relevant to an account like the one by Peter Carruthers. The simple argument is very much ammunition for his account: but on the other hand, it quite dramatically changes the rationale for holding it. Carruthers believes that the reason that judgments are system one is a contingent fact of mental architecture, but if the simple argument is right and if system two processing, as Carruthers holds, is essentially active, then this is not about architecture, but follows conceptually from the simple argument.

Another way to avoid having to take the simple argument into account would be to take the above as an argument that proves that dual process theories must be wrong. As already discussed in the section on dual systems, the jury is still out on whether dual systems accounts are indeed helpful in understanding human cognition. It is certainly possible to use the previous chapters as arrows in the armoury of the dual systems critique. However, making this move has a snag.

The simple argument is framed in terms of dual processing accounts, but its key message is not exclusively a two systems problem. Intentional control of our thinking not only plays a prominent role in dual processing theories. Notions like cognitive control and executive function do not only exist in dual processing accounts, and the same argument would apply to them, too. If doxastic involuntarism is true, then judgments or decisions cannot be described in the language of cognitive control or executive function. So, while it is true that dual systems accounts rely more heavily on the notion of intentional control and effort than many others, it is also true that the problem of the intuitive importance of intentional action for cognitive processes like judging and deciding does not go away if we give up on such accounts.

Therefore, the most important and much more general point of the simple argument is that it forces any theorist to clarify their position on the nature of rationality and cognition and its relationship to agency.

Let us unpack this a little by looking first at a mistake that it might be very tempting to make at this juncture: one natural reaction to the simple argument could well be to argue that dual processing theorists understand the notion of control for system two judgments to be more akin to the idea of evaluative control as defined by Hieronymi. This could be tempting, because evaluative control is defined as rational control and it is very popular to associate system two with both agency and a specific form of rationality. The problem with this approach is that evaluative control is explicitly not intentional control. *A fortiori*, using intentional control in the process of acquiring new doxastic states is alienating the rational agent from her thinking, according to proponents of evaluative control like Moran and Hieronymi. As discussed in the case of Pascal (Chapter 2), if an agent brings it about intentionally that they acquire a doxastic attitude, then that attitude does not integrate with the rational belief network. It is not an expression of the rational understanding the agent has of the world and remains alien to the agent. It is like the kind of belief Moran discusses in the psychiatrist case: the agent can acknowledge its existence, but does not have the special authority over it that we seem to have over our normal beliefs.

Therefore, in short, it is not possible to simply combine evaluative and intentional control. This brings us back to the alternative discussed above: to accept that intentional control is not evaluative control, but that it is nevertheless crucial in bringing about different forms of beliefs. The problem with this move is that once we accept the distinction between the different forms of control, it might well still be true that intentional actions are important causal antecedents of cognitive events proper, but the only control that is *directly* responsible for doxastic attitude acquisition is evaluative control. All across the spectrum of mental actions there is agreement that thinking, the production of new content (Strawson), and rationality (Moran, Hieronymi) are all associated with evaluative control and not with managerial control. If we accept the distinction between the different forms of control, then no intentional mental process ever gets to be a constitutive part of cognition understood as the direct acquisition of new doxastic attitudes.

Nonetheless, an objector from the cognitive sciences can simply hold out and ask the question: so what? It might be the case that in philosophy, people would want to define rational acts in a certain way, but for the cognitive sciences this is simply impractical. When we study real-life psychological creatures nobody cares about these old chestnuts and we simply define things differently.

Indeed, on some level, it certainly seems right to say that arguments should not just be about terms. If people in epistemology and cognitive science simply mean something different when they use the term 'rational act', then that is not a major disagreement.

In this case, however, it is at least not clear that this really is just a terminological issue. Arguing that the intentional manipulation of the mind in the right kind of way simply is what cognitive scientists mean by a rational act has consequences that are surprisingly radical. As the next chapter will show, rejecting the idea that only evaluative agency is rational agency and claiming that intentional mental actions can literally be part of the cognitive process makes it very hard to resist the move that intentional physical actions can also be literally part of the cognitive process: in other words, the position entails accepting that cognition literally can extend into the environment.

The deep message of the simple argument is, therefore: there are only two very different options that one has in characterizing the relationship between agency and rationality. Either one accepts doxastic involuntarism and accepts thereby that intentional actions are never constitutive parts of rational agency. Alternatively, one can argue that cognition in cognitive science needs to be understood as something more than the process that directly leads to the acquisition of doxastic attitudes, because in actual cognitive systems intentional behaviour does play such a crucial role. But then, it becomes very difficult to resist the move that physical actions could also literally be part of cognition.

The next chapter will aim to unpack this seemingly radical claim. It will begin by looking at an argument by Yair Levy that makes a very strong case against drawing any deep distinctions between physical and mental actions (Levy 2019). Levy, however, does not distinguish between evaluative and managerial mental agency. Once the distinction is introduced, it turns out that his argument now suggests that there is no deep functional difference between managerial mental actions and physical actions, but that evaluative agency is very different and does not extend.

There are good reasons to be sympathetic to the extended mind project, so the conclusion of the book is not against holding a position that understands intentional actions as potential part of the cognitive process. Rather, what the book objects to is the claim that intentional mental agency is part of the reflective process and therefore very different from physical intentional actions, which are only tinkering with or manipulation of the mind. The simple argument insists that if intentional mental actions can be a constitutive part of cognition, then physical tinkerings also can be. If intentional actions ever are cognitive, then our minds are tinkering minds.

4
Extending and Shrinking Agents

1. Levy's Argument

In his 2019 article 'What Is a Mental Action' Yair Levy argues that the doctrine of the extended mind can help to understand the nature of mental actions better (Levy 2019). More specifically, Levy argues that understanding the mind as extended can be used to defend the idea that mental actions are simply like physical actions.

However, Levy does not distinguish between evaluative and managerial mental agency (Hieronymi 2009). Once this distinction is applied, his argument leads to some surprising consequences that Levy does not envisage. Although Levy is indeed right to claim that there is no functional difference between purely internal and environment-involving *managerial* mental actions, it is difficult to contend that there could be *evaluative* mental agency that is environment-involving, because it is about the direct formation of occurrent states, and even many defenders of the extended mind do not think that conscious mental processes extend.

We should note at this point that Levy himself stresses that his argument is about mental actions but says nothing about the truth or falsity of the doctrine of extended cognition.[1] However, once we amend the Levy argument to include the distinction between different types of mental agency, a choice is forced on us on how we can understand cognition coherently. Either we stick to the traditional view that physical intentional actions are not ever constitutive parts of cognition, but then we have to accept that the same is true for internal managerial actions, or we insist that managerial mental actions are cognitive, but that forces us to accept that cognition literally extends into the environment, because physical intentional actions fulfil the same functional role as managerial mental actions within the skull.

---

[1] The text gives conflicting evidence on this issue. In footnote 11 Levy asserts that he is not focusing on cognition but just action, but on page 984 Levy asserts that agential cognition extends.

To understand this point in depth, it is necessary to have a look at this argument in a bit more detail, beginning with a reconstruction of Levy's argument from the extended mind. Andy Clark and Dave Chalmers (1998) argue in their seminal paper that we should accept the principle that cognition literally loops into the environment in those cases where the environment plays a role that we would not hesitate to call cognitive if it had taken place within the skull. They contend that not doing so simply seems to amount to an unjustified bias against processes outside the skull. They call this the 'parity principle'.

In their most famous example, Otto, who suffers from mild Alzheimer's disease, finds his way to the MoMA by checking his trusted notebook that he always carries with him, because he cannot rely on his biological memory. Clark and Chalmers argue that this notebook fulfils for Otto exactly the same function as a biological memory trace. The mere fact that Otto has to access the trace outside his skull seems functionally irrelevant. Clark and Chalmers argue that Otto has a dispositional belief about the location of the MoMA because of the information stored in his notebook in the same way that other people have a dispositional belief because of a biological memory trace. In this way, the information in the notebook literally becomes part of Otto's belief and the vehicle of that belief extends into the environment.

This argument for the extended mind is as celebrated as it is controversial. Apart from the fact that it is highly counterintuitive to think of a notebook as a constitutive part of somebody's mind, there are a number of philosophical worries about the plausibility of the claim. Probably the most famous worry is the one about so-called 'cognitive bloat', which is that once one accepts that the mind literally extends in cases like the Otto scenario, it is impossible to find any good principled reasons to not allow much less plausible extreme extended belief cases. It has for example been suggested that agents in this case would have extended beliefs about all numbers in a phonebook, or even about all the content available on the Internet (see prominently e.g., Rupert 2004; Adams and Aizawa 2008; Sprevak 2009).[2]

Levy discusses a number of ways in which his claim is allegedly more moderate than Clark and Chalmers, but probably the most important one is that it avoids cognitive bloat, because intentional actions are, according to him, always conscious. That means there is no equivalent to the worry about

---

[2] Clark has a number of other arguments to deal with cognitive bloat (2007), but they are not directly relevant in this context.

the numbers in a phonebook or the entire content of the Internet which undermine the standard story.

This is an important point and requires some attention, especially because in the literature many are convinced that conscious mental states simply do not extend. Brie Gertler (2007) has used the cognitive bloat worry as an argument that taking the parity principle seriously in cases like Otto and his notebook should not lead us to say the mind extends into objects, but rather that dispositional beliefs are never part of the mind irrespective of whether they are stored within a notebook or the brain. According to Gertler, the only part of the cognitive machinery that should be called the mind is the conscious mind—or to be more precise, the only states that should be called mental states are occurrent states. In other words, the only belief states that are mental states are the ones that are *consciously entertained* by the subject. With this definition in place, Gertler then argues that no part of the mind extends, because all plausible cases of extension, such as Otto's notebook, only work for dispositional mental states and those are not properly part of the mind on her understanding.

Gertler's argument is one of the most powerful ways to make sense of our intuitive scepticism about the extended mind, but it does come at a very high price. On Gertler's definition, all unconscious states of our psyche are simply not part of the mind. That does not seem to chime very well with contemporary views in psychology and the neurosciences. This is why Clark and Chalmers reject this view in their approach to the issue and work on the assumption that understanding of the mind obviously should include dispositional states.

Levy seeks to avoid this controversy in a different way, by arguing that he only needs to hold a significantly weaker version of the claim in order to use it for his argument that there is no deep difference between mental and physical actions. He writes:

> ExM is evidently taken by the bulk of its supporters and critics alike as promoting the extension of both mental states and mental acts or processes [...] In contrast, the present suggestion proposes a more moderate extension of only the latter category. On this suggestion (call it Mod-ExM), some mental acts supervene on the subject's extrabodily environment.
> (Levy 2019: 977)

The kind of acts Levy has in mind here are things like calculating on paper, sketching a drawing, reading Braille, and so on. All these actions seem like perfectly ordinary intentional actions and yet all of them clearly seem to be mental actions at the same time.

However, Levy accepts that there is one way in which his moderate claim invites the same worry as other forms of the extended mind. This worry is the so-called causal/constitutive worry. According to this worry, it is obviously true that the environment often plays a crucial causal role for our cognitive processes. A cognition machine requires inputs it can operate on. Perception, for example, is clearly enormously important for cognition, but this does not mean that the perceptual inputs to the machine should be seen as part of the processes of the machine itself. Levy refers to Adams and Aizawa's (2009) neat bowling example: while it is certainly true that the spinning of the bowling ball is causally dependent on the presence of the bowling alley, this does not mean that the alley is part of the spinning process. It is a causal condition for it but not a constitutive part of it.

Applied to Levy's extended mental action claim, this worry becomes the idea that it might be possible to divide such actions into a mental and a physical part. The physical part of the action—which obviously happens outside the skull—is simply seen as causally connected to the mental action, which happens fully within the head. For example, if an agent calculates the product of 2,338 and 567 on a piece of paper, one could argue that the writing down of the numbers is a physical action, but all actual calculations are still done in the head. The numbers on the paper simply provide inputs for the calculations. These inputs might well be necessary for the calculation to take place. The agent might well not be able to multiply 2,338 by 567 in their head, but this does not mean that writing down the numbers is any more part of the cognitive process than the bowling alley is a constitutive part of the spinning bowling ball.[3]

Levy's answer to this worry is very much the same as the one Clark uses against his critics. He writes:

> When developing one's ideas by speech or in writing, the ongoing process continuously loops backwards and forwards between the 'outer' scribbling and the 'inner' thought; it is not as though one first thinks out the idea in one's head, and then proceeds to write it down or say it out loud. The

---

[3] Note the similarity between Levy's point and the discussion of deliberation as a skill in Chapter 3.

writing/speaking and the 'inner' thinking are far more integrated than that—indeed, so integrated as to prompt the thought that one's writing/speaking just is one's thinking (hence the expression, 'thinking out loud').

(Levy 2019: 980)

In other words: it is impossible to neatly distinguish between the contributions made by the intra and the extra cranial to a specific action and because of that, the physical action can legitimately be regarded as a constitutive part of the mental act of, for example, calculating.

Clark himself (2007) has developed a nice example to make the same point. He imagines first the scenario where the rain against his Edinburgh window helps him think. In this case, he agrees that the contribution the rain makes to his cognitive process is merely causal, because it is coincidental and simply a background against which cognition happens. The situation is very different from a robot that is designed to spit water at a plate and to use the auditory signal that the spitting generates to time its cognitive operations. Here, Clark holds that 'those self-maintained cognition-supporting signals are surely part of the cognitive mechanism itself. A neural clock or oscillator would count after all' (2007: 37).

In such examples where it is not just 'mere' coupling between environment and brain, but where the outputs of the agent produce new inputs that actually drive cognition, it seems odd to say that these loopings cannot count as part of the cognitive process, merely because they happen outside the skull. Insisting that the difference exists without any further argument is according to Clark, quoting Hurley, to commit 'the "causal constitutive error" error' (Clark 2007: 36). Adams and Aizawa are right to insist that there must be a boundary between a system and its environment, but we need to have good reasons for why we put the boundary in a certain place. Functional integration is such a reason, while the simple fact of being located inside or outside the skull is not.

2. The Inverse and the Negative Parity Principle

With this jigsaw piece in place, Levy can then proceed to argue for his next point. He wants to show that his account can disable Strawson's (2002) argument that there are no real mental actions. Levy focuses specifically on Strawson's argument that one cannot have an intention to think a specific new content, because in forming the intention, one would have thought the content already.[4] All one can have is an intention to think some unspecified new content, but producing the specifics always has to be automatic.

Levy invokes what he calls the inverse parity principle to counter this argument. Just like Clark and Chalmers argued that we should accept that a process outside the head should count as cognitive if we would have had no qualms calling it cognitive if it had happened inside the head, Levy assumes that everybody would share his intuition that calculating on paper would be called an intentional mental action. Levy then argues that if we have no qualms about calling calculating on paper an action, we should also be happy to accept that functionally, the same process is an action if it happens inside the head. Levy's argument actually chimes well with the literature in claiming that intentional physical actions that serve a cognitive purpose are functionally equivalent to intentional mental actions.

For example, in their much-cited work on epistemic action, Kirsh and Maglio define epistemic actions as physical actions that make mental computation easier, faster, or more reliable (Kirsh and Maglio 1994: 514f). They then say that it is widely assumed that it is uncontroversial that such epistemic actions are very normal when doing algebra on paper, composing music, or marine navigation—all tasks that require the manipulation of symbols (515). What this means is that Kirsh and Maglio assume to be the case what Levy thinks he needs to establish, i.e. that physical actions like calculating on paper can at the same time be mental actions. They see their work in showing that non-symbolic skill-based actions can also belong to this group of actions. In their paper, Kirsh and Maglio discuss the physical manipulation of Tetris blocks as such an example: manipulating blocks on a screen is not symbol manipulation, but it confers a cognitive advantage on the agent. Kirsh and Maglio want to argue that this is sufficient to support the claim that this is a true mental action. It is their work that Clark and Chalmers (1998) take their inspiration from when they discuss Tetris in their extended mind paper to argue that there is no functional difference between rotating a Tetris block in your head or using mouse clicks for the purposes of facilitating computation.

Some recent work goes even further. In his work on mental action from a Predictive Coding perspective, Thomas Metzinger writes:

---

[4] As discussed in Chapter 1.

> We can conceptualize cognitive agency (CA) as an abstract mental simulation of embodied actions, first executed using the physical, non-neural body. Such actions could have been the manipulation of discrete symbolic tokens in the external world, the use of gestures or bodily sign language, or even full-blown speech acts. (Metzinger 2017: 26)

Thus, for Metzinger, not only is it possible that internal epistemic actions are functionally the same as physical epistemic actions, he also believes that the physical actions might well have come first, and that the internal mental actions are simply a simulation of what used to be done externally. In a similar vein, Tom McCleland (2017) claims that there are mental affordances for cognitive phenomena like multiplication and again, the argument for this claim is derived from the idea that doing multiplication in one's head is very much like doing multiplication on paper.

Hence, Levy seems to be very much in line with the literature in arguing that there is no functional difference between physical and internal intentional actions. Except unfortunately, neither Levy nor anyone else in this literature distinguishes between evaluative agency and managerial mental actions. Once this distinction is introduced, Levy's argument, and with it the standard use in the literature, gets turned on its head. To see why, let us look again at Levy's assertion that when we use pen and paper to work out a difficult mathematical puzzle, we literally calculate on paper. If we apply the distinction between evaluative and managerial agency here, then it is obvious that we are dealing with two distinct forms of agency in this example: there is the managerial action of writing down the numbers and there is the evaluative agency, which uses the added provided input to understand the calculations.

However, we already encountered Levy's reply to the similar objection that we could split calculating with pen and paper into a mental and a physical action. Levy's reply to this is that, in cases like calculating on paper or perhaps even stronger, in reading Braille, there is too much looping to justify the distinction between different individual actions. The calculating only works because of the constant interaction between brain and environment.

To answer this point, let us remind ourselves of the case of deliberation and skill.[5] Deliberation seems to be an intentional action that is somehow

---

[5] As discussed in Chapter 3.

intimately intertwined with an evaluative agency. Does this mean that after all there are intentional evaluative actions?

As we have seen it does not, because it remains a fact that there is a clearly describable part of the overall intentional action which is non-intentional, and everything that is *directly* responsible for the acquisition of a new belief is in that part. All we need to add here to use this argument for the Levy case is that this evaluative part also does not extend. In fact, we can revert here to the fundamental difference between intentional actions and cognitive (mental) actions, which Levy attributes to Strawson and which can also be found in varying forms in Mele 2009, Proust 2013, Vierkant 2013, Hieronymi 2009, and Wu 2013, to name but a few, i.e. that one cannot have a specific intention about what to think, because in forming the intention, the task would already have been achieved.

Thus, describing calculating on paper as an intentional cognitive action is a little misleading. In reality, calculating on paper consists of two types of agency that are closely intertwined: there is the intentional action, which is the writing down of symbols; and there is the evaluative agency, which allows the agent to understand what it is that they are doing.

Levy is therefore correct in claiming that there is no fundamental difference between mental and physical actions when we are talking about managerial actions. However, it is at the very least misleading to say that these actions are actions like thinking, or that the absence of a difference in this case provides arguments against Strawson. The argument against Strawson only works if we buy into extended cognition. In that case, it would still be true that mental actions are what Strawson calls shepherding actions, but obviously because of the entangling between intentional shepherding processes and non-intentional evaluative processes, one legitimately could call the whole action a cognitive process.

If we do not want to commit to extended cognition, then Levy's claim about managerial actions is fully in line with Strawson. The kinds of actions that are under discussion in that case are exactly the kind of things that Strawson described as non-cognitive shepherding.

Levy's approach illuminates a couple of very interesting points. First, we cannot use his reverse parity principle as long as we do not commit to extended cognition. However, we now have instead something like a negative parity principle. If something is clearly not cognitive if done outside the head, then it also should not be considered cognitive if done inside the head. If in calculating with pen and paper, the cognitive part is always a different process to the physical one, then the same argument should hold for parity reasons for the intentional parts of deliberation, i.e. they are not truly cognitive. Intentional mental actions can be extended, because there are no intentional mental actions in the sense of cognitive mental actions in the first place. The lesson from the extended mind literature here is not that there clearly are intentional cognitive actions inside the head, because there are intentional cognitive actions outside the head, but that there are no intentional cognitive actions inside or outside the head.

This is in fact reminiscent of a point made by Clark about the problem with seeing the skull as a significant boundary between the cognitive realm and the merely physical. Taking this boundary for granted, according to Clark (2007), is not only problematic because it artificially rules out cognitive ongoings outside the head, but it also obscures the fact that many ongoings inside the head might not necessarily be cognitive. Intentional mental actions are just such a case. Whether they happen inside or outside the head, they are not constitutive parts of the cognitive in this scenario.

3. Where Are We Now?

As discussed at the end of Chapter 3, where this argument leads us very much depends on what we mean by cognitive action. Obviously, one could deny that the distinction between evaluative and intentional agency is relevant in the cognitive sciences, but in this case, Levy's argument now seems to hold and the implication of that argument would be that there are extended intentional cognitive actions. If, on the other hand, one is convinced that the distinction between evaluative and managerial mental agency is an important one, then one also has to accept that cognitive agency is only ever intra cranial. For intentional actions, the skull boundary still seems of no great functional importance, but this is now because neither intra cranial nor extended intentional mental actions are cognitive.

Looking at extended cognition allowed us to emphasize the point that was already made by the simple argument: intentional mental actions are not like evaluative mental agency, but like physical intentional actions. This does not mean that there cannot be good reasons to call them cognitive, but only if we allow that intentional actions outside the skull are also cognitive.

Making this choice has consequences: it defines what makes the agent rational. If one goes for intentional action being a constitutive part of at least some rational processes, then this means that a rational process is about being able to initiate or stop applying the rules of logic—but one has to accept that cognition in this sense says nothing about understanding or evaluating the result of these processes. Therefore, cognition on this definition is not specifically about whatever it is that brings about acquisitions or changes of doxastic attitudes. In addition, this choice means that the control of cognitive processes does not have to happen in the brain to be cognitive, but that controlling your thinking by means of physical actions should now also be called cognitive.[6]

If, on the other hand, one goes for evaluative agency as the sole rightful place for cognition, then intentional action can only ever be catalytic. On this reading, cognitive control is not about controlling first order attitudes with second order attitudes in the way one controls changing one's socks, but control consists in an influence of the rationality of the higher order states.[7] Clearly, both options have costs as well as advantages: but should we not aim to decide which is the better option?

An unambiguous position is obviously a virtue of theoretical enquiry, but there are cases where it seems adequate to leave the choice to the reader. To see why, let us take a short look at the pertinent example of Clark's discussion of whether the extended mind makes for better cognitive science.

Extended mind sceptics worry that the parallels between processes outside the skull and inside the skull only exist at a very coarse-grained level, and that cognition can only be understood at a more fine-grained level, where processes inside the skull do not mirror the processes that loop into the environment. The note in Otto's notebook might well play the same function as biological memory would on a coarse-grained level, but once we look at the details of biological memory, it becomes clear very quickly that the notebook works quite differently. Biological memory traces change over time and is subject to various recall phenomena that do not apply to the notebook. See prominently e.g., Rupert 2004, Adams and Aizawa 2008, and Sprevak 2009.

Clark (2007) has an answer to these worries: he denies that the extended mind approach fails, despite the fact that there are fine-grained differences. He argues that it seems oddly 'speciesist' to insist that all cognition should be

---

[6] I have presented this option as one that seems mainly attractive in the cognitive sciences, but there is very interesting recent work in moral psychology that seems to be attracted by the idea that the looping between intentional and evaluative components in maintaining beliefs is so intricate that this control over one's beliefs can be called intentional (see e.g. Chrisman 2018 and Tumulty 2020). I think these arguments are very plausible, but they also do not escape the consequence of our argument. If intentional mental actions are literally constitutive parts of belief maintenance, then the same can hold for intentional physical actions.

[7] See Chapter 1.

required to mirror all the contingent features of human cognition. While it is true that recalling information from a notebook is not subject to, for example, recency effects like biological memory, this does not seem to be a valid argument to claim that it is somehow not 'real' memory.

But Rupert (2004) has a second worry: he argues that opting for the coarse-grained functional level that the extended mind seems to require makes for worse cognitive science. Let us take the example of working memory: the extended mind theorist might want to argue that there is no difference between external and internal storage, as long as it is readily available. But this does not do justice to the role of working memory in many cognitive tasks. Rupert imagines a conversation where one of the interlocutors uses a written external store to keep track of the conversation instead of using internal working memory. Clearly, such a conversation would be enormously cumbersome. In general, the high-level similarities between external and internal stores can make it difficult to see how the details of implementation matter.

Clark's reply brings us to the relevant point in the context of this book (2007): he argues that there is no reason that we could not take on board what Rupert says about the importance of biological structures for the study of biological memory, but that this does not mean that there might not be important questions for cognitive science, for which it might be more helpful to look at extended systems. In other words: Rupert is right to emphasize that there are some questions where it is important to focus on internal resources, but in other cases understanding cognitive ongoings appropriately requires taking extracranial resources into account as well. Our definition of what does or does not count as part of a system and what is only a causal contributor can vary relative to our explanatory interest.

This is particularly the case because the brain itself is what Clark calls 'cognitively impartial'. The brain always chooses the most efficient way to solve a problem and it does not care whether the solution uses internal or external means. This is nicely demonstrated by the experiments of Gray and colleagues. In these experiments, subjects had to retrieve a piece of information. The information was presented in a window on the screen and was available either by simply looking at the screen or only after subjects removed an opaque cover with a mouse click. Subjects also had to memorize the information presented in the window. Subjects used the external information if it was readily available but used the stored memory if accessing the external information required the extra mouse click.

These experiments, according to Clark, nicely demonstrate that there are real cognitive phenomena out there which are investigated by cognitive scientists and which use soft assembled structures in order to maximize efficiency. Therefore, it seems right that successful cognitive science cannot exclusively focus on long-term stable structures. At the same time, Clark himself has a worry about this move: while empirical research seems to support the claim that the brain is *cognitively impartial*, it still is always the *brain* that chooses the resource (Clark 2007). This suggests that the brain *does* indeed have a privileged position, and that in turn casts doubt on the claim that external resources have the same cognitive status as the brain.

It is at this point that the discussion of the extended mind in cognitive science displays an interesting similarity to our discussion surrounding cognitive agency. This is because the selection process in the Gray experiments discussed by Clark looks very much like a process equivalent to evaluative agency. Like the cognitive agent, it is the brain that evaluates the best course of action, and the execution of this action might well be environment-involving.

Does this mean that Clark agrees that there is after all such an important asymmetry that it makes sense to deny that cognition really extends? Unsurprisingly, that is not how Clark interprets the point about the selecting brain. In answer to the cognitive impartiality worry, Clark suggests that we should distinguish between different explanatory targets: when it comes to the assembly of the cognitive processing device, the brain does indeed play a special role, but once the system is up and running, there is no functional difference between the use of intra- or extracranial resources.

In summary, Clark's argument is: selection is different from execution, because the brain does have a privileged role in selecting, but this is not a good reason to claim that there is no such thing as extended cognition, because once up and running, the processes that solve cognitive tasks do extend. From a science perspective, it seems perfectly acceptable to decide what constitutes a cognitive system relative to the explanatory interest of the research programme.[8] Clark's discussion in a way replicates what we said

---

[8] In addition, while selection does not normally extend, in contrast to the cognitive agency case, this seems to be a contingent fact. It is entirely imaginable that in some future sci fi world there might be artificial systems that automatically select the most appropriate tool to solve a cognitive problem. The further down the ladder of cognitive complexity we go, the less deep the difference between execution and selection seems to be, at least in terms of it being cognitive. In fact, this very idea of an extended sub-personal selection process is one of the reasons why Gertler (2007) wants to restrict the mind to the conscious mind. She imagines a scenario where

already in Chapter 3: whether or not we want to call intentional mental actions doxastic actions might be a definitional question, but if we do opt to call intentional mental actions cognitive, that would imply that there are extended cognitive mental actions. Clark's discussion adds a reason for why we might want to define terms one way or the other, i.e. specific research interests such as stable selectors or transient execution coalitions. As he very succinctly puts it: it seems perfectly permissible to define cognitive systems here in a way that helps scientific progress. As long as successful cognitive science is the guiding principle, it is okay to let a thousand flowers bloom (Clark 2007).

4. Is It Really True that Accepting Extended Mental Actions Means Accepting Extended Cognition?

Suppose we go for the first option and accept that there is no difference between intra cranial and world-involving actions when we acquire a new doxastic state, but we still want to insist that there can be intentional mental actions. Does this mean that the world literally becomes part of the cognitive process? On the face of it, this does seem to be the consequence of Levy's argument. But perhaps there is a way out? Perhaps we could accept that there can be intentional mental actions that are world-involving, but that in all intentional actions only specific parts of the action are the proper agentive part, and perhaps that part is also where the cognition happens? If this were the case, then there could be intentional world-involving actions that are cognitive, but the cognition would nevertheless never happen outside the head.

Just to be clear: this is not the same move as Levy's argument, which stated that calculating on paper can be separated into a physical and a mental action, but rather, here the claim is that all intentional actions really happen inside the head, i.e. the agentive part of intentional actions is

---

Otto has a computer in which he has saved his desire to make banana bread on Tuesday. This computer also controls a robot which is also part of the extended Otto system. So, one morning, while the organic part of Otto is fast asleep, the computer sends the robot to fetch the ingredients and bake the bread, so that the organic part awakens to the smell of banana bread. Gertler uses the example as an argument against the extended mind, because obviously, the very strong intuition here is that Otto did not make the bread, but Gertler argues that Clark and Chambers will struggle to explain why this should be the case. But for our question, the main point to emphasize here is that it is not obvious that selection always happens in the brain, so that selection is not sufficient for cognitive agency.

reducible to tryings, whereas the stuff in the world is just a consequence. So even the physical writing of the numbers is really only an action because there are mental tryings underpinning it, and these are in actual fact the only essential part of the action.

The position that all intentional actions are at heart really intracranial tryings is also not even that unusual. In fact, it is quite intuitive and was even once the dominant position in philosophy. This position goes by the name of volitionism and was held by Descartes and many others in the philosophical tradition. Indeed, there are also good arguments for holding such a position. In his excellent article 'The Province of Human Agency' (2016), John Ford discusses three:

> First of all, intuitively our knowledge of our willing and our control of our tryings are more secure than the knowledge and control of our bodily movements. It is easy to imagine that my hand moved when in fact it did not and much harder to imagine the same thing in the case of trying to lift my hand.[9] Secondly, there is separability. Even if I try to move my hand, my hand might not move because somebody is holding it down, but it is hard to imagine that I try to move my hand and somehow do not try to move my hand at the same time. Finally, there is etiology. Moving my hand intentionally depends on me trying to move my hand, but not the other way round, so trying to move my hand is etiologically prior to moving it.
> (Ford 2016)

Modern technology might also seem to provide us with an additional argument for volitionism. Brain computer interfaces (BCI) allow people to act intentionally without moving their bodies: a computer is programmed to recognize specific brain patterns and can move a robot accordingly. Steinert et al. describe the use of BCIs in the following way:

> In active BCIs, the user intentionally performs a mental task that produces a certain pattern of brain activity, which the BCI system detects for processing. A commonly deployed mental strategy in active BCIs is motor imagery. The user imagines moving parts of her body, without actually performing the movement. The imagination of the movement of different body parts corresponds to different activations of the primary

---

[9] This is what makes Wegner's work so counterintuitive.

> somatosensory and motor cortical areas. For example, imagining right-hand movement activates a different cortical area and results in different activation patterns than imagining left-hand movement or movement of the foot. These different activation patterns picked up by the BCI and is translated into signals to control an application (for more on motor imagery see Graimann et al. 2009, 11–13). For example, via active BCIs participants were able to command a robotic arm orthosis to assist drinking (Looned et al. 2014), to control a robotic gait orthosis (Do et al. 2013), drive a wheelchair (Galan et al. 2008), and control a spelling application (Perdikis et al. 2014). (Steinert et al. 2018)

Thus, it can be contended that the existence of BCIs suggests that bodies are no more than contingent and replaceable elements of actions like drinking, walking, and writing.

Given these strong arguments in favour, is volitionism a threat to the claims advanced so far? Theoretically, yes—but in reality, the worry posed by volitionism is rather minor, for two reasons. The most important one is that volitionism, despite its early popularity, really is quite implausible. But suppose we found the consequences of the argument advanced so far too unappealing and decided to endorse volitionism, in spite of the very good reasons against holding it. This would still require a very specific reading of volitionism—indeed, one that is even more implausible than a standard account—to really create a threat for our argument here. Let us take a quick look at this second point, before looking at the arguments against volitionism in general in a little more detail.

Volitionists hold that the element of trying is the only essential component of an intentional action, but all the potential arguments for considering intentional actions as truly cognitive are interested in what these actions achieve. It is not the trying element of inner speech that makes it potentially cognitive, but the act of succeeding at inner speech acts that makes it possible to focus on specific bits of content. It is not the effort we make to solve a puzzle that makes the action cognitive, but the fact that this effort succeeds. In order for volitionism to be a threat for our argument, one would have to endorse the argument that what is truly cognitive is the trying, while finding the solution is, as Strawson puts it, simple ballistics. In contrast to Strawson's account, this specific brand of volitionism would be forced to claim that the ballistic part—that is, the direct cause of the acquisition of a new doxastic attitude—is not cognitive. Acquiring and changing doxastic attitudes would become a non-cognitive automatic process. That seems very implausible.

If volitionism were the only game in town, then perhaps it would be worth exploring ways to make this work, but it is not. In fact, rather the opposite is the case, as Ford nicely explains: there are two alternatives to volitionism, namely corporealism and materialism.

Corporealism is the dominant position in the philosophical literature and argues that basic intentional actions do include the movement of the body but not distal action effects, while materialism argues that these distal effects can also be essential parts of the action.

Ford favours materialism over corporealism because he argues that the very same arguments that can be used by corporealists against volitionists can also be used by materialists against corporealists, and that the only arguments that corporealists could use against materialists could then in turn also be used by volitionists against corporealists, rendering corporealism unstable. Ford's argument here is very convincing, but for our purposes it does not matter whether corporealism or materialism is correct, all we need is the arguments against volitionism.[10]

There are three of them: the first one is pre-theoretical practical thought. Ordinarily, we do not understand our actions as mental pullings of bodily strings, but we simply move our bodies, or we even experience ourselves as making the coffee or driving the car. Both corporealism and materialism do more justice to our natural pre-theoretical way of understanding actions than does volitionism. The second argument against volitionism is about embodiment. Volitionism suggests a picture where the human mind is like a computer, a disembodied calculation machine, and the body is simply a piece of equipment the mind uses for moving. But in reality, we are indeed embodied minds and as Ford points out, not only are our minds embodied, but our bodies are not simple effectors either: we understand them as having natural functions, which enable them to deal with the world.[11] Legs are for walking, hands are for grasping, and so on. The final argument against volitionism is animality. Volitionism seems to struggle with the naturalistic thought that we are part of the animal world. Animals do not care about or understand doxastic states but are firmly focused on coping with their

---

[10] Having said that, our earlier discussion of BMIs provides another strong argument that corporealism will struggle with. While materialism finds it easy to integrate BMI actions, the same is not obvious for corporealism.

[11] Empirical research seems to back this up. Researchers who argue for so-called event coding show that we are much better at executing complex behaviours if we understand them in terms of their distal effects rather than in terms of the movements required to achieve the effects (Hommel et al. 2001; Mechsner et al. 2001).

environments. But if this coping is what is essential about animal agency, and we are animals, then presumably it is exactly this coping with environments that defines our agency as well (Ford 2017: 705).

To summarize: volitionism might be a theoretical threat to our argument, but it is an implausible position to hold. Even if one is tempted by it, one would need to hold a particularly implausible form of volitionism to undermine the argument here, so that the threat really is minimal.[12]

5. What Happens to Deliberation if Only Evaluative Agency Is Cognitive?

While the simple argument does force us into accepting the radical philosophical position of extended cognition if we want to allow for intentional mental actions, it actually also throws up some very tricky questions for philosophers like Gertler, who want to hold that the conscious mind does not extend. This is because once we accept that there is no functional difference between intentional actions inside the head and ones that are world involving, and argue that cognitive mental actions do not extend, we now have to accept that the parts of reflective deliberation that are intentional are not cognitive, but are just shepherding actions like using a notebook or going to the library.

The evaluative core of deliberation that remains is now obviously no longer intentionally controlled. In fact, the processes that bring about new cognitive content look surprisingly automatic. This seems in conflict with some assumptions that Gertler would also like to hold. Again, we have to remember that at no stage so far was it completely clear exactly what

---

[12] Thinking about volitionism is also helpful in order to get a clearer grip on Strawson's argument about the passivity of the mental. Wayne Wu (2013) argues that Strawson's argument about mental actions being ballistics leads to a reductio, because the same argument could also be used about shepherding and bodily intentional actions. All the agent could do is set an action up, and then the rest of the action is ballistics. If this interpretation is correct, then there are no intentional actions at all, a position that is clearly absurd. Interestingly, what Wu says here would be absurd seems to be the position that volitionists would like to embrace. If volitionism were right, then 'we never do more than will: the rest is up to nature' (Ford 2017, 705). Thus, for volitionists, strictly speaking there are no making coffees and lifting arms, only mental tryings to do these things, and the effects of these tryings in the world. This is quite different from Strawson's point. Strawson has nothing to say about the question of whether or not the physical lifting of the arm is part of the action of raising the arm; what he wants to insist on is that the thinking of new mental content is not in the same way related to the trying to think new content as a physical movement is related to the mental trying to perform that physical action.

cognitive agency is: philosophers like Moran (2001), Hieronymi (2009), McHugh (2011), Mele (2009), Toribio (2011), and Wu (2013) have argued that they exist, and they are all agreed that they are very different from ordinary intentional actions. At the same time, some philosophers like Strawson have taken the very same arguments to show that there simply are no cognitive mental actions, because these processes look so different from ordinary actions.

This might be a problem for people like Gertler, because it is unclear that cognitive agency in this sense really has very much to do with reflective reasoning or deliberation as ordinarily understood. Often when we talk about deliberation in ordinary discourse we do mean the conjunct intentional action that contains both shepherding and the cognitive action proper, but once we focus on that cognitive action itself, it is not really clear any more what distinguishes it from what Gertler calls 'brute processing'.[13]

Furthermore, as discussed at length, it is not only the folk who think that reflective reasoning is the intentional action of deliberation that contains the evaluative episodes: some philosophers, such as Frankish (Frankish 2009), even go so far as to simply identify this intentional deliberative process with personal level reasoning.[14] Therefore, according to Frankish, all non-intentional reasoning is sub personal. One argument for this might be that for a personal level reasoning process, the reasoning process needs to be transparent, i.e. it can't be ballistic and mandatory (Mandelbaum 2014).[15] However, cognitive agency in the evaluative sense seems to be exactly that, because it can't be intentionally initiated or stopped.

There is the beginning of a radical argument here: if we accept that cognitive agency has to be on the personal level, and if personal level reasoning requires a transparent process, then there is no cognitive agency in the evaluative sense. Now, it is surely uncontroversial that agency has to be a personal level phenomenon. Doxastic voluntarism is about voluntary action, and that is clearly a personal level ability, and usually doxastic involuntarism is supposed to be an alternative on the same level of analysis. In order to escape this eliminitavist argument against doxastic agency, it is

---

[13] Or at least, it is no longer clear in which sense it is agency (see Chapter 1).
[14] Jesse Prinz (2004) uses the notion of organismic control (which is the voluntary control of mental content) as a necessary constituent of all cognition. However, in personal communication, he has recently told me that he is now suspicious of this notion.
[15] See Chapter 3.

necessary to argue that transparency of process is not necessary for a personal level process.

6. Intuitive Judgments and Social Reasoning

Yet perhaps the above is not as big a problem as it might perhaps seem at first glance. For example, over the last decade Hugo Mercier and Dan Sperber (2017) have developed a position on human reasoning that seems to chime very well with the strictures of the simple argument.

According to Mercier and Sperber, human judgments and decisions are always intuitive. They define intuitions as judgments 'that we make and take to be justified without any knowledge of the reasons that justifies them' (2017: 64). In other words, Mercier and Sperber think of intuitive judgments as intransparent. Intuitions on their account are nevertheless quite special. All animals make lots of inferences, i.e. extrapolate new information that goes well beyond that available to the senses, but most inferences are automatic and unconscious. Intuitions are special because their outputs are conscious. Moreover, intuitions are not experienced as mere guesses, but come with a graded sense of certainty. Sometimes we are absolutely sure that our intuitions are correct and sometimes much less so. Intuitions come with a metacognitive sense about how reliable they are.[16] But particularly relevant in our context is what Mercier and Sperber claim next:

> Intuitions also come with a sense of authorship or agency. While we are not the authors of our perception, we are, or so we feel, the authors of our intuitions, we may even feel proud of them. (2017: 66)

Mercier and Sperber do not talk about what the reason for this sense of authorship over intuitions may be, and they also do not address the question of whether it is justified. But as they do think that something that is intuitive is also special and not merely automatic, because it is metacognitive, one could at least suspect that the sense of authorship has something to do with its metacognitive nature. Perhaps one could even understand their account of intuition as an explanation of the sense of evaluative agency? We will come back to this thought in Chapter 7, where we will discuss the role of

---

[16] We will have a lot more to say on this in Chapter 7.

uncertainty for an evaluativist account of metacognition (Proust 2013). For now, we first need to look at what Mercier and Sperber have to say about reasoning.

Interestingly, Mercier and Sperber argue that system two reasoning is not a human special privileged way to get at the truth, but that it mainly exists for communicative purposes. In that respect, their position aligns quite nicely with the conclusion of the simple argument that intentional mental actions are not for the direct acquisition of beliefs. However, Mercier and Sperber are more radical than the simple argument. The latter shows that intentional actions do not directly lead to new doxastic states, but I was at pains to point out how important these indirect tinkering actions are nevertheless for the cognitive process. Mercier and Sperber, on the other hand, argue that the function of reasoning is not at all for the finding of truth, but rather, has a mainly communicative function. That their position seems to chime so well with the main conclusion of the simple argument is one good reason to look at their position more closely, but additionally, Mercier and Sperber frame their position as an alternative to two systems theory, and this alternative framing will take us to the last central topic of this book that so far has been neglected, namely metacognition.

Here is what Mercier and Sperber have to say on dual systems approaches:

> The whole dual process approach of Evans, Kahneman, Stanovich [...] has at its core the assumption that intuitive inference and reasoning are achieved through two quite distinct types of mechanisms. We disagree. One of the main claims of this book is that *reasoning is not an alternative to intuitive inference; reasoning is a use of intuitive inferences about reasons.*
>
> (2017: 133)

Let's unpack what is being said here: according to Mercier and Sperber, reasoning is not a different process that leads to judgments, but it is a form of intuitive judgment with a specific content. Reasoning is about using intuitive judgments about reasons. For example, one might judge that the field is probably yellow, because the farmer is growing oil seed rape. The whole statement is an intuitive judgment, but the conclusion is not intuitive, because the reason for the conclusion is transparent. Hence, the whole intuitive judgment is about the fact that the reason that the farmer planted rape is a reason for the embedded conclusion that the field is yellow.

According to Mercier and Sperber, reasoning is making intuitive judgments about reasons. But what about the rule of logic and probability theory that one standardly associates with reasoning? According to Mercier and Sperber, these play a far smaller role than the standard dogma would allow. Their main reason for this surprising claim is that the alleged superiority of using such tools relies on the idea that logical arguments are fully explicit, but Mercier and Sperber point out that all logical arguments ultimately rely on implicit intransparent inferences. Here is their neat example of a mischievous Sherlock Holmes to illustrate the point: Holmes might say to Watson that either the butler stole the diamond or the gardener did. The butler didn't. So, the gardener stole the diamond. This is clearly a sound syllogism, but if Holmes already knew in advance that the butler was not a suspect, then the fact that he did not steal the diamond is as little an argument for the claim that the gardener did it as would be the claim that the pope or E.T. or whoever has not stolen the diamond. The soundness of such a syllogism simply does not provide any evidence for the conclusion of the argument.

In order for the syllogism to be a general argument, it needs to be the case that the butler was one of the suspects. But this has nothing to do with the quality of the syllogism according to the rules of logic. As Mercier and Sperber put it:

> The common wisdom is that most arguments ordinarily used in conversation are, in fact, truncated syllogism. [...] What we have just shown is that arguments consisting just of a syllogism, even a fully explicit one, are themselves truncated arguments: they implicitly convey that their premises are not just true but provide genuine reasons to accept the conclusion. There goes the alleged superiority of explicitly laid-out syllogisms over informal statement of reasons; both, in fact, provide incomplete arguments.
>
> (2017: 158)

If reasoning is not a new independent process to arrive at judgments but is rooted firmly in intuition, what then is the role of reasoning on that account? According to Mercier and Sperber, reason is mainly a social competence. Producing explicit reasons for your conclusions is not important to gain new knowledge but to convince others of your position.

Mercier and Sperber's account is too rich to discuss in full here (but it will come back a number of times in the chapters to follow), but it has already provided us with an excellent link to our next chapter. What their account makes very clear is that perhaps what makes human thought special might not be a special process as assumed by dual process theory, but a special type of content of human thought. It is forms of thinking about thinking or metacognition that are crucial both for intuitive and reflective thought, according to Mercier and Sperber, and as that also seems to fit incredibly well the Frankfurtian idea that agency might be about higher order thought, it is to this which we will now turn.

5
Metacognition

1. Thinking about Thinking

Before we can turn to the applications of the results of our discussion so far there is one more point that needs to be addressed. Since Chapter 2 when the notion of managerial control was introduced, most examples of intentional control of the mind discussed were examples in which the agent was aware that they were acting in order to control their cognition in some sense. As we have seen, according to many philosophers these managerial actions are not as directly relevant to the acquisition of new beliefs as evaluative processes are. In the previous chapter this led us to the claim that there is no deep difference between intentional actions that happen inside the brain and intentional actions that use the environment for shepherding purposes.

However, while it might be true that mental actions that happen inside the head are not qualitatively different from intentional physical actions with regard to the directness of doxastic state acquisition, perhaps we have neglected a difference between the two that is crucial, especially for human cognition. This crucial difference is the ability of humans to think about their mentality. Humans, but arguably no other animal, can think about their beliefs and understand that they are states with intentional content that can be right or wrong. This feature of human rationality is centrally important in many philosophical and cognitive science accounts. In dual systems theory, for example, one key feature of system two is that it is metacognitive, which, as the name suggests, means that it concerns thinking about cognition (see e.g. Carruthers 2009; Stanovich 2011).

The so-called mindreading literature takes as a starting point the question: 'at what age do children acquire an understanding of false belief?' This is because it is assumed that understanding false beliefs requires an understanding of the nature of representation, or in other words: metarepresentation (see Lavelle 2019 for an introduction). Grice (1957) held that there could not be language without an understanding of communicative intentions, which are famously defined as being complex metarepresentations. To end this by no means exhaustive list, philosophers like Clark (2006) and

Bermudez (2003) argue that language enables second order cognitive dynamics, which is their word for metacognition, and that these might well be one of the features of distinctly human thought.

Perhaps the deep difference between intentional mental actions inside the head and intentional actions that shepherd the mind by manipulating the world is that only the former are mental actions at all, in the sense that they are actions that are about the manipulation of cognitive states, whereas the latter have a cognitive side effect, but they do not have a cognitive goal.

Pursuing this line of thought also throws up a very interesting connection to the issue that this book started with. In Chapter 1, we looked at the work of Harry Frankfurt and Stanovich's rendering of Frankfurt's idea that specifically human rationality is rooted in our ability to think about and control relevant parts of our mentality. As Hieronymi then pointed out, we should not think of this control as normal intentional control on pain of becoming homuncular and introduced instead the notion of evaluative control. It was at this point that we left Frankfurt behind, on the understanding that his ideas could not be read as advocating intentional higher order control of the mind and in the following chapters, looked into the question of how work on two systems does or does not take into account the difference between these two types of control.

But perhaps there is an issue here with Hieronymi's criticism that deserves more attention than we assumed? Perhaps there is a way in which Frankfurtian hierarchical control can be thought of as intentional control that is not homuncular, but at the same time really is at the heart of what human rational agency is all about. This could be because managerial control might be what second order cognitive dynamics are all about.[1] Only humans understand that they have propositional attitudes and are therefore able to target them intentionally. So, while it might well be true that managerial actions are parasitic on evaluative agency (see Chapter 2) and that they do not lead to the direct acquisition of doxastic states, they are nevertheless a unique tool of human rationality.

Perhaps if this is the case, there might be an argument here to resurrect the boundaries that separate intentional mental actions inside the head from intentional epistemic actions in the environment (Kirsh and Maglio 1994).

---

[1] Managerial control gives the agent the freedom to create the mind they want, independent of their first order evaluations, by means of manipulation (Vierkant 2013).

What is special about managerial actions in this case might be that they are directed at states that we normally assume to be inside the head.[2]

In what follows, we will see that there is indeed a way in which one could understand intentional mental actions as being at the heart of human rational agency, but we will also see that this is no argument for resurrecting the boundaries between brain-bound and environment-involving mental actions.

2. Metarepresentation and Mindshaping

As already mentioned, the term metarepresentation is most used in the so-called mindreading literature. The representations this literature is interested in are mental representations—mainly beliefs—and the question this field is centrally concerned with is how do we attribute beliefs to others (and perhaps to oneself)? During the first years of the debate, some of its founders assumed that it was obvious that in order to be able to attribute beliefs one would need to understand the concept of belief, and that coming to understand the concept of belief would require a theory about what beliefs are. This position is called 'theory theory' (TT) and for a while it was dominant enough that the whole field of research was called 'Theory of Mind'. The field is not called this anymore, because in the meantime, the exact role of theory in mindreading has become highly contested (for a useful introduction to the debate see Lavelle 2018.

At the same time, nobody in the mindreading debate denies that it is possible to attribute mental states using theory. In our context, the importance of understanding metarepresentation also seems obvious: only an agent that understands the concept of belief can have intentions about beliefs.

But while this seems obvious, there is one important complication here. As already mentioned, the mindreading literature is interested in understanding the ability to attribute beliefs and so, when people talk about metarepresentation in this literature, they normally mean that an agent is capable of understanding the concept of belief. But as for example Mercier

---

[2] Obviously, if beliefs can also be stored in the physical environment, as the extended mind theory holds, then this is not the case. However, the point under consideration here is whether thinking of mental agency as intentional agency forces one to accept the extended mind, and obviously that is not the case. In fact, it seems perfectly natural to assume that what makes managerial control different from other intentional actions is that it targets internal states.

and Sperber (2017) point out, beliefs are not the only representations in this world. There are also numerals, language, reasons, and many more. It seems at least possible that one could understand metarepresentation only for some, but not for all types of representation.[3]

Mental representations are different from other representations in two important ways, however. First, they are invisible.[4] We can only observe the behaviour that is caused by beliefs, but we cannot observe beliefs directly as they are hidden inside the skull. This is one reason why TT is so popular. Paul Churchland, one of the early key proponents of TT,[5] argues that beliefs are the unobservable theoretical postulates of folk psychological theory that are needed in order to predict the behaviour of other people.

With characteristic conviction, Churchland states that this is something everybody should easily be able to agree on:

> Not only is folk psychology a theory, it is so obviously a theory that it must be held a major mystery why it has taken until the last half of the twentieth century for philosophers to realize it. The structural features of folk psychology parallel perfectly those of mathematical physics; the only difference lies in the respective domain of abstract entities they exploit— numbers in the case of physics, and propositions in the case of psychology.
> (Churchland 1981: 71)

One consequence of TT is as follows: if in order to think about representations one needs a concept of what representations are, then obviously once one has this conceptual understanding it will apply to all types of representations. In this way, understanding mental representations in a TT way allows one to understand the representational nature of all other representations as well.

A second consequence is that only mental representations are supposed to have intrinsic content. Linguistic representations, on the other hand, like all other types of representations, are derived representations. They are representational only insofar as they are understood by an agent that has

---

[3] In fact, in line with many others, I have argued that language is probably the vehicle that first gave humans the ability to think about representations (Vierkant 2012; Bermudez 2003; Clark 2006).

[4] Apart from extended beliefs at least.

[5] Even though he obviously thinks that ToM is a bad theory, see Chapter 1.

mental representations. This might lead one to think that in order to really understand the nature of representation one needs to understand mental representation, because in the end all representational power is derived from them.

But while this thought might be one important reason for pursuing TT, it might nevertheless be a red herring, because it begins with the idea that in order to understand representation, one has to have a theory about invisible representational entities. Perhaps, beginning to think about representations does not begin with beliefs, but with representations that use visible vehicles.

The most obvious vehicle here is language. Words, especially in written form, are in a format that enables a whole host of cognitive operations that are far more difficult to achieve with invisible and fleeting beliefs. In his 'Magic Words: How Language Augments Human Computation' (1998), Andy Clark suggests a number of ways in which language provides tools for thinking. Language augments memory, when we for example write shopping lists. It helps to simplify the environment, for example by using signs to help us find directions. It also helps coordination, reduces the need for online deliberation, controls attention, and enables data manipulation. All of these, while vastly magnified in power by natural language, are possible in embryonic ways for non-linguistic creatures (Bermudez 2003) and they all do not require a theoretical understanding of the nature of representation.

Clark has a neat example of how this can work. He discusses the numeral-trained chimp Sheba. In an experiment, Sheba is allowed to decide which of two unequal piles of food a conspecific will get, after which she will get the other one. Even though Sheba hates the result, she always points at the larger pile and gets the smaller one herself. However, once the food is put in labelled containers, she is able to get the bigger pile of food for herself. The symbol puts some distance between the agent and the desired object, allowing the agent to more effectively pursue her desire.

Sheba can transform her thinking from two BANANAS to TWO bananas, just by looking at the symbol instead of looking at the bananas. The symbol simply constantly keeps the twoness of the bananas salient independently of the tendency of the animal to focus on their juiciness. The symbol simplifies the environment, controls attention and reduces the need for online deliberation (Clark 1998).

It is not clear exactly what cognitive capacities Sheba needs in order to be able to use these symbols, but one thing is clear: Sheba does not need to have a concept of belief. In fact, it is not even obvious that what Sheba is doing is in any recognizable sense linguistic.[6]

If metarepresentation requires the understanding of beliefs, then Sheba is not a metarepresenter, yet on the much more permissive understanding of metarepresentation proposed by Mercier and Sperber, she might well be.[7]

By using symbols, Sheba can focus away from the automatic behavioural tendencies that the stimuli elicit and instead concentrate on the task-relevant domain. The symbol is a visible intermediary between Sheba and her world. Once this is achieved, the animal can begin to focus on specific higher order properties of the stimuli. In this context, Clark relates experiments from Boysen's lab where once trained, chimps learned to apply the categories of same and different to completely new stimuli.

In some sense, this training clearly demonstrates that the chimps are thinking about thinking or metarepresentation, because they use symbols in order to solve problems that require a certain distance from lower order stimuli. On the other hand, these animals obviously do not need to understand that representations can misrepresent, or to understand what propositions are, or that they can be true or false, or indeed to have even the faintest grasp of aspectuality—all essential features of the belief concept.

Emphasizing the visibility of material symbols as tools to aid cognition is also one of the major inspirations for a relative latecomer in the mind-reading literature. Ironically, the name mindreading, picked as a neutral term between theory theoreticians and its main challenger (the so-called simulation theory), has turned out to be less neutral than intended. Mindshapers argue that attributing mental states to self and others is not something we do to predict people's behaviour in the first instance, but to shape it.[8]

---

[6] Clark (2006) says yes, Bermudez (2003) says no. According to Bermudez, symbol use is not enough, because language requires compositionality. There is also a chicken and egg issue here, because many people believe that using language requires an understanding of metarepresentation (Grice 1957).

[7] It is not 100% clear that Mercier and Sperber would be fully on board with the permissive understanding of metarepresentation I attribute to them. They do list the many representational domains mentioned here, but they talk about mental representations of numerals. In this case, they could either mean that users think about the different structure of the representational vehicle, or that they understand them as mental representations with a particular vehicle. The latter would not fit with the argument advanced here, but it also seems implausible that it would be possible to understand numerals as mental representations without understanding the concept of belief.

[8] On mindshaping in general see Zawidsky (2008) or Hutto (2012).

In the context of this book, specifically interesting is the work by Victoria McGeer, who focuses on the dimension of mindshaping that consists in the voluntary regulation of beliefs. Material symbols facilitate what Phillip Pettit and Victoria McGeer (2002) call content attention, i.e. a way of making and maintaining features of content salient independent of ongoing mental effort. In the above discussion of Clark's material symbols, we have already seen how attending to the material vehicles of symbols does have an effect on the kinds of cognitive operations a mind can perform. Through these symbols, the concept of sameness or difference becomes computable for the chimpanzees.

In the next section, therefore, we will have a closer look at different levels of behaviours that have a shaping effect on the mind to see what forms of metarepresentation are important for which kind of shaping.

3. Metarepresentation and Shepherding

Let us begin by looking at the most basic ways in which behaviour shapes cognition and consider whether such processes seem to require any form of metarepresentational awareness. The clear answer to this question seems to be a resounding no!

Obviously, it is possible to influence cognition without being aware that this is what one is doing. When a deer turns around to see whether there is a wolf behind it, this will enable it to acquire a new belief about the presence and the location of wolves that it could not have acquired without looking. If all that is required for an action to be shepherding is that it enables some form of cognition that would not have been possible without it, then the deer has shepherded its cognition by turning its head. But the deer is obviously not interested in beliefs at all, simply in the presence of wolves, so on this understanding of shepherding metarepresentation is clearly not necessary (see Vierkant 2012, Vierkant & Paraskevaides 2012.

The above example demonstrates that understanding shepherding very liberally is implausible. In fact, we can strengthen this point by pushing shepherding even further down the evolutionary ladder. If managerial control is defined as behaviour that enables new forms of cognition, then this also works for a bacterium turning around because it senses a higher concentration of sugar. Indeed, it is quite banal to state that behaviour will change input and in so doing, will have an influence on the potential cognitive operations the organism can perform on that input.

In the bacteria example, there is also an easy way of explaining why its behaviour is not managerial control. Managerial control is intentional control: bacteria do not engage in managerial control because they do not act intentionally at all. This seems a very fair reply, inasmuch as bacteria are concerned, but things get slightly more complicated with the head-turning deer. One could try to take the same line here and argue that deer do not act intentionally either but simply behave and therefore, the head turning of the deer cannot be a managerial action, because it is not an intentional action at all.

There are some philosophers (e.g. Davidson 2001) that might be tempted by this answer, because it does seem right to say that deer do not have language and probably do not think about their own thoughts. If either language or second order cognitive dynamics are a necessary condition for intentional action, then deer do not act intentionally. Most people, however, feel that imposing such highly intellectualist conditions seems too strong a line to take in relation to a condition for a plausible definition of intentional action. But is there another way to argue that a deer can behave intentionally, despite it not being linguistic or a metarepresenter?

Tim Bayne (2013) has one suggestion for how to avoid this unpalatable conclusion. He suggests that it makes sense to distinguish between hardwired and inflexible instinctive responses on the one hand, and more flexible and goal-directed behaviour on the other. This type of behaviour can then be attributed to the agent, rather than to a sub-system, and can thus be referred to as 'voluntary action' (2013: 164).

This seems like a much more plausible definition and we will adopt it for our context, although there is an obvious problem with it. Even if we accept that intentional action is the behaviour of the agent rather than of a subsystem the question remains: how it is possible to know whether a behaviour was agentive or not? In the human case there are two ways to find out: one is to see whether the behaviour looks similar enough to other behaviour that clearly is intentional; the other is to simply ask the individual concerned. But in the animal case, the second route is not available, because animals do not report anything. Obviously, the first route is treacherous as well, because it is very hard to know what exactly it means for a behaviour to be clearly intentional, or to know whether there could not be a more conservative non-intentional explanation for the behaviour.

Nevertheless, Bayne argues convincingly that this should not lead us to a sceptical stance with regard to intentional action in animals, because (a) it is not obvious why the first kind of evidence cannot be sufficient and (b) there is more than enough evidence that introspective evidence is not as reliable as one might think (for the detailed argument, see Bayne 2013). Using the first route, it then seems to make sense to say that on the whole, the more flexible and cognitively integrated a behaviour is, the more likely it is that it is intentional. There are clearly enormous differences between simple reflexes and the complex behaviours of animals (think e.g. of the coordinated behaviour of hunting lionesses) and pre-linguistic human children.

Finally, this rule of thumb seems to chime quite well with the literature on language evolution. In this literature, it is often claimed that gesture must be at the beginning of human language because it is under voluntary control, while vocalizations are not (Corballis 2003). In line with Bayne's rule, the evidence that gestures are voluntary is typically that gesturing is more flexible and less stereotyped. Given that the Bayne heuristic makes excellent sense not only of our intuitions in general but also of the specific literature, and given also that it is clear that we very much need a distinction between inflexible instinctive behaviour and flexibly controlled voluntary behaviour to adequately describe these phenomena, we will continue to apply his heuristic here.[9]

To return to the example of the deer: if we accept that deer might well act intentionally when they turn their heads to look out for a wolf, then the question becomes, whether this intentional action is also an act of shepherding. Importantly, here we will also need to establish whether this is because of the type of behaviour that the deer is engaging in, or the mindset it has while doing so. Clearly, not only deer but also humans occasionally turn their heads in order to help their cognition.

In fact, one might argue that the kinds of behaviours that Kirsh and Maglio are talking about are not very different from the head-turning deer. They defined an epistemic action as a physical action that makes mental computation easier, faster, or more reliable (Kirsh and Maglio 1994: 514f). It is undeniable that the deer can perform different and more reliable computations about the presence of wolves by turning its head. Actually, Kirsh and Maglio would probably be willing to accept that re-orientating sensors is an epistemic action. In fact, they argue that in robotic research this is something that was being investigated, but they were particularly interested in actions that did not simply reorient sensors or attention, but help to make tasks easier by structuring the environment in helpful ways. As real-life examples,

---

[9] For an excellent overview of the many different aspects of voluntary action see Krisst, Montemayor, and Morsella (2015: 25–62).

they discuss for example actions like sorting nails, or placing a key in a shoe. But again, behaviour like this neither seems to require any understanding of the nature of representations, nor does it seem to be uniquely human. Beavers building dams or dogs leaving scents show, alongside countless other examples, that intentional behaviour that has the function to shepherd the mind in some sense does not have to be metarepresentational.

Perhaps this is the reason why most thinkers are in this respect more conservative and demand, as for example Metzinger (2017) does, the manipulation of symbols in the external world for any truly epistemic action. Most thinkers demand metarepresentation at least in the liberal Mercier and Sperber (2017) sense, where it means no more than the ability to manipulate external symbols for epistemic intentional actions. Manipulating external symbols is also what allows Sheba to solve her problem and it is behind many of the epistemic advantages Clark identifies for the use of material symbols.

The theory that probably makes most use of such intentional epistemic actions is one approach to mindshaping especially prominent in the work of Victoria Mc Geer. She argues that the crucial advantage of material symbols, in contrast to propositional attitudes like beliefs, is that they are under the voluntary control of the agent. As discussed in Chapter 2: coming to believe that p is not a voluntary affair, whereas asserting p or writing down p most definitely is.[10]

Pettit and McGeer make this point by stating that language enables belief regulation.[11] Language also allows you to overcome any natural but fallible evaluative tendencies that you might have. Pettit and McGeer discuss a practical example of this: the pilot who can overcome her natural evaluation of whether the plane is going up or down that stems from her proprioception by focusing on the instruments.

Yet this is just one neat example: language does so much more. It allows you to rehearse arguments, to focus on specific dimensions of a problem, to

---

[10] This is the point that Frankish uses for the creation of his super beliefs in Chapter 3.
[11] There is an interesting link between what has been said here about mindshaping and Joelle Proust's account of procedural metacognition. Metacognition is often understood as mindreading for self: once we understand what minds are, we then begin to try to read and influence them. In the case of others, this comes under the heading of mindreading and in the case of self, under the heading metacognition. Joelle Proust, probably the philosopher who has contributed more to the philosophy of metacognition than anyone else, has always argued that this understanding is a mistake. According to Proust, what she calls procedural metacognition is primarily about self-evaluation. These evaluations often do not involve the capacity to self-attribute mental states. Instead, they operate e.g. with noetic feelings like fluency to monitor ongoing cognitive activity (Proust 2013).

make evidence more easily available, and so on. Most of the actions we have discussed since Chapter 1 are enabled by language, and most of them do not necessarily require that the agent understands that they are a psychological creature. When the small child learns behavioural rules in nursery rhymes, she does not have to understand beliefs in order to do so. Even adults do not need to contemplate any facts about intentionality or intensionality in order to know that going to the library or googling might help them to find the solution to a specific problem they want to solve.

The other obvious domain for cognitive self-regulation that language opens up is communication; talking to others is one, if not the most powerful, tool in the human cognitive armoury and as we have already heard, according to Mercier and Sperber, communication is what reasoning is for. Indeed, they have stressed that it is not necessary to understand psychological concepts in order to use reasoning.[12]

As should have become clear in these few paragraphs, the intentional control of material symbols, be it for self-directed mindshaping purposes or communication, is a critical turning point for the evolution of human thought. In fact, there are very many thinkers who hold that being able to use material symbols in one way or another is what makes humans different from other animals. Nonetheless, despite its enormous importance, use of material symbols is not typical managerial control as we introduced it in Chapter 2. In that chapter, managerial control was introduced as being attitude directed. In a typical managerial action, the agent treats their mentality as an object and manipulates it in the same way as they would an ordinary object in a physical action. However, given the liberal understanding of metarepresentation we took from Mercier and Sperber, and despite the fact that manipulating material symbols is a form of thinking about thinking, being able to manipulate material symbols does not require the agent to have the faintest idea of what a mental representation is. In fact, the beauty of material symbols is that they are much more accessible and easier to grasp than the invisible propositional attitudes (Vierkant 2012).[13]

In view of the discussion above, one might now ask what is so important about the ability to think about propositional attitudes themselves if material symbols so handsomely deliver all the cognitive goods?

---

[12] Another powerful voice for the importance of social mind-shaping practices is Tad Zawidski's (2008) work.
[13] For a recent version of this link between language and intentional epistemic agency see Fairweather and Montemayor (2017).

The simple answer is that despite the enormous power of the manipulation of material symbols, there are certain problems that are not solvable as long as one does not understand the psychological nature of the manipulated representations. Material symbols are excellent tools for attention to content, but they do not help the agent to focus on the mental states from which their intentionality derives. They are therefore great tools when it comes to deliberation about first order problems, but they do not automatically enable an understanding or even an awareness of psychological states. For most problems this does not matter, because after all, representations are mainly useful because their content represents some fact in the world. Clearly, however, not all cases fall into this category. Only if one can take what Moran in Chapter 3 called the theoretical stance toward one's own mentality is it possible to solve puzzles like Pascal's attempt to believe in God without any evidence for God's existence. As long as we are merely focused on deliberating about the evidence for the proposition that God exists, we cannot take into account reasons that we might have for simply holding the belief. It is rather obvious that if one wants to form intentions about beliefs, then one needs to have the concept of belief.

A more practical example for the importance of the theoretical stance is the case of Parfit's (1984) young communist I discuss in my article 'What Metarepresentation Is For' (2012. In this example, a young communist judges that the right thing to do would be to give his inheritance away, but he also knows as a general psychological fact that by the time he is 40, his values might well have changed and he would probably achieve more happiness in his life overall if he kept the money. Importantly, Parfit does not say that the perspective of the 40-year-old is the correct one, but that it is very difficult for the young communist to take the perspective of his older self into account. Given that he believes very firmly that the right thing to do is to give the money away, accepting that he will believe the opposite is almost Moore paradoxical. He has to be able to believe that it will still be right in 20 years to give the money away, and at the same time believe that by then, it is very likely that he will believe that it is not. Understanding this is only possible once he shifts out of the deliberative stance, where the belief that p is transparent to p in to the theoretical stance. Only once he has done so can he then deliberate on whether he should follow his current value system or maximize utility over his lifetime.[14] This is why future directed self-control is one of the key examples of the importance of intentional attitude directed actions, and we will look at this in detail in the next chapter.

This regulation of belief qua attitude is very different to the regulation of cognitive states that is possible via mind shaping. Pettit and McGeer's pilot example shows that material symbols can easily be used to regulate beliefs, but what is different in this case is that the mindshaper simply learns that one form of evidence is less reliable than another. She does not need to leave the deliberative stance, whereas managing current beliefs has the paradoxical flavour of intentional self-deception: the agent is trying to make themselves believe something, despite the fact that she strongly believes that this specific belief is not supported by the evidence.

4. Is Metarepresentational Managerial Control an Argument to Uphold the Distinction Between Brain-Bound and Environment-Involving Actions?

As we have seen over the course of the previous section, the notion of managerial control is surprisingly unclear. The standard examples of managerial control as attitude-directed control are highly sophisticated in their metarepresentational requirements, but on the other hand, intentional shepherdings of the mind happen not only in such cases but also with much weaker metarepresentational capacities and without metarepresentational abilities. Finally, we can even talk about behaviour shepherding cognition in cases where there is no action at all, because there is not an agent. Cognition and behaviour are interwoven at all levels.[15]

Second, despite the fact that the prototypical managerial action is one where the agent is targeting an attitude with their intention, it is not these actions, but the manipulation of the material symbols of language, numbers, and reasons that are the ones that are most important for the development

---

[14] Parfit himself by the way does not use this example to show that the young man should keep the money, but to demonstrate that there is something wrong with a theory that only focuses on utility maximization over the course of a lifetime.

[15] Given that this investigation is interested in intentional mental actions, the fact that cognition and behaviour are also closely interwoven at the sub-personal level is not a core issue for this book, but it is worth keeping this in mind, because this interwovenness is most prominent in so called 4E approaches (Newen et al. 2018). Thus, it might not come as a great surprise that understanding intentional mental actions as part of cognition also aligns well with an acceptance of extended cognition.

of a distinctly human rationality. Both Clark's and McGeer's work provides us with evidence for why intentional, mindshaping actions might be what human rational agency is all about. Pettit and McGeer are very explicit here. According to them, human minds are best characterized as self-regulating minds, because of their ability to manipulate material symbols in the external world, in contrast to the routinized minds of other animals who lack this ability. Indeed, the very fact that material symbols are outside the head and thereby easier to grasp and to manipulate is what has made them such powerful scaffolds of internal cognitive processes. Furthermore, as we have also seen, it is not necessary for an agent to use these tools to first develop a theory of mental states.

Oddly enough, this is even true if the agent does learn to perform these actions inside the head. When we try to remind ourselves for example of the 12 times table, our goal is to have a series of numbers before our inner eye: we do not need to possess the concept of belief, or indeed of any propositional attitude, to do so. However, despite all this, it is also true that there is a special trick that works only by targeting psychological attitudes. This is the case whenever we need to switch from the evaluative to the theoretical stance (Moran 2001). This happens in cases like Pascal's or Parfit's young communist, where the agent is interested in the attitude as an attitude, rather than as the bearer of some content. This is what Hieronymi (2009) has in mind when she discusses managerial actions.

In these cases, there really is a need for an understanding of inner mental states. Nevertheless, while it is true that this is special in terms of the target of the intentional action (it is truly attitude directed) and these attitudes seem to be inside (if we do not buy into the radical extended mind), managing them clearly often uses actions that are realized via the environment—Pascal, for example, suggested going to mass or praying rosaries to change the belief.

Finally, while it is true that real attitude-directed actions do target internal states, it also seems quite likely that learning to target propositional attitudes develops because of external scaffolds, as discussed in Chapter 4 (see e.g. Fernández-Castro and Martínez-Manrique (2020); Metzinger (2017); and McCleland (2017).

On the whole, then, it seems fair to conclude that metarepresentation does not provide an argument for a special category of internal mental intentional actions that are more closely connected to cognition than environment-involving actions.

Nonetheless, looking at metarepresentation was very useful. It has taught us that tinkering is not only 'under the hood' (Moran 2001). Not only can shepherding the mind be done outside the head, it can also be done without any awareness that propositional attitudes exist. If this is correct and environment-involving actions are managerial actions which often do not even target attitudes, then tinkering with the mind also happens in the external world. Given that everybody agrees how important this kind of thinking about thinking is for the uniqueness of human rationality, one might wonder whether it really is the understanding of psychological attitudes that makes human minds special. Even in the cases like Pascal where metarepresentational abilities are necessary, we have seen that the biggest effect on cognition is not direct but via management, and what is more, management that often involves the environment.

This is important because it does now give us a different reading of Frankfurt. Hieronymi was very dismissive about changing attitudes like your socks, but perhaps the ability to do so is actually a quintessential part of human cognition?

PART II

SYSTEM TWO AND THE MORAL MIND

In this second part of the book we will come full circle. The investigation started out by identifying the puzzle of mental rational agency in moral psychology as one that had important lessons for the philosophy of cognitive science. In this part, it will now become clear how the lessons learned from the discussion of the rational mental agency problem in the cognitive science context can be in turn used to derive a better understanding of a number of fascinating phenomena in moral psychology.

Many authors in both philosophy and psychology have argued that the effortful control of the mind in system two is crucially important for human moral agency. This part will discuss the work of two prominent writers in this field, Richard Holton and Neil Levy, and evaluate what the lessons from the simple argument mean for their work.

Richard Holton is a towering figure in the discussion of the will and like Levy, Holton is an expert on the empirical literature on the relevant issues. More specifically for our purposes, Holton endorses the influential (if controversial) mental muscle view of willpower developed by Baumeister, Tice, and Vohs (2008), which is firmly based on a two systems approach.[1]

In the next two chapters, we will look at Holton's account of willpower and choice that seems particularly interesting in the context of the discussion of this book. Holton (2009b) himself singles out these two phenomena as the two items of the mental inventory that are critically involved in the phenomenology of freedom and mental agency. He argues that the

---

[1] Just to be very clear here. Holton endorses Baumeister but this book does not. The mental muscle theory which Baumeister defends seemed convincing when Holton came up with his account but has been severely damaged by the replication crisis (e.g. Vohs et al. 2021). As we will see at the end of the chapter in actual fact the issues discussed in this book can be seen as ammunition for critical questions about the Baumeister approach.

philosophical debate on free will between incompatibilists and compatibilist positions, while interesting, probably does not capture the main ingredient that makes ordinary people attribute freedom of the will to themselves.

Incompatibilists hold that freedom of the will is not compatible with determinism, while compatibilists think that it is possible to be free under the conditions of determinism. There is a large literature by now on the question whether or not lay people are intuitive incompatibilists or not (Nahmias et al. 2007; Nichols and Knobe 2007; Vierkant et al. 2019), but Holton suspects that it is quite likely that what people really mean when they talk about not being determined is a much more local determinism than the universal determinism that is usually in play in the philosophical free will debate. He argues that the experience of freedom stems from the sense that we are not fully determined by our beliefs and desires, rather than the universe at large, and from the experience that we can act to influence our choices or whether we stick to our intentions. We as mental agents can shape our choices and act to make sure that we follow through on the resolutions we form.

Famously, standard compatibilist accounts have a problem here. They seem to leave no room for choices made by agents. All that has to be done for a decision is to execute a weighing process of the relevant beliefs and desires. The process that leads to the choice does not look agentive at all, but as R.J. Wallace (1999) aptly puts it, 'hydraulic'. It is as if one could hear the whirring of cogs and imagine the pumps operating to produce the intention. Such a process, whatever else it may be, seems to have very little to do with choices in the ordinary sense.

Choices in everyday language are actions taken by agents and they feel genuinely open. It does not feel to the agent as if choices only require the execution of a calculation process that leads to a determined outcome. What I want to call the agency problem of compatibilism that Wallace points to is very similar to the core problem of this book. Mental agency can be understood as the workings of the rational mind, represented in this debate as the belief desire calculus, but even if we were to accept this form of agency as sufficient for free will and moral responsibility, as the compatibilists seem to suggest, it still seems inadequate to capture our intuition about what it is to be an agent.

David Velleman suggests a solution here that is Frankfurtian in spirit, because it postulates a second order desire to be rational.[2] As we have seen,

---

[2] It should be noted here that his solution does not satisfy Wallace who argues that Velleman's account is also hydraulic.

moves like this are popular, but as Hieronymi points out, they obscure the relationship between the second order desire and first order states. At first, this relationship appears to resemble something like intentional control, but on a closer look it becomes clear that this cannot be true. Instead, the control in play here is simply a form of reason responsiveness.

As we have seen in Part I, while this might still be enough to justify the attribution of responsibility to creatures who possess this form of agency, it does not convince philosophers like Strawson that this is enough to make thinking or choosing an action in the intuitive intentional sense.

This is why Holton's solution is so intriguing. He takes seriously the idea that the agency that the pre-theoretical intuition refers to is intentional agency. Making a choice and sticking to one's intentions is intuitively an intentional action, just like lifting one's arm.

There is much that is important and right in Holton's thoughts about mental agency, but Holton is also influenced strongly by dual systems accounts in psychology and especially his account of choice makes use of the mental architecture provided by such approaches. Applying the lessons from the first half of the book will allow us to develop Holton's insights and to see some interesting implications that were obscured by the unclear standard picture of system two as the rational and intentional system.

On the one hand, the following chapter will focus on Holton's argument that exercising willpower is an intentional action. This is interesting because Holton, as well as most philosophers, would also want to argue that there is a deep difference between true willpower and so-called 'tying to the mast' strategies, where the agent uses intentional actions to manipulate the environment and so achieve the self-control effect that willpower achieves by sheer mental force. However, if we apply the lesson from Chapter 4 that there simply cannot be a deep difference between intentional actions inside the head and ones that involve the environment, then we can see that if willpower is an intentional action, this deep difference is not coherent.

Second, Holton's discussion of choice is also very relevant for the purposes of this book. Holton argues that choice brings the intentional agent into the rational decision-making process. However, we have seen that intentional agency can only play an indirect role in the bringing forth of new content. Holton's solution to this quandary is ingenious, but his account is underdeveloped in one crucial respect. Bringing in the lessons from the first half of the book, Chapter 7 will fill this lacuna.

6
Willpower and Epistemic Agency

Odysseus was able to listen to the Sirens unharmed, even though their song was such that everybody else who had heard it before jumped off their ship and died in the sea. This episode is certainly one of Odysseus's finer achievements, but it seems very odd to say that it is one where Odysseus showed great strength of will. Odysseus manages to achieve his goal by having himself tied to the ship's mast by his sailors before they get close to the Sirens. The sailors then put wax in their ears and so are able to row the ship past the Sirens, because they cannot hear them. Odysseus can, but he can't give in to his desire to jump overboard, because he is tied to the mast. Because he is tied, he cannot decide to give in to temptation. He is not free to do what he wants to do at the moment when he hears the Sirens, and therefore, it makes little sense to praise him for his strength of will in this case.

Willpower does not seem to play a role in this particular scenario. Odysseus is clearly praiseworthy, because he is clever, because he is a good judge of his own mind and he is capable of thinking of ways that will ensure that he will behave in the way that is best for his long-term interests, even if the temptation to not do that is incredibly strong. But even though his cleverness has the same effect as an act of willpower, insofar as it allows him to withstand temptation, it seems obvious that it achieves that effect by fundamentally different means.[1] In fact, the Odysseus strategy is used to describe a whole class of self-control strategies that achieve their control aim without apparently having to use willpower, i.e. so-called 'tying to the mast' strategies. If an agent uses willpower to withstand temptation, they use their capacities as agents to not be tempted, while tying to the mast strategies temporarily disable agency for the period when one might be tempted. Willpower is about defeating temptation head on as an agent, tying oneself to the mast simply makes it impossible to give in to temptation, whatever the

---

[1] See Heath and Anderson 2010 for an argument to the effect that Odysseus should count as a case of willpower and Paglieri 2012 for an argument that uses the move discussed in the text to dismiss this.

agent would want to do at the time. The agent is simply not free to do otherwise, in even the weakest and most uncontroversial sense of this term.

But this intuition is mistaken. *If we take the lessons of the first half of the book seriously, then it can be shown that there is no qualitative difference between the way tying to the mast strategies defeat temptation and the way someone defeats temptation by using willpower in the more standard sense.* This is because, if we understand willpower along the same lines as Holton (2009a), then willpower operates in a way that is structurally identical to a tying to the mast strategy. *In both cases, the agent performs an intentional 'tying to the mast action' and the ties put in place by that action stop the agent from giving in to temptation.*

Alternatively, if we translate the vocabulary used in the debate on willpower into the jargon of the first half of the book, tying to the mast actions are nothing other than the shepherding or stage setting or managerial mental actions of Part I of this book. They are intentional mental actions that influence evaluative processes without being evaluative themselves.

If willpower consists in intentional mental actions, then the only difference between the specific tying to the mast strategy Odysseus uses and the use of standard willpower lies in the strength and durability of the ties that are put in place by the tying action. Obviously, they are extremely stable in the Odysseus case and they are relatively flimsy in the standard willpower case.

As in the cognitive case, there is no difference between intentional mental actions that happen inside the head and ones that utilize the environment. The only way to understand willpower in a way that would put a qualitative difference between willpower and tying to the mast strategies would be to understand willpower as evaluative agency, which, as Chapter 5 showed, does not extend. Understanding willpower as a form of rational agency has been quite commonplace in the literature and so the tradition might not feel too troubled by the argument that follows. However, as we will see in the next section, there are very good reasons for why one should understand exercising willpower as an intentional action. The clearest exposition of the arguments for this position can be found in Richard Holton's work.

1. What Is Willpower?

In order to get the argument off the ground, we first need to gain an understanding of what willpower is supposed to be according to Holton.

Crucially, Holton holds that acts of willpower consist in intentional actions, rather than in exercises of practical rationality, as was traditionally understood to be the case. On Holton's picture, willpower works in the following way: at some point in time an agent forms an intention to do something in the future, but knows that she might not want to do it once the time comes. She might for example form the intention to go for a run on Sunday morning on Saturday, but know that she will not be very keen when Sunday morning comes along. Holton calls such intentions which the agent forms, despite knowing that their judgment may be in danger of shifting about them by the time they have to be implemented, 'resolutions' (2009a: 9f).

Once an agent has formed a resolution, they can now use that resolution in the face of temptation in the following way: when the agent notices that they are tempted not to act in accordance with the resolution, they rehearse the reasons for not giving in to temptation and in that way strengthen their resolve. Crucially however, this rehearsal is not an exercise of deliberation but instead an intentional action that actually prevents the agent from engaging in full-blown practical deliberation (2009a: 121f.).

According to Holton, practical deliberation is undesirable in tempting situations, because if the agent were allowed to fully deliberate, they would come to the conclusion that they should give in to temptation. This is exactly what happens when an agent is weak willed. Weakness of the will is a consequence of too much deliberation under temptation. Thus, willpower is necessary when our deliberative capacities are in danger of being corrupted by temptation (2009a; Chapters 5 and 6). Willpower is not about preventing oneself from acting against one's best judgment,[2] but about stopping the rational mind itself being corrupted. The rehearsal in this account is therefore not a full-fledged exercise in practical rationality, but rather a tool to prevent such an exercise. The agent rehearses in order to stop herself from deliberating, because deliberation would lead to a judgment shift that would rank giving in to temptation higher than pursuing the long-term goal. Rehearsals feel like a struggle, because the mind is constantly drawn to the now very salient reasons why one should give in to temptation.

---

[2] Holton reserves the term akrasia for cases of acting against one's best judgment. Holton does not deny that akrasia exists as well, but he does not think that these are the cases that are described as typical weakness of the will situations in ordinary usage. Thus, strength of will is the ability to resist unwanted judgment shifts.

But why should we think that this is the correct account of willpower? Unfortunately, there is not enough space here to give a full defence of Holton's view, though we can at least discuss Holton's two main reasons for holding this account. Both reasons seem so plausible that it seems worthwhile exploring the potential implications of the account. On the one hand, Holton points to the phenomenology of exercising willpower. Resisting temptation feels like a mental struggle, something we have to try to do again and again, and we have only limited resources to keep up the fight. His account captures this intuition very well, but it seems that all accounts that rely on practical rationality rather than intentional action will struggle to explain this phenomenology. Holton calls his stalking horse here 'augmented Humean accounts'. According to such accounts, resolutions work like promises. The agent promises herself not to give in to temptation and if she does not want to be someone who breaks her promises, then she now has an extra reason to stick to her long-term goal because of the resolution.

The problem with such accounts is that even after the promises, the exercise of willpower is still simply about evaluating what the best action would be. The resolution does change this calculation and might therefore help to avoid temptation, but it is difficult to see why willpower could feel effortful if this account were right. Either the agent evaluates that she should give in to temptation or she evaluates that her future goals are more valuable to her, but whichever way she decides it seems that there should be no need for any struggle after the evaluation. The agent will simply do what she thinks is best.[3]

Additionally, as discussed in detail in the first half of the book, evaluations seem not to be the kind of thing that we can do intentionally anyway (Hieronymi 2009), while effortful actions always seem to have an intentional component. So, on the plausible assumption that the phenomenology of willpower clearly does contain a mental struggle, evaluative accounts will not be in a strong position to explain this phenomenology.

The second reason for Holton holding his account ties in nicely with the first. It seems that the Holton picture fits the wealth of empirical data that have recently been accumulated from developmental and social psychology (2009a: 120). Holton refers on the one hand to studies of delayed

---

[3] The only possible struggle here could be between what the agent wants and some motivational force that she is alienated from, but weak-willed actions are supposed to be full-fledged actions by the agent rather than compulsions where the agent cannot stand up to an irresistible psychological force outside the agent.

gratification tasks in developmental psychology (Mischel 1996), where subjects are confronted with a choice between a small reward now (one cookie) or a large reward (two cookies) ten minutes later. In these studies, it could be shown that children perform much better when they engage in the kind of rehearsals that Holton talks about. More importantly even, in social psychology, Baumeister (e.g. 2008) and colleagues have produced an impressive body of work that seems to indicate that there is a special faculty that humans use to achieve self-control aims. The most prominent finding here is the phenomenon of ego depletion. Baumeister and colleagues could show that resisting temptation seems to require the usage of a mental resource that is strictly limited. Trying not to eat the cookies will affect the performance on an unrelated task that requires the same resource, like gripping a handlebar as hard as you can some time later. They could also show that it is possible to train this resource, leading them to the very intuitive metaphor of willpower as a mental muscle that can be trained and exhausted. Obviously, this work provides great empirical support for Holton's phenomenological observation that willpower is characterized by a mental struggle.[4]

2. Why Willpower Is a Tying to the Mast Strategy

According to Holton, in a willpower case the agent disables her rational evaluation capacities temporarily by rehearsing the argument in order to not give in to temptation. At this point it is worth reminding the reader of the conclusion we reached in Chapter 5. There, we showed that we can understand rational mental agency only either as evaluative agency, in which case there were no rational intentional mental actions, or we could argue that there are intentional mental actions, in which case there would not be a difference between intentional mental actions like rehearsals and environment-involving mental actions. Holton's account is very much in line with the first interpretation. Rehearsals are described as intentional actions that are not part of rational evaluative agency, but rather impede it. But if this is correct, then it is not the case that in contrast to the Odysseus case agents using willpower fight temptations using their rational agentive (i.e. evaluative) powers, but instead they do exactly what the Greek hero

---

[4] It has to be noted here that the Baumeister work is involved in the replication crisis and there is an ongoing debate about the ego depletion model (see Baumeister et al. 2018) for a reaction to his critics.

did—they intentionally bind themselves to a (in their case mental) mast. In this case, the ties consist in the rehearsal that makes it impossible for the agent to evaluate the situation neutrally. As the evaluation is what constitutes the mental agent, disabling evaluation disables mental agency.[5]

This is the core of the argument, but a lot needs to be said to make it really clear and plausible. First of all, some clarifications are in order: Holton does acknowledge that our ordinary language use does not clearly distinguish between cases where the agent ties him- or herself to the mast mentally, by distracting him- or herself, and cases where the agent uses rehearsals. However, Holton believes that only the latter should be thought of as agent involving. Following on from this view, Holton legislates that only these cases should be thought of as 'real' willpower (2009a: 127).

Furthermore, my interpretation of Holton's story differs at a crucial point from his own. Holton argues that rehearsal is not arational (2009a: 147), as I have claimed here. However, if the rehearsal is *not* arational, then it looks as if we can have our intentional action account of willpower and be mental agents at the same time. Holton's reason for saying that rehearsal is not arational is that, in contrast to an arational strategy, rehearsal does allow the agent to remain moderately reason-sensitive. If, for example, it turned out that on Sunday morning there was a snowstorm and it would be dangerous to go outside, then the agent would still be able to appreciate this danger, despite the fact that she had just got herself out of bed by rehearsing her reasons for going for a run. This is in marked contrast to the Odysseus scenario, where it would not help Odysseus at all if he recognized a couple of miles before the Sirens that his sailors were about to hit an underwater rock. His ties are truly arational and Odysseus would not be able to react flexibly to this new situation: if the ship sank, he would go down with it.

But even though this sounds very plausible, what is being said here is actually very unclear. The Odysseus case is slightly misleading, because it creates the impression that the crucial difference between a tying to the mast case and 'real' willpower is that a tied agent loses all agentive powers and becomes entirely passive, but most external ties are not like that, as even a very moderate twist to the story can show. Suppose the Sirens do not bring instant death but would nevertheless be able to overcome Odysseus's clear long-term preference to get home to Penelope, and imagine also that

---

[5] Obviously according to the lessons from Chapter 5, one could also accept that intentional actions can be a constitutive part of rational agency. But in that case, we would have to accept that tying to the mast cases are also cases of real willpower.

Odysseus has his leg chained to the mast in order to avoid being able to fall for the Sirens' song, because even while listening to the Sirens he would still prefer having his leg to being with the Sirens. This set up seems relevantly parallel to the original story. Odysseus still manages to listen to the Sirens without endangering achieving his long-term preferences, because even though the Sirens' song will switch his preferences for the time that he hears it, he is not able to do something about it, because the only way that he could do something about it would entail doing something that he does not want to do (chopping off his leg), even while hearing the Sirens' song.

Although the scenario does appear parallel in many respects, there is an interesting difference between the two: in this second scenario, if Odysseus sees that the ship will hit a rock, he does have the option of cutting off his leg to avoid going down with the ship. Does that mean that the chaining to the mast has now become an intentional action that preserves rationality and is perhaps even an act of willpower, because in this scenario some agentive powers are clearly preserved? To argue this would be a very strange move for a defender of a position that emphasizes the difference between tying to the mast strategies and 'true' willpower. Odysseus is still passive with regard to the chain that stops him from jumping overboard and presumably the defender of real willpower will say that this means that there is no willpower necessary at all, if the chains ensure that Odysseus is not tempted to jump, because he does not want to cut off his leg in order to be able to do so.

But if one accepts that this change to the story does not make the Odysseus case a case of willpower just because some reason responsiveness is preserved, then the example clearly shows that the mere fact that the agent is still reason responsive cannot be what distinguishes a rehearsal from a tying to the mast action: rehearsals must be special in a way that is more than just the fact that the agent stays reason responsive.

In the next two sections we will look at potential ideas which suggest what this specialness might be. We will examine whether rehearsals are special because they contain an element of struggle, or whether they might be special because they help to confront temptation. What we will discover, however, is that there is no way in which rehearsals are fundamentally different from mental tying to the mast strategies like distractions. Once this core point is accepted, it will become much less obvious that there could be a clear line between willpower and any tying to the mast strategy. Pushing this line as far as possible brings us back to the claim that there is no obvious clear line between even Odysseus cases and real willpower.

3. Where Did All the Struggle Go?

One of the main reasons to endorse the Holton account was that it got the phenomenology of willpower right. As Holton points out, the exercise of willpower seems to be characterized by effortful intentional tryings to do the right thing, and Holton argued that the main rival accounts are not able to explain this phenomenology adequately. For the purposes of this chapter, this was assumed to be correct. The chapter then proceeded to argue that the intentional tryings in the exercise of willpower are nothing other than tying to the mast strategies, which are structurally identical to the Odysseus scenario.

There seems to be a major problem lurking here, however. If tying to the mast strategies really are like willpower, then it seems that the struggle cannot be an essential component of willpower. Odysseus might struggle against his ties, but not because he wants to resist temptation, but because he desperately wants to give in to it. More generally, the very point of ties seems to be to take the need for a struggle away. So, if willpower really consists in tying to the mast strategies, then the phenomenology of the struggle must be mistaken. This in turn seems to make the whole position unstable, because it was built on the assumption that Holton's account is plausible, yet this plausibility rests to a large degree on the plausibility of the phenomenology of struggle.[6]

Answering this very powerful objection will need some careful preparation: first of all, there should be a concession. The Odysseus case might be the archetypical tying to the mast scenario, but it is not the archetypical willpower scenario. However, this is not to concede that it is qualitatively different from 'true' willpower cases. The concession simply states that Odysseus is a limiting case of the huge variety of intentional strategies to control the mind.[7] It is a limiting case because the way the story is told, the control by the environment imposed in this case is maximally inflexible and installed long before the moment of temptation. In order to get a better picture of the claim, it is at this stage necessary to get a clearer idea of the strategies which have a much higher flexibility.

We have seen already that even relatively small tweaks to the story can make quite a difference to the intuition that tying to the mast strategies

---

[6] Thanks to Mike Ridge for pointing this worry out to me.
[7] For a discussion of the different varieties of intentional strategies to control the mind see Vierkant 2012 and Vierkant & Paraskevaides 2012.

automatically disable all agency. Instead, what they do is restructure the environment so that the options for the agent are systematically changed in such a way that the desired option is the one that will likely be the most attractive one for the agent. Still, in the tying to the mast case discussed, it is still the case that the chain is very durable, the cost of getting out of it is very high, and most importantly, the chain is clearly outside Odysseus's head.

Because of all of these factors, all defenders of a deep gap will probably be very confident that my second scenario is not a case of willpower either. All that the scenario could demonstrate was that the difference between tying to the mast scenarios and true willpower cannot consist in the mere fact that a tied agent is not at all able to act on reasons. Odysseus with his leg tied is clearly able to act, but equally clearly, the intuition that this situation is not one where he needs to use willpower remains unchanged from the scenario where he is fully chained to the mast.

But, all of the conditions which make these cases seem so different from real willpower cases are not present for all tying to the mast scenarios. Tying to the mast actions can create flimsy ties, breakable at a relatively low cost, and they can happen entirely inside one's head.

Think for example of distraction cases. An agent trying to lose weight might have formed the resolution not to eat too much at the lunch buffet, but when the time comes, and he is standing next to the buffet, he is very tempted by the lovely cakes on display. Now, in order to not give into temptation, he might try to engage a colleague into a discussion about some departmental gossip, because he knows that this will take his mind off the tempting cakes. Even better, if no colleague is at hand, then the agent could simply look the other way and try to work out a tricky objection to his paper. In these cases, the agent again does something intentional (chatting to the colleague, turning away, concentrating on the puzzle) that brings it about that the agent does not give into temptation. This is achieved by focusing the attention of the agent on something else. Now, according to Holton, such cases are clear tying to the mast strategies, rather than instances of true willpower, because the agent uses the intentional action to avoid temptation, rather than in order to confront it.[8]

Yet it is of note that in such cases, quite a few things are different from the Odysseus case. If the building were to burn down, then it seems not impossible for the agent to abandon the conversation or the objection and

---

[8] For a very similar argument see Paglieri (2012).

to leave the building. In these cases, this does not even come at a very high cost. Even more importantly, the gossip might not be that interesting and the objection not that pressing, so that it might take the agent quite a lot of cognitive effort to keep concentrating on it. In these cases, the phenomenology of effort will be very plausible. The less successful the distraction, the more effort it will take to maintain it.

Obviously, the upshot of this is that effort and tying to the mast strategies are not mutually exclusive. That being established, it is now quite easy to explain why Holton's observation about the phenomenology of willpower is at least compatible with the idea that willpower is nothing more than a tying to the mast strategy. This can be done either in a conciliatory way or through a more hardnosed approach. On the soft line, the argument would be to accept that Odysseus is not about willpower, because a struggle is a necessary condition for willpower, but to maintain that willpower and distraction-like cases are simply a sub-class of effortful intentional self control. The only difference between them and Odysseus-like cases is that they happen in tempting situations. Taking a hard line, one could deny that Holton's phenomenology argument requires us to accept that willpower always involves struggle. Instead, Holton's argument would still work, if it were the case that it *typically* involves a struggle. As all the distraction cases[9] fulfil the struggle condition, it would then be possible to be hardnosed and to claim that Odysseus-like cases are simply untypical cases of real willpower. Either option can maintain the bulk of the argument, but as the soft option seems slightly ad hoc, we shall proceed here assuming the hardnosed reply and claim that Odysseus is a—albeit limiting—case of willpower.

4. Confronting and Avoiding Temptation

From the discussion in the last paragraph, it should have become clear that tying to the mast strategies very often can involve a struggle in the face of temptation, but does this really fully lay to rest the worry that they are not qualitatively different from real willpower? One might, for example, object that even if it is true that tying to the mast strategies can require effort in the

---

[9] Note that it will not do here to claim that the qualitative difference between tying to the mast cases and willpower-like cases is the difference between ongoings inside or outside the head. The ties in distraction cases (TV, book, etc.) are very often outside the head, but seem to have exactly the same function as the rehearsal.

face of temptation, they are still fundamentally different from real willpower, because the effort is used to achieve fundamentally different things. In the distraction cases, the effort is used to achieve the goal of diverting attention away from temptation, thereby making agential control less arduous. Part of the control effort is taken away from the agent and loaded on to the environment. In true willpower cases, on the other hand, the effort is used to confront temptation, but with a mindset that does not allow re-evaluation. In other words, it does not seem as if the agent in these cases relinquishes any control. In fact, the very opposite seems to be the case: the agent puts her evaluative system, as it were, on a short leash and that allows her to confront temptation without being corrupted by it.

Again, this seems very intuitive and we will need to construct another distraction case to see what is wrong with it. Suppose our agent at the lunch buffet does not avert his attention from the buffet, but instead he stares right at a small bit of jelly on one of the sandwiches which he finds disgusting in order to curb his desire to give in to temptation, or he sets himself the job of arranging the mini pies in such a way that they could represent the proposition of the objection that he wants to think about. What these examples show is that it is entirely unclear what exactly is meant by the idea that someone is confronting temptation. Our agent in this scenario clearly is orientated toward the buffet and has his full concentration on it. On the other hand, he equally clearly isn't thinking of the buffet as a temptation that he has to resist, but manages by means of a lot of cognitive work to transform it into something disgusting or a puzzle. This seems parallel to the rehearsal case. It is true that in one sense the agent confronts temptation head on, by repeating his reasons for not giving in to it. But this is very much only one side of the coin. The crucial aspect of the rehearsal, as Holton states himself, is the thought that it will prevent the reopening of a real deliberation of the merits of not giving in to temptation. This is nothing else than an avoidance strategy. The agent does not confront temptation in its full force and reason with it. The very point of willpower, according to Holton, is that the agent is worried about being corrupted and prevents this from happening by avoiding letting himself fully appreciate the force of temptation.[10]

---

[10] One might ask here whether there could not be cases where the agent is aware that his long-term goal is worth more to him, but needs rehearsals so that he is not swept away by a brute motivational force that he does not agree with. One might think that in such cases rehearsal does contribute to deliberation. Cases like that do surely exist, but they are (a) not cases of willpower on the Holton definition, because there is no judgment shift and (b) even

The general point being established, it is time now for a clarification that amounts to a small concession. I have shown that rehearsal cases are indirect in the same way that distraction cases are indirect. What I have not shown, however, is that distraction and rehearsal are always the same thing—but that they are two different variations on the same theme. What is more, there is a very simple explanation for why Holton thinks that rehearsals but not distraction cases are real willpower: rehearsals on average seem to be harder. It is intuitively very plausible that rehearsing your reasons for not giving in to temptation is harder than simply averting attention, and this intuition is also borne out by the empirical evidence.

In the developmental evidence that Holton discusses, children found it much easier to distract themselves from the cookies than to repeat the reasons for not eating the cookie (Mischel 1996). In addition, there are also fascinating studies with chimps that show that chimps can use distraction techniques in order to master delayed gratification tasks, but find it impossible to simply stare down temptation, as it were (Evans and Beran 2007). Thus, it seems empirically plausible that rehearsals are more difficult than the employment of some distraction strategies. However, all this shows is that some distraction strategies do require less cognitive strain than rehearsals, presumably because they are more like looking away from the buffet, rather than trying to transform the buffet into a puzzle. The ties in such cases are more durable, because the tempting stimulus is simply removed, rather than transformed.[11]

5. Tying and Being Tied

So far, I have tried to establish that the rehearsal strategy is nothing other than a distraction strategy. This is already an important result, but it invites a possible argument against my overall claim that willpower is nothing more than a tying to the mast strategy. The sceptic could concede that it is right that distraction cases and rehearsal cases are structurally identical, but insist

---

more importantly, even in these cases the rehearsal does not contribute to deliberation, but simply ensures that the outcome of the deliberative process is what the agent will do. Thanks to Rob Rupert for raising this worry.

[11] This leads to an empirical prediction against the Holton account. If Holton is right, then strategies like transforming the buffet into a puzzle should not deplete the mental muscle as they are not true examples of the use of willpower. On my account, however, the prediction is that they will, because the effort is explained exclusively by maintaining the ties.

nevertheless that all that this shows is that even in rehearsals, not the whole process is about willpower. She could accept that even in such cases, the effect of the mental ties achieved by the rehearsal are not part of the exercise of willpower, but simply a consequence of it—and if this were the case, then the same could be said about distraction cases. Bringing about the distraction can be an exercise of willpower, but being distracted cannot be. This has the advantage that willpower seems to again reside purely in an intentional action, as well as seeming to be much more closely linked to the exercise of agentive powers.[12] It seems right as well with regard to the phenomenology of struggle: it seems right that averting attention from the tempting stimulus in order to achieve distraction is hard, but once attention is on something else, no more real work is done by the agent until attention, for whatever reason, is drawn back to the tempting stimulus.[13]

This seems very powerful, but again we have to carefully unpack what is being said in order to evaluate the force of the objection. First of all, it should be emphasized again that this is already a very important concession. It allows that intentional actions that have the purpose of achieving the avoidance of temptation count as willpower. This is the stated aim of this chapter, so the concession admits defeat on the main point of contention that there is no qualitative difference between willpower and tying to the mast actions. Without further qualifications, this would even allow that Odysseus action of tying himself to the mast is willpower, even if the tied stage is not part of the exercise of the capacity. In order to rule out such cases, we need not only accept that the action of distracting oneself counts as willpower, but also an extra condition on what willpower is. The obvious candidate here could be that willpower requires that the intentional action takes place in the tempting situation itself and not beforehand. This move would clearly exclude the Odysseus case. But even with this condition in place, it is still not obvious that willpower can consist only in the tying stage.

To see why, we need to think about rehearsal again. The idea is that rehearsing the reasons for not giving in to temptation might have the effect that we do not reconsider in situations where this reconsideration is likely to go wrong. But why do we not reconsider in such situations? At a very general level, presumably because the rehearsal has some effect on our psychology—i.e., it is the psychological effect of the rehearsal that brings about the desired

---

[12] An account that argues for a position like this might be e.g. the one defended by Sripada (2020).
[13] Thanks to Marcel Brass for raising this worry.

result. So what is the potential difference between rehearsals and distractions? If anything, it presumably is the effect these actions have on the system. In fact, the struggle will be a function of the effect. Rehearsals could have long-lasting or short effects. The effects could be stronger and weaker, they could be specific or unspecific, they could be additive or not. But if it is the case that the character of an act of willpower is systematically dependent on the effect it has on a cognitive system, then it becomes quite ad hoc to claim that willpower consists only in the act but not in the effect it is having.

So, it seems that willpower, on this more subtle picture, is a complicated interaction between the tying and the tied-up part of the mind. But if this is the right way to think about willpower, then it is just not possible to have a deeper understanding of willpower, if we do not examine the nature of the ties, as well as the act of tying—and this in turn means that the final objection to this account fails. Whether it comes as a rehearsal or a distraction, willpower is willpower because it is an intentional action that has a self-control effect, and if we want to understand a specific act of willpower, then we will have to examine the ties as well as the tying.[14]

6. System One and System Two

It is time to bring the specific discussion of willpower back to the overall theme of the book. The obvious place to begin doing this is one last worry that could be raised against the account. Holton argues that an exercise of practical rationality should not feel like a struggle, but to readers of Baumeister, this may seem surprising. Baumeister thinks in the two systems terminology: conscious deliberation according to him is a system two activity and hence effortful.[15] This seems worrying for the Holton account,

---

[14] The same goes for a related distinction. It might be claimed that the real dividing line is between ties that disrupt deliberation (rehearsal and distraction) and ties that disrupt acting on the consequences of flawed deliberation (both Odysseus scenarios) (thanks to Rob Rupert for pointing out this worry). But even here it is not clear that we can uphold the distinction. Distraction might normally occur during deliberation, but it also works after a judgment shift has occurred.

[15] From here, it looks as if a worry about Holton's account could be constructed. Perhaps whether something is a struggle has less to do with the question whether it is an intentional action, but whether it is system one or system two controlled. A similar argument has in fact been put forward by Neil Levy for cases of weakness of the will (2011). Levy argues that strength of will is not a specific faculty (as Holton would have it), but simply requires system two resources. Holton is aware of Levy (see p. 134) and does not think that this is a problem for him.

because if practical deliberation is always effortful, it appears that one of the main reasons for rejecting a deliberative account of willpower does not work anymore.[16] The phenomenology of struggle is explained by the fact that rational deliberation is a system two activity.

Obviously we know by now that there is a problem with understanding exactly what deliberation in system two is. If it is understood as the intentional actions that guide cognitive processes, then it is very true that system two deliberation is effortful, but in that case, as we have seen in Chapter 5, environment-involving actions that guide cognition can be thought of as part of the cognitive process too. So, the only way to keep deliberation safely inside the head and to distinguish it clearly from intentional stage-setting actions like rehearsals, as Holton aims to do, is to understand deliberation as evaluative agency.

However, taking this step also entails the consequence that now Holton is very much a target of the worries raised by the simple argument. If deliberation is evaluative agency, then it is no longer clear in which sense it is system two—if, as Chapter 2 argued, system two processing is all about intentional control.

To be fair, Holton is not the source of the problem here. Baumeister (2008) himself understands deliberation in system two as rational and effortful. In fact, it seems the ability of the agent to intentionally control their cognitive processes that makes system two rational, according to Baumeister. Obviously, though, the arguments in this book demonstrate that this is at least misleading. Either we argue that intentional actions can be constitutive parts of cognition, in which case willpower and all tying to the mast strategies could be proper parts of deliberation, or we argue that willpower, like all tying to the mast strategies, is an indirect non-rational way to control practical deliberation.

Thus, the worry about 'effortful deliberation' is not a worry for the stance taken in this book, but clarifying what one can sensibly mean by this phrase is the reason that it had to be written. Once this clarification is achieved, we can then combine Holton's insight that the exercise of willpower has an intentional agentive phenomenology with the lessons from the simple

---

He is simply happy to accept that strength of will is probably a system two phenomenon, and doubts whether it is clear that Levy has a strong argument that it is not a specific faculty within this system.

[16] Thanks to Robin Scaife for this worry.

argument to show that *willpower and tying to the mast strategies must have the same cognitive status*.

7. Round Up

At the end of this chapter, it might be worthwhile reminding ourselves why it made sense to look at the Holton account of willpower in the first place. One reaction one might have to the discussion on the previous pages is to see them as an argument that Holton's account is simply wrong. After all, the vast majority of philosophical accounts of willpower and weakness of the will do not give any big role to intentional managerial actions, but instead think of the issue as a problem of rational decision making.

There is nothing in the arguments that were discussed in this book so far that would make this an implausible move, apart from the general problems identified for the concept of evaluative agency in Chapter 4. In fact, it was argued at length that it is supposed to be a strength of the book that it leaves it to the reader to decide whether they want to think that intentional action is an integral part of cognition or not.

However, while this is also true in this case, because I do not want to convince the reader that the phenomena discussed in this chapter are an expression of rational agency, I will at least say the following: the self-control phenomena in this chapter are very much the ones discussed in the psychological self-control literature and in this literature, action is understood as *intentional* action. This means that in this literature, very much in line with Holton, willpower is often understood as the inhibition of impulses to give in to temptation.

It seems to me a very important result to show that there is no deep difference between inhibition and other intentional self-control strategies—particularly because it is becoming ever clearer in this literature that inhibition is probably not the best, but the least effective self-control strategy. Below is a quote from a recent paper which very nicely makes the point that willpower understood as simply toughing it out or inhibition is the least effective self-control strategy:

> Recent research has proposed that self-control is most effective when exerted as early in the process as possible (Fujita 2011; Hofmann and Kotabe 2012; Mann et al. 2013; Gillebaart et al. 2016). For example, individuals at a pub with friends who see other customers smoking may

themselves experience the desire for a cigarette. Although this scenario does not automatically represent a self-control dilemma, it can do so for individuals who are trying to break the smoking habit. Although the first and most proactive approach is to avoid such a tempting situation (situation selection) in favor of others that support long-term goals, once the desire has arisen, the second approach is to shift attention away from the problematic situation (attentional deployment) and toward non-tempting stimuli or thoughts such as thinking about the next holiday destination. The third and fourth approaches are to alter the meaning of the cigarette (reappraisal) – for example, to a source of bad smelling clothes and hair or cause of cancer – or simply inhibit the desire to smoke inhibition.

(Nielsen et al. 2019)

The emerging picture here makes clear what is so important about the Holton account. While it is obviously possible to defend a philosophical account of willpower that is not affected by my arguments, it seems clear that such an account would be less in touch with the psychological literature than Holton's. When it comes to self-control, intentional actions do play a critical role, not only in psychology but also pre-theoretically, and this is why a philosophical account that does justice to this is so powerful. But if the crucial reason to buy parts of the Holton account is that it intuitively understands that intentional action is an integral part of willpower and the psychological literature, then that also suggests that at least at this point, the option to understand all kinds of intentional actions as willpower, whether they involve the environment or not, is the one that looks most plausible.

7
How Choices Can Be Actions

Choice is intuitively one of the key ingredients of human mental agency. Choice is a central theme in both the Bible and Homer, with their various stories of apples,[1] in modern popular culture in films like *The Matrix*, and in some of the great tropes of moral psychology like Sartre's young man or Sophie's choice (see below). Human choices are deeply fascinating, because almost nothing else says so much about the human condition than the ability and necessity to make choices.

It is therefore quite surprising that in the most influential current accounts of philosophy of action, as well as in the free will literature, there seems to be little room for choices. As we already discussed in the introduction to the Holton part of this investigation in Chapter 6, the agency problem of compatibilism does not seem to leave any room for choices, because after the weighing of reasons, there is nothing left to do for the agent. On the other hand, the agency problem of compatibilism[2] obviously did not come about because compatibilist philosophers simply did not realize that a belief desire calculus might not feel agentive enough, but because they were impressed by a version of the homunculus problem.

As Velleman writes about the philosophers who do believe that a belief desire calculus is sufficient for the will:

> Those who believe the story [of the belief-desire calculus adding up to the will] will of course contend that the events recounted in it add up to the agent's participating in his action, as components add up to a composite. The story doesn't mention his participation, they will explain, simply because his participation isn't a component of itself. Complaining that the agent's participation in his action isn't mentioned in the story is, in their view, like complaining that a cake isn't listed in its own recipe.
>
> (Velleman 1992: 462)

---

[1] In Homer the young Trojan prince Paris has to decide which Goddess he wants to give the apple to. In the Bible, Eve chooses to eat from the tree of knowledge.
[2] See the introduction to Part II.

In other words, the belief desire calculus cannot be an intentional action controlled by the rational agent, because the rational agent is at heart nothing more than the belief-desire calculus. Alternatively, we can phrase this as Strawson put it in Chapter 1: the agent in this case is Kantian spontaneity.[3]

There is a second major reason why so many philosophers have decided to bite the bullet of the agency problem: the problem of 'picking'. Picking refers to a 'choice' between items that are qualitatively identical and where the consequences of picking one rather than the other are negligible like, for example, tins of tomatoes on the supermarket shelf.[4] If choices are intentional actions, the worry is that they might be no more than arbitrary pickings. In these cases, the choice element is not supposed to be reducible to any specific reason for the choice, but rather, is an arbitrary action without an underlying reason or combination of reasons. If a choice is not fully determined by a reason or combination of reasons, then the only alternative seems to be that it is made arbitrarily. However, to think of choices in this way is obviously deeply unattractive. It is clear that if we wish to maintain the huge importance that choices are supposed to have for the agent, then choices should not be reducible to picking. Agents are supposed to be responsible for their choices and have to consider the consequences of choosing one way rather than another: if choices would be reducible to pickings, then it seems hard to see in which sense agents could be meaningfully responsible for them.

In the literature on choices, philosophers tend to focus on so-called 'hard' choices. These are choices where it is impossible to simply 'calculate' the right answer, but which are also not reducible to picking. The most famous cases discussed in this context are Sartre's story of the young man who has to decide whether to look after his old and frail mother or whether to join the resistance and fight the Nazis and 'Sophie's choice'—the harrowing account of a mother in a concentration camp forced to decide which of her two children will live and which will die. However, even in these cases, on the face of it there seems to be only two options of how we can understand these choices. In Sartre's story, either the young man has better reasons for prioritizing his mother above fighting the Nazis or vice versa, in which case it seems that there is no need for a choice, or he does not, in which

---

[3] As discussed in the introduction to Part II, Velleman's own solution fares no better here.
[4] For the distinction between picking and choosing, see Ullmann-Margalit and Morgenbesser (1977).

case it looks as if his choice is dangerously close to picking.[5] The same holds for Sophie, either there are reasons to choose one child, in which case it is clear what she has to do even though it is obviously extremely horrible, or it is the most awful but still arbitrary form of picking.

The notion that picking cannot be real choice is also one reason why so many especially compatibilist philosophers are very dismissive of psychological attempts at experimentally operationalizing choice. Famously, many have argued that the Libet experiments discussed in Chapter 1 say nothing about free will and choice because they are mere random pickings of a moment to move in a situation where the subject has no reasons to prefer any particular moment. Recently, there have been very interesting attempts to create more meaningful choices in an experimental set up (see Maoz et al. 2019),[6] but at best, these scenarios can look a bit more like Sartre's hard choices. As we have seen, the principled problem does not disappear, even for those.

It is to this seemingly intractable problem that Holton has an ingenious solution. This solution makes it possible for him to argue that choice is not reducible to picking, while at the same time, allowing him to claim that he can solve the agency problem, at least on the phenomenological level.

Holton (2009a) has three intuitive desiderata for a phenomenologically satisfying account of choice. First, choice is not fully determined by our beliefs and desires. Second, choices are sufficient for actions and, in contrast to other psychological states like beliefs and desires, choices are directly linked to actions. Finally, and most importantly in this context, choices are intentional actions. He writes:

> Choice is an act. It requires time, concentration and a certain amount of effort. (Holton 2009a: 54)

In order to make it possible that his account of choice can fulfil all these desiderata despite the obvious problems, Holton draws on a two-systems account and some metacognitive hunches. Holton's account of choice is a great example of the key issues investigated so far, and his discussion of the issue is extremely insightful. However, as we will see, there are some weak

---

[5] For an in-depth discussion of hard choices see e.g. Bratman (2003) and Smith (1994).
[6] Maoz et al. made subjects choose between two charities, telling subjects that the one they chose had the chance to get real money. They then tested for the readiness potential when subjects made these choices.

points in his account, which the second half of this chapter will aim to patch up with the arguments developed in the first half of the book.

1. Holton's Argument

So how does Holton's argument work? The first step of his argument points out that there are very many situations in an agent's life where it is not obvious what the right course of action is.[7] Now, obviously, not every action is like that. Often in life, when faced with two or more options, agents don't need to make a choice that could be characterized as a distinct action. Often, agents simply know which action they prefer and the question of whether to do that or something else instead is quite simply not deliberated. The action is selected automatically; nothing takes place which could be characterized as an act of choice.

Equally common are situations where the agent is faced with two options, where it is not immediately obvious which is the better one. Sometimes, a bit of deliberation will resolve the issue, and as soon as an agent reaches a judgment[8] that one option is clearly the better one, this option will be selected without anything that is recognizable as a separate and distinct act of choice.

But in some cases, even a bit of deliberation will not resolve the issue completely. As we are finite human beings and not doing anything is often worse than doing either A or B, we often have to pick one of two options, even though we do not really know which of the options is the better one. In contrast to the mechanical weighing of reasons, simply picking one of two options is a very typical instance of an intentional mental action. Indeed, it is intuitively possible for the agent to pick A or B just as easily as it is for the agent to lift her arm or not.

However, there is also a problem with acts of choice. The way the story has been told so far, these acts of choice seem very much reduced to random picking, with no particular decisive reason for the agent choosing one option

---

[7] Importantly, Holton does not want to restrict choice to true incompatibility (Bratman 2003; Smith 1994). Instead, he focuses on the much more common phenomenon that we simply don't know in the time available for the decision what the better course of action would be.

[8] As is standard in the literature, Holton assumes that judgments are system two. Obviously, this is not something that we would want to endorse here. However, at the same time Holton clearly accepts that judgments are not voluntary actions in the same way that choices are, because according to him, if choices were judgments that would trigger the agency worry, because judgments are just about weighing reasons.

over another. While these choices look like real intentional actions it is unclear whether they really deserve to be considered an act of choice.

This is where Holton's second step comes in. He argues that choices feel like they are random to the conscious subject, but that they are in fact not random at all. The subject has the impression that she simply picked one of two equal options, because she does not have access to all the information that she has picked up. Unconsciously, the agent might well 'know' which option to prefer, but the conscious subject does not know why she is attracted to the option she chooses.

With these two elements, Holton now has an account where choice is very clearly an intentional action and the decision is fully arbitrary at the conscious level, but at the same time, it is not just random picking, because the agent makes her choice on what we might call a hunch, i.e. on information that she has access to unconsciously but that she can't use for conscious deliberation.

This is a neat idea and it is very much in the spirit of this book. On Holton's account, the role of intentional action looks very much like setting the stage. The choosing agent does not evaluate content by making a choice, but rather, by applying brute force, simply stops the process of deliberation. At the same time, the account does not have the problem that this might be no more than picking because of the evaluative biasing in system one.

Obviously, this is not really achieving the goal that Holton set out to achieve. The idea was that we could show that a choice is an action, and not reducible to a judgment, or simply an act of random picking. Holton achieves this aim, but only by pushing the evaluative weighing of evidence out of sight, as it were. However, as soon as one zooms out a bit, the agency problem seems to be back. Now, it is the evaluative calculus of the whole psychology of the agent, including the unconscious, that decides the matter. Holton can simply reply to this by claiming that he is interested in the phenomenology of choice, and the fact that it should feel as though choices are genuinely open to the agent. If we approach the problem a little more globally, this goal can be achieved, even if it is the case that the choice is not really open but determined. This is exactly what Holton argued from the very beginning: it is the local determinism of conscious beliefs and desires that laypeople find implausible (see the introduction to Part II). It clearly seems false that our conscious beliefs and desires always fully determine how we choose. In general, people tend to have far less of an opinion about the mechanisms outside consciousness that bring about their conscious choices.

Holton's account also chimes very nicely with what has been argued in this book. The intentional control exercised in system two is not problematically homuncular, but simply shepherds the agent to make decisions, and the evaluation of which decision to take is clearly not intentionally controlled. Nonetheless, there is an important problem with Holton's account. Investigating this problem will permit us to get a clearer picture of how shepherding works in decision making. The most difficult problem will be to understand what exactly the nature of the shepherding action is. Here, we will make use of the distinctions on the various forms of metacognition introduced in Chapter 5.

2. Holton's Choice Complications

Holton's account of choice seems like a neat way to have your rational cake and intentionally eat it. But on closer examination, there is a serious problem with this account, and it is not even that difficult to uncover. Let us look at Holton's argument that it is unproblematic if choices are biased by unconscious calculus, because his account is about conscious choice, a little more closely.

Holton does not tell us how it is that the unconscious judgment influences the conscious picking. Perhaps he thinks that there simply is no experiential echo at all. The influence on behaviour would in that case be a bit like blind sight (see famously e.g. Weiskrantz 1999).[9] In this much discussed phenomenon, patients who are cortically blind are still able to perform above chance in visual tasks, such as discrimination in their blind field, despite reporting not seeing anything in that part of their field of vision. Importantly, these patients would never initiate an action with regard to the stimuli in their blind field, but if prompted to do so by the experimenter, they can perform with some success in the task.

If choice really were to function in the same way as blindsight, this would fit well with Holton's emphasis on picking, in which the agent feels that a choice is completely random and could just as well be decided by the throwing of a coin. Holton could even allow that we can learn a lot about our attitudes from choosing, even though the causes of our choices are hidden to us, because we could do so by simply observing our choices. We observe what we do and infer something about our mind from these observations, and perhaps even something about the world that the

---

[9] Thanks to Robert Deutschländer for this apt comparison.

unconscious part of our mind had picked up on.[10] If we find ourselves picking one option rather than another, we can often infer that we did have a reason for our choice, even though we might not be consciously aware of it. Even if there is no experiential echo of the unconscious judgment at all, this does not mean that the information cannot reach consciousness after the choice has been made.

However, if it were the case that the only way to access the information that biased our choices would be to access them after the event, this would also mean that the conscious agent would have no access at all *at the time of the choice*. In that case, we would have to consider ourselves lucky that we do not often really use randomness generators to make these choices, because presumably that would render the useful and completely unconscious biasing null and void and we could not use all the information it provides.

So, are choices really like blindsight with absolutely no experiential echo of the unconscious judgment as Holton seems to suggest? I want to argue that this is unlikely and in fact, even the cases Holton uses as examples for his argument seem to suggest, contrary to his account, that there is some form of access to the unconscious judgment.

One of his key examples involves a fireman who can consciously see no reasons why he should leave a house where they are fighting a seemingly harmless one-storey fire, but who has the strong sense that he needs to get out and retreats. Here, it turns out that the feeling saves his life, because minutes later the house collapses. In this case, there is a very intense conscious experience that makes the fireman leave the house. The thing that is different to an ordinary conscious judgment is that the fireman does not understand the reasons for why he has the feeling. However, the fireman does have an experiential echo of the unconscious judgment, and it is this hunch that he trusts, even though he does not know the reasons for having it.[11]

---

[10] Obviously, sometimes this can go wrong and in these cases, we end up confabulating a rationalization of our behaviour. According to Holton, this is what happens in the seminal Nisbett experiments, where subjects defend their picking the garment on the right of a row of identical items, a choice which is actually caused by an unconscious bias to the right, by inventing quality differences between identical garments to rationalize their choice (Holton 2009: 67).

[11] I discuss this also in (Vierkant 2011). There, I make a distinction between explicit and aware, i.e. the fireman is aware of his feeling of knowing (FOK) but cannot put into words why he feels it. But in actual fact, this issue is even more complicated. In Holton's scenario, the fireman does know and can express in language that he has a FOK and trusts it, perhaps because

Why does Holton insist in his theoretical account that the conscious choice is an intentional arbitrary picking action, if even his own example suggests that the action is not arbitrary at all even on the experiential level, but consists in following a hunch? One reason might be that once we accept that the conscious hunch is a sufficient reason for the choice, it now does not seem any more as if the choice is an intentional yet arbitrary picking. At this point, either Holton has to lose his intentional picking component or he cannot allow that the hunches are conscious.

3. Choice as Managerial Control

Is it possible to save Holton's idea of choice as an intentional action while at the same time allowing for an intuitively plausible scenario where the choosing agent is aware of the hunch that leads to the choice?

The solution I would like to propose lies in thinking of Holton choices as managerial acts: what I want to argue is that the phenomenon of choice that Holton describes (intentional action, but still not random) can best be understood as a managerial action in Hieronymi's terminology. Choices are actions that shepherd the deliberation process, by enabling or inhibiting evaluative intention formation processes.

Before we can look at the detail of how this proposal could work, we need to address a major problem in combining Holton and Hieronymi. Hieronymi thinks that forming an intention is a cognitive act. But isn't the formation of an intention and a choice the same thing? If we were to assume that forming an intention is the same as making a choice, then it seems that choices on Hieronymi's picture cannot be managerial actions at all, because managerial actions are always intentional and cognitive acts are never intentional.[12]

However, the problem disappears once we look more closely at what forming an intention actually means for Hieronymi. According to Hieronymi, intention formation is nothing more than a practical judgment about what the best thing to do is, all things considered. Intention

---

he has reasons to trust it, even though he does not know why he has the FOK: but there could also be a scenario where the fireman is aware of and acts on his FOK without recognizing it as such.

[12] Thanks to the anonymous reviewer who pressed me on this point.

formations are cognitive acts because they are a form of judgment. In contrast, as already discussed, for Holton choices are acts that agents perform, especially when they are insecure about what the right cause of action is. In other words, they are the weapon of choice when the agent is uncertain about what to do and has no obvious means to dissolve the uncertainty, and can therefore not form an 'all things considered' judgment about the best cause of action.

Holton describes a phenomenon that Hieronymi does not explicitly discuss in her work. As discussed in Chapter 3, in situations where the evidence does not favour either option, the agent cannot simply form a judgment either way, but they can accept that they need to act as though they believe that one of the two options was the better one. Obviously, this is something that can be done voluntarily.

However, given the preceding discussion about hunches, presumably choices are a bit more complicated than simple pickings. First, let us think about the phenomenology of choice again. As Holton rightly points out, choices often require considerable effort. It is hard for an agent to decide which option to pick, if she doesn't know which option is the better one. But in a way this is surprising, if Holton's account is correct. If it really feels to the agent as if it is in the end all the same no matter which of the options she picks, then doing so should not be difficult: it should be as simple as throwing a dice. What makes choosing hard are the attempts to inhibit a constant reopening of the question once one feels that further deliberation would be counterproductive.

Once the agent has decided that they need to pick one of the options, despite not having any evidence that this particular option is any better than the alternatives, they then can engage in any number of managerial actions that stop the mind from evaluating the situation further. One can stop new inner speech by telling oneself that the decision has been made now, or actively try to think about other things, or even simply rehearse the decision. This is very similar to the kind of strategies discussed in the previous chapter on willpower.

Obviously, this does not mean that in these cases there are managerial acts without evaluative acts. These intentional acts of attending to the question and of inhibiting the reopening of deliberation obviously only happen if the agent feels that it is appropriate to attend to the problem and to inhibit further deliberation. They are dependent on prior cognitive acts. They are intentional acts which are employed for the purposes of managing the cognitive process and which are directly caused by a prior evaluation that such management is appropriate.[13] Thus, cognitive acts remain the basic category of mental agency, but what is special about the evaluative acts that initiate the managerial actions that choices consist in is that these are evaluative acts that are not about evaluating what to do in the world, but about evaluating how to manage a difficult decision process where the evidence is not sufficient to decide the matter.

That all choices on this account are rooted in a metacognitive judgment could be perceived as posing a problem for Holton's account: after all, he insists that choices can happen before judgments and that is certainly not true on this picture, because choices are the direct consequence of metacognitive unconscious judgments. However, as discussed before, Holton is willing to concede that choices might be the product of unconscious judgments, as long as they do not depend on conscious ones.

With this solution, we can identify a workable explanation for why choices can be thought of as intentional actions. However, what we do not obtain from this solution is an important role for picking in choice. It is clear that choices in this sense don't need to be acts of picking to be described as intentional. Holton thought that choices could only be intentional actions if they are pickings, because the real business of choice, which is to evaluate which is the better option, is done by an evaluative process that cannot be intentional.

Yet once we introduce managerial control, there is another option. If we understand choices as managerial acts, then it is easy to see why choices are intentional actions and why they have been traditionally understood as 'decisions to': they are not about evaluating what is best, but about cajoling the mind into following through on its evaluations, to produce the best possible conditions for the evaluation, and to actively inhibit responses if the evaluation is not yet 'safe' enough.

As the evaluative acts that cause the managerial acts are unconscious, this account can also explain why these choices can feel like pickings to the agent.[14]

---

[13] My account of choice here is in many ways similar to Shepherd's (2014) account of decisions as intentional actions. However, while I agree with Shepherd that deciding can be understood intentionally, I want to insist that this only works if we understand it managerially in the sense discussed here as well. In this case, the decision itself has no rational dimension. For more discussion of this see Chapter 3 and Vierkant (2015).

[14] However, as I discuss in section 2, it is not the case that all choices feel like pickings in any case. Often, choices are more about gut feelings that make one option more salient for the agent, but where the agent cannot put into words the reason for her being attracted to that option.

Holton is right that choices often feel like no more than picking for the agent, but while this is true, it is a red herring to describe this experience as an important reason for choices being actions.[15] Choices are actions because they work exactly like ordinary intentional bodily actions. The only difference is that while bodily actions have a world-directed intention, the intentions that guide choices are attitude-directed.

We now have an account of choice that does explain the phenomenology of picking and effort in choice, but one where the importance of picking is illusory. Instead, what makes the choice in this sense intentional is simply that it is an act of managerial control.

Where does this leave us? Like Holton, the account can explain that choices feel like intentional actions (because they are) and also feel like pickings (because the agent is not aware of the rational acts that cause the managerial ones). Like Holton's account, the one suggested here does solve the issue of the agentive phenomenology of choice, but in contrast to the Holton account, it does not have to rely on picking to deliver a solution. This seems like a good result. However, there is one important catch here. Obviously, for the account to work, it has to be possible to understand properly how the intentional actions that make up our choices really can be thought of as managerial control.

4. A Problem: Is Choice Really Attitude-Directed Managerial Action?

I have argued that we should think of choice as managerial control. However, this might seem surprising given the definitions suggested earlier. Managerial control in Hieronymi's sense is supposed to be attitude-directed, but choices seem not to be about attitudes at all, but rather, about what to do (see also Vierkant 2013, where I first raise this issue). How is it possible that there are intentional actions that control attitudes when the agent is not at all interested in attitude control, but simply tries to achieve world-directed goals? In other words: how could it be possible to have a form of control that is dependent on thinking about thinking, when all the thinking involved is aimed at achieving something else?

---

[15] This is important, because it means that Holton's project of introducing the intentional agent into compatibilism is reduced to an explanation of why the experience of picking is associated with being a mental agent, even though everything that makes a mental agent a mental agent is based on the (albeit unconscious) weighing of reasons.

Luckily, we already have an answer to the question of how to understand the notion of managerial control in the context of a revamped Holton choice: we just need to go back to the discussion of the various forms of thinking about thinking in Chapter 5. There, we discussed that while attitude-directed thought in Hieronymi is a form of thought by human adults who understand psychological concepts and can consciously think about them, there are many other forms of thinking about thinking that do not require explicit attitude-directed thought. In Chapter 5 we drew on the arguments of McGeer and Clark to show how we can use language to self-regulate, and it became clear that we do not need to be able to understand the nature of psychological states to do so. Language allows us to attend to content.

This, I would suggest, is what might well happen in many choice scenarios: after deliberation, one might for example choose a holiday by the sea, instead of a holiday in the mountains. This choice might consist in an inner speech act of saying to oneself: 'That's it! Decided! This summer we will go on holiday by the sea!'. This voluntary speech act could either express an involuntary judgment, or it could simply be an act of acceptance without an actual judgment having been made. But in either case, it will trigger further managerial acts of inhibiting thoughts about the wonderful views from mountain tops, lead to a focus on the details of the holiday by the sea, and so on. All of these actions will have mindshaping effects that will lead to or shore up the sincere judgment that the holiday by the sea is the best thing to do all things considered (see the discussion in Chapter 5).

Once it is clear that choices are managerial actions in the wider mindshaping sense, it then becomes clear that the crucial point we made about this wider category is also true about the specific class of actions that we call choice. As in the case of all these actions, it makes no difference whether the self-management happens purely inside the head or is environment-involving. There is no deep difference between internally rehearsing the arguments for going to the sea or writing them down on paper to have them constantly available. Both are, in exactly the same way, abilities that enable the agent to manage their evaluating mind.

Interestingly, seen like this the difference between willpower and choices becomes quite small. Both are intentional mindshaping actions which give stability to the evaluating mind. Willpower does this for intentions that are stable now; but where the agent foresees uncertainty in the future, choice is a tool to create stability in the present by managing the mind on the basis of hunches.

5. Metacognitive Feelings and Uncertainty

Although mindshaping is one essential metacognitive component of choices as managerial action, there is another one that has so far not been discussed. To understand this issue and how it interacts with our account of choice, it is worth returning to our discussions in an earlier part of the book. As was outlined in Chapter 2, all managerial actions depend on two acts of evaluative agency: the first is the act of the agent forming the intention to perform the managerial action; the second is the evaluative agency that is influenced by the shepherding action. An agent can for example form the intention to go to the library, or focus on a problem, then perform the relevant action and will then have a new evaluative step because she is in the library or because she has focused on the problem, and so on.

When we say that mindshaping enables metarepresentational thinking, the second instance of evaluative agency is the interesting one. By providing the evaluative system with a persistent vehicle, for example a word, the shepherding (mindshaping) action makes it much easier to attend to the content in that vehicle and by manipulating the vehicle, different aspects of the content can be highlighted.

What is not emphasized in this story is the role of the first instance of evaluative agency in this metacognitive process. However, one can argue that intentional mind regulation not only is possible without possessing mental state concept but also does not necessarily rely on using material symbols to enable thinking about thinking at the second evaluative step. Instead the process can also be understood as metacognitive if we weaken the condition for metacognition of the first evaluative step. In the full-blown version of managerial control, the agent forms an intention about the attitude they want to target, but in order to form such an intention, it seems natural to assume that the agent would need the concept of the attitude that the intention is supposed to target. However, some philosophers have argued that it is sufficient if the agent has an epistemic feeling that signifies a mental state non-conceptually, and which has the function of enabling regulation of that state by means of mental action.[16]

---

[16] In Proust's account, mental action is defined as an action that aims at regulating mental states. This is obviously narrower than e.g. the Kirsh and Maglio definition.

The metacognition in question is Joelle Proust's evaluativist account.[17,18] In order to understand both her account and how it relates to choice in more detail, we can draw on some of the experiments she uses as a neat illustration of her account: an example of this phylogenetically very early form of metacognition[19] can be found in a series of much discussed experiments by David Smith and colleagues (2003), who tested uncertainty monitoring in macaques. In this experiment, the animals had to decide whether a screen presented to them was densely or sparsely pixelated, with an arbitrary cut-off point set at 1,500 pixels: any higher, and the animals had to rate the picture as dense; any lower, they should rate it as sparsely pixelated. Obviously, solving this task becomes progressively more difficult the closer to the arbitrary cut-off point the screen displayed is, and at some point the task becomes impossible to solve.

The connections between this experiment and our discussion of choice are not difficult to work out. The monkeys are asked to make a 'choice' between two options (dense or sparse). They are rewarded with food if they get it right and penalized with waiting time until the next trial[20] if they get it wrong. The macaques are very good at solving this task if the pixellation is relatively far away from the cut-off point. The interesting trials are the ones where the pixel number is very close to the cut-off point: here the choices become nothing more than arbitrary picking, because the macaques do not have the resources to make such a fine-grained distinction.

These two scenarios present both horns of the traditional dilemma of choice. If it is possible to know whether the screen is sparse or dense, then the choice seems mechanical and there is no need for intentional action in the process of choice but rather, it seems that the actions are simply reactions to the stimuli. If, on the other hand, there is no discernible reason for the animal to make a choice either way, then the choice seems to be no more than arbitrary picking.

---

[17] See Fernandez-Castro and Martinez-Manrique (2020) for a discussion of how mindshaping and evaluativist accounts are competing accounts of metacognition.

[18] For an in-depth analysis of Proust's account and a fascinating embodied variation of it, see John Dorsch.

[19] There is a debate about whether this is metacognition at all, because it does not require any understanding of mental state concepts (Carruthers 2008). I want to remain neutral here about what the right use of the term metacognition is, if there is one. Important in our context is only that the macaques seem to have a special ability that allows them to have this new form of choice behaviour.

[20] They love doing these tasks.

The interesting thing about these experiments is that the researchers introduced a third option into the mix. The macaques could not only press dense or sparse, but they were also offered a third option, which would simply give them a new trial, without waiting time, but also without reward. The researchers interpreted this button as the 'I don't know button'. The researchers found that the macaques can learn to use this button efficiently, but they also found that this is a very rare ability in the animal kingdom. Most animals will ignore the button, and this is even true for very close relatives of the apes, like capuchin monkeys.

Smith and colleagues concluded from these experiments that in macaques we have the first tender shoots of metacognition. The apes not only try to understand the world, but they also monitor the cognitive tools that they are using to perform world-directed tasks. In other words, they monitor their own mentality, or have attitude-directed states in some sense.

The researchers have a plausible interpretation, according to which the experiments very nicely show that at least some non-human animals do have a way of dealing with their own uncertainty. On this reading of the results, what is interesting about the experiments is that by introducing the 'I don't know button', the researchers give the animal the possibility not only to be uncertain but to show that it is aware of its own uncertainty. The researchers think that in the experiment, they are able to demonstrate that the ability to use the button transforms what used to be arbitrary picking into a choice informed by a monitoring of one's own cognitive performance. On some level, the macaques seem to be aware of their uncertainty: they have a feeling of not knowing the right answer and it is this feeling which allows them to use the 'I don't know button'.

This monitoring of cognitive performance, in contrast to deliberating with metarepresentations, is at the heart of Proust's evaluativist proposal of metacognition. According to this proposal, there is a form of metacognition that works without an understanding of metarepresentation, because of epistemic feelings that allow the monitoring of cognitive performance. Epistemic or noetic feelings, such as a feeling of knowing or in the macacque case, a feeling of uncertainty 'predict potential success or error in the current task (prospective noetic feelings, e.g. feelings of knowing)' (Proust 2013: 318).

What is interesting about this proposal in terms of this chapter is that on Proust's account, the hunches that bias Holton's choices are in Proust's sense already metacognitive. If feelings of confidence and uncertainty are metacognitive feelings, then presumably the hunches in the Holton story are too. Choices on our amended Holton account are metacognitive in two distinct ways: first, they are triggered by metacognitive feelings; and second, these metacognitive feelings lead to intentional actions that allow the agent to regulate their thinking using material symbols.

A clarification is in order at this point. What I am suggesting here is to combine Proust's account of metacognition with Hieronymi's account of managerial action to explain the two metacognitive elements of Holton's choice. But this seems odd, because Proust and Hieronymi have competing accounts of mental action (Proust 2013: 7–8). Where Hieronymi argues that metacognition is a specific category of mental agency, i.e. evaluative agency, Proust argues that metacognition in the form of epistemic feelings is a necessary component in all mental actions. These two different definitions of mental agency come down to the two choices offered by the simple argument: Hieronymi wants to insist that cognitive agency is only ever evaluative, whereas Proust sees intentional mind-regulation as part of the cognitive process. As stated before, both options are possible, and this book does not want to adjudicate between them.

Nonetheless, there is one interesting point we can draw on from our discussions thus far in this book that could be used by a Proustian supporter of intentional mental actions. In Chapter 4, the arguments of Mercier and Sperber are presented, which contend that intuitive judgments are metacognitive, and the sense of metacognitive that they employ is exactly the same one used by Proust. Intuitive judgments are metacognitive because they are guided by epistemic feelings of uncertainty and confidence. In the context of this book, however, the really fascinating point is that Mercier and Sperber also claim that intuitive judgments give us a sense of authorship. We observed at the time that they do not say anything about why this might be and whether it is justified, but we speculated that it might provide us with an explanation of the sense of evaluative agency. Connecting their work to Proust's might give us such an explanation.

On Proust's account, these feelings have the function of triggering mental actions, if mental actions are understood to be intentional actions that have the function of regulating the mind. Perhaps intuitive judgments feel agentive because their function is to trigger mental actions in the Proustian sense? Now, obviously this is not what philosophers like Hieronymi have in mind when they argue that evaluative control is agentive! For her, evaluative control is agentive because it is ultimately the activity of the rational mind that is what makes humans rational agents, rather than any specific connection to forms of intentional action. But as one of the strong points of such an account is the intuitive plausibility that judgments and decisions are agentive, it is interesting to see that it might be possible to explain this intuition by drawing on the intimate connection between epistemic feelings and managerial actions.

6. Conclusion

We looked at Holton's account of choice because it is a wonderful example of how to deal with the core problem of mental agency that has concerned us throughout the whole book.

Human decisions feel agentive, and that seems to imply more than a mechanical weighing of reasons. At the same time, however, choices do not seem random, but are influenced by reasons. Initially Holton's account looked impressive in doing this intuition justice. It seemed that Holton had come up with an account of choice that was both intentional and not arbitrary. Holton argued that the conscious system two experiences choices as intentional pickings. For the agent, the experience is one of an arbitrary picking of one option over the other, much in the same way as one would choose between qualitatively identical tins on a supermarket shelf. As we have seen, however, choices are not mere pickings, because while the agent experiences them as such, they are informed by an unconscious biasing. The system does evaluate one option as better as the other, but the information is not accessible to the conscious agent.

At the same time, Holton's account did leave open some unanswered questions. While his account does do a good job of explaining the phenomenology of intentional agency in choice, we have seen that Holton's account is misleading in its emphasis on picking. Experimental philosophy studies suggest that picking does have a role in the phenomenology of choice (see Vierkant et al. 2019)[21] and that the lack of access to the reasons for this choice might well play a significant role in the reasons for humans having such a phenomenology. Nevertheless, Holton's own account of how the system one information biases the choice was unsatisfactory, because it was not clear whether he thought that these were fully unconscious, or whether they were something resembling conscious echoes in the form of

---

[21] The notion of arbitrary intentional picking is also very prominent in experimental attempts to implement free will (see e.g. famously Libet 1985).

hunches. His theoretical account suggests the former, while his examples suggest the latter.

As a result, it became clear that the examples created a more convincing picture once the account was slightly tweaked. On this amended account, choices are not arbitrary pickings, but managerial actions triggered by epistemic feelings. The phenomenology of picking is explained by the fact that these feelings do not provide the agent with first order reasons that would allow her to form a judgment, but simply make managerial actions that favour one outcome feel right. Once we think of choice as managerial control triggered by epistemic feelings, it is possible to retain the Holton architecture of an experience of picking caused by an unconscious judgment, but to give a more plausible explanation of why intentional actions matter for choice.

The most important insight from thinking about Holton's choice account was a better understanding of the various ways in which different forms of metacognition play a role in the two choice elements of evaluative hunch and self-regulating intentional action. First of all, it became clear that the managerial intentional actions involved in choice should not be thought of as actions directed at attitudes, but more like McGeer's self-regulation discussed in Chapter 5. On McGeer's account, choices are metacognitive in the sense that the intentional actions triggered by the hunch allow the system to self-regulate, so that for example deliberation is not reopened once one has claimed in inner speech that a decision has been made. The metacognition in this case consists simply in the fact that the inner speech item, like all language, allows the system to attend to the content of the speech act in ways that are not possible without perceptible vehicles.

On the other hand, it became clear in our analysis that choices really consist not of one but two metacognitive elements. This is because there is a different sense in which the hunch is metacognitive. Proust's work on metacognition in the evaluativist sense understands hunches as epistemic feelings that allow the system to evaluate its confidence or uncertainty with regard to the options of a choice situation.

Whether one should locate the action of choice in the metacognitive hunch or in the mindshaping intentional action is, as stated above, not something that we want to adjudicate between. Nonetheless, combining Holton's choice account with the lessons from the first half of the book gives us a way of understanding choice that does justice both to our pre-theoretical agentive intuitions as well as a theoretically plausible account of what might explain them.

8
Diachronicity
Intentional or Rational?

1. Introduction

Over the previous two chapters we looked at two key phenomena of human agency—self-control and choice—and explored why intentional action plays a key role in explaining both. In this chapter, we will now look at a more general reason as to why self-control and choice might be so important for human agency: diachronicity. Contending that diachronicity is a key feature of moral agency, because it unites the moral agent, is not very controversial. Velleman (1992), Bratman (1987), Gerrans and Kennett (2010), Levy (2014), and many others have argued for this claim. In his 2014 article 'Consciousness, Implicit Attitudes and Moral Responsibility', Neil Levy succinctly explains the central reason for this being the case:

> Moral agency, I have claimed, is a diachronic property: it is only insofar as we are able to pursue plans and projects across time that we are moral agents. Such agency requires that our mental states be relatively unified, so that we are able to pursue our plans across time without later person-stages undercutting the projects of earlier person-stages. (Levy 2014: 19)

However, exactly what it is about the human mind that makes this diachronicity possible is less clear. For Levy, it is the conscious mind and the control that we have over propositional attitudes. He writes:

> Explicit attitudes, when they are utilized as premises in effortful reasoning, generate contents in ways that are guided by the rules the agent (implicitly) accepts as normative. Because the contents of a belief are structured in this way, explicit beliefs can be utilized as premises in reasoning. They have contents that are assertible, and they can be used to generate further contents in ways that are justified. These contents, because they are constrained by norms of reasoning, are linked with one another in ways

that are coherent, and therefore can impose coherence on the agent herself. Effortful reasoning can be used to generate plans and policies by which the agent guides her behavior. Equally, when the content of a plan is explicit it entails a consistent set of actions aimed at fulfilling it. (Levy 2014 13)

By now, the question that this quote poses will look familiar. Is it the intentional control in effortful reasoning or is it the rational structure of the conscious mind that enables the diachronicity required for moral agents?

Over the course of this chapter we will look at Levy's account more closely and attempt to answer this question.

2. Levy's Argument

Intuitively[1] it seems very plausible that our explicitly held attitudes in system two are in a special sense relevant for moral responsibility, in a way that system one attitudes, such as gut feelings and implicit biases, are not. However, this view is challenged by findings from research in the cognitive sciences, which seem to suggest that we are systematically mistaken about the attitudes that we really hold. Matt King and Peter Carruthers (2012) have argued that these findings demonstrate that conscious explicit attitudes cannot be what makes us responsible agents, because there are no conscious explicit attitudes that have the right causal profile to control our behaviour (e.g. decisions, intentions).

In reply to this work, Levy (2012) has tried to articulate in which sense consciously held attitudes in system two could be special for moral responsibility after all. Levy contends that it is not consciousness that separates explicit reasoning from implicit attitudes, since we may be aware of our implicit biases as 'gut feelings'. Instead, Levy suggests that a better way to understand the difference is that while implicit processes and attitudes may be propositionally *described*, only explicit beliefs are propositionally *expressed*. For example: we can *describe* our implicit biases as being processes that cause us to act *as if* we were sexist, while we *express* the explicit belief that we think men and women are equals. In this respect, gut feelings (like e.g. phobias) and implicit biases fall on the same side of the explicit/implicit divide. We are very much aware of our spider phobia for example,

---

[1] The following three sections are a version of Vierkant and Hardt (2015).

but this does not mean that the phobia expresses our belief that spiders are dangerous, just as our knowledge that we have an implicit bias against some group does not express a negative belief about that group. Obviously, there are many important differences between the two categories. For example, we are aware of gut feelings introspectively, whereas often we know about our biases only because of a theoretical approach to our own psychology. For our purposes, however, what is crucial is that they both do not have what is critical for our explicit attitudes according to Levy—i.e., they do not express beliefs and they are not integrated within a web of reasons.

Levy argues that consciously held attitudes that are explicit in this sense unite us as moral agents in a special way that other attitudes do not. This is because we have a special kind of control over our explicit mind. It is available for the effortful syntactical manipulation of propositional thought in system two. It is this mechanism which explains the importance of consciousness for the moral agent.

3. Why Assertibility Matters

In order to understand Levy's idea, first of all we need to make clear exactly what Levy has in mind, because not all attitudes that we are conscious of are ones that can be controlled in this specific way. You might well be aware of your spider phobia, but this does mean that simply deliberating about the fact that there are no dangerous spiders in the Northern hemisphere will make your phobia disappear. Thus, it is not just the fact that you are aware of having an attitude that makes it a candidate for the specific control that we are interested in here.

In response to this worry, Levy distinguishes between attitudes like phobias and ones that are controllable in the right kind of way. Levy claims that only very specific kinds of attitudes, but not phobias and not implicit attitudes, can be expressed in propositional form and can form the premises in a rational argument.[2] This difference matters according to Levy, because it is these two characteristics of explicit attitudes that explain why these attitudes have a special role in integrating the agent. For Levy this is

---

[2] Levy presents this distinction as a response to King and Carruthers (2012), who argue that cognitive science shows that we are never directly conscious of our attitudes and that they should therefore not have a special status for moral responsibility. Levy's response is to assert that this special status is not attributable to the direct access, but to the functional role attitudes

important, because as already discussed, he argues that moral responsibility depends on the diachronicity of the agent. In turn, this is why we are held responsible for mental states that unify us.

Levy also writes that 'insofar as consciousness underwrites the unification of behavior it underwrites moral agency' (Levy 2014: 7). Thus, Levy argues that we pick out which cognitive processes we can be held responsible for on the basis of whether they have a role in constituting us as moral agents.

But what does Levy mean when he says that some explicit attitudes can be expressed in propositional form and can form the premise in a rational argument? The example of the spider phobia can clarify this: in the case of such a phobia, the sufferer will often be very aware of the fact that they are suffering from it, and often they will also know how they are disposed to react in the presence of a spider. They will even know what kind of mental states the presence of a spider will produce in them. They know that they will feel fear and experience the spider as threatening and dangerous. Nonetheless, even though they possess all that knowledge, they would not be able to sincerely assert that they believe that spiders are dangerous. Even though the spider produces such a comprehensive set of integrated emotional states and response dispositions, it does not produce the equivalent assertible belief. On the contrary, the typical assertion from a phobia sufferer will be that they know that spiders are not dangerous in the Northern hemisphere, but that they can't help feeling threatened by them anyway.

Levy contends that it is exactly this ability to sincerely assert the content of a mental state that makes some explicit states special for moral responsibility, and it is exactly the lack of this assertibility—e.g. in the case of phobias—that explains why some states are not special in this sense, even if the subject is conscious of having them (Levy 2014: 12).

The question now has become, why does assertibility matter? In what he calls a first pass (Levy 2014: 5), Levy argues that it might be because only asserted beliefs can be, as it were, cast in a different medium (language), and this new medium allows a whole set of operations that are only possible in language. What Levy has in mind here looks a lot like the mindshaping discussed in Chapter 5: language allows self-attribution of mental states and this allows the agent to pay attention to and interpret the states so attributed and in turn, this will have a unifying effect on the agent. Once the agent

---

play when we are conscious. While I agree with Levy's argument in principle, but I am not sure that he has demonstrated that explicit states really do play the functional role that he attributes to them.

ascribes mental states to herself, she can use those states to construct a consistent practical identity around them.

However, the mere fact that asserted beliefs have linguistic form and can be self-attributed does not always distinguish them from phobias, for example. Obviously, the agent can also put the content of a phobia in a sentence using natural language. The important difference is that in the case of a phobia, the agent does not thereby express a belief, i.e. they would not agree that the proposition in question e.g. 'spiders are dangerous' contained in the sentence is true. Because of that, they will not feel either that they have to believe anything that follows rationally from the proposition contained in the sentence. This is in sharp contrast to the case where the agent can assert their belief sincerely. In this case, as the assertion expresses the agent's belief, they are bound to accept all the logical entailments that can be made explicit by manipulating the assertion according to the laws of logic. This, in turn, has a hugely unifying effect on the beliefs an agent will hold, because the fact that they are manipulable means that it is far easier to bring individual beliefs in contact with each other and to spot potential incoherencies.

In Chapter 5, it was argued that language enables different levels of intentional self-regulation of the mind. The mechanisms described there are roughly the same as those described in what Levy refers to as his first pass. He does appreciate the power of linguistic representations which can be used to create focal points that help create consistent psychologies, but Levy thinks that this cannot be all there is. He wants to show that we need more control and according to him, only asserted expressed beliefs have a strong enough unifying potential to answer King and Carruthers's challenge.

4. What Is the Problem?

Unfortunately, Levy's account is less clear than it might at first appear. The first problem is that the story about described phobias and expressed beliefs invites us to buy into a false dichotomy. It seems very plausible to say that attitudes such as a spider phobia are not part of the responsible agent in the same way as e.g. an explicitly endorsed fear of criminals. The phobia might well have a powerful influence on the behaviour of the agent, but it does not play a role in how the agent understands the world, insofar as the agent does not feel that stating the content of her phobia expresses her world view. She is simply afraid of spiders, but she does not believe that the attitude requires justification and she would not feel the need to give reasons for why it is right to have this attitude, because 'rightness' as such is not a criterion for holding it. This is very different to the explicitly endorsed fear of criminals: in this case, the agent claims that she is afraid of criminals and she can present good reasons for that fear. In asserting her fear, she can claim that there are criminals out there, and that she has good reasons to fear them. If she were confronted with rational evidence that her fear is not justified, then she would be under normative pressure to feel less fear, or she would have to accept that her fear is phobic.

The phobia case is intuitive, because the gut feeling is not only clearly in contrast to what the agent would want to assert, it also is extremely insensitive to evidence. This seems very plausible. On a closer look, however, it turns out to be far less obvious than we might have thought. The spider phobia case is quite special, because it is one of the few cases where the agent is very sure that the gut feeling experienced is just about their psychology, but not about how the world really is. In most cases where gut feelings compete with judgments that we have formed on the basis of explicitly available reasons, this is not the situation we find ourselves in.

A famous literary example might help us to see this more clearly.[3] Huck Finn's conscious deliberation leads him to the judgment that he should betray the runaway slave Jim to his owners, but at the same time, Huck has a strong gut feeling that there is something wrong with this course of action. Huck does not have reasons for this feeling that he is able to express, but this does not mean that he perceives his gut feelings as something akin to a phobia. Instead, in the end he decides to act in accordance with his gut feelings, even though he is fully aware that in so doing he is violating what follows from the explicit reasons available to him, because he feels that what his reasons tell him to do is in some indescribable sense wrong.

Huck's balance of assertible reasons for or against turning Jim in leads him to the judgment that he ought to return Jim to his rightful owner, but this does not mean that he can assert that he is convinced that it is overall the best thing to do according to the conclusion he can reach by means of deliberation on his assertible reasons. The strong gut feeling that something is wrong with his reasons leads him to decide to act against the conclusion derived from those reasons, and instead, to act in line with his gut feeling. Hence, Huck's gut feeling is in an important sense an expression of a deeply

---

[3] Arpaly (2002) includes an in-depth discussion of the philosophical relevance of the Huck Finn case.

held conviction, even though it does not at all cohere with the assertible reasons available to him.

The worry generated by Huck can be generalized. In fact, Huck's gut feeling looks very much like a prime example of a hunch as described by Holton in Chapter 7. Very often, we do not have very good reasons for what we think is the right thing to do, and sometimes all the reasons even seem to point in the wrong direction, and yet, we still somehow know that it is wrong to do what we think we have good reasons to do.

This is not a rare phenomenon. There is a substantial literature that demonstrates that decisions made on the basis of gut feelings are often superior to ones where the agent tries to figure out by deliberation which decision she should make on the basis of the best reasons available to her (e.g. Dijksterhuis and Van Olden 2006). It is also the key message of the highly influential work by Noemi Arpaly (2002).[4] Thus, what we can establish from this discussion is that the distinction between gut feelings and explicit reasonings can clearly not be about the one expressing our understanding of the world, because often gut feelings express this understanding in the same way or even better than our explicitly held beliefs.

5. Logic Entailments

Even though it seems to be true that the clear distinction between assertible judgments and merely describable gut feelings is less clear than Levy seems to think, this fact on its own only does limited damage to Levy's claim. It still seems to be true that sincerely asserted beliefs create strong normative pressure to accept their entailments, and this still seems to be a unique feature of explicit beliefs and a powerful tool to generate unified agents. Gut feelings might well express something important about the agent, but they don't seem to lend themselves to deliberation, and they are not governed by the laws of logic.

While it is very intuitive that deliberation and logic are the tools that make explicit beliefs held in system two special, we have already seen that even that is not uncontroversial. It is not clear how independent of intuition

---

[4] This leads Richard Holton (2009a) to use Huck Finn as an example for a distinction between weakness of the will and akrasia that he favours. According to this distinction, Huck Finn is weak willed, because he does not follow through on his resolution to turn Jim in, but he is not akratic, because by the time he has to execute his resolution, he is no longer convinced that it is the best thing to do, even though he still does not have good assertible reasons why it is not.

reasoning is, or how powerful it is. In Chapter 4, Mercier and Sperber introduced us to the idea that reasoning is not an alternative to intuitive inference, but that reasoning is a special form of intuitive inference, i.e. intuitive inference about reasons. In addition, on their picture, the use of logic, while a feature of explicit reasoning, is not what makes for good arguments.[5] While we don't have to commit to their radical claim that reasoning is mainly for communication, the arguments discussed in this book do entail at least that Mercier and Sperber are right that all reasoning, insofar as it is understood as the intentional activity of providing reasons, is ultimately anchored in intuitive, intransparent, and non-voluntary judgments. All of this does not mean that logical entailments are not a special feature of explicit beliefs, but it does mean that they are highly dependent of intuitive judgments.

In addition, for the structure of explicit beliefs to matter for moral agency it would be important that they actually do guide behaviour. However, this does not seem obvious.

The literature on confabulation (e.g. Wegner 2002; Hirstein 2005 demonstrates that in very many cases, people are not aware of their real motives for acting and use explicit reasoning only post hoc to rationalize their behaviour. Perhaps the impression that explicit reasons are action-guiding stems only from such rationalizations. In that case, it would not be surprising that we accept belief and entailments sincerely, because we only rationalize what the explicit belief is that entailed the action after we performed the action for unconscious and often entirely unrelated motives.

Whether this really is how we should think of the role of conscious deliberation in action guidance is obviously disputed (it is worth noting here though, that this literature was the reason for Carruthers (2007) to doubt the existence of conscious action guidance). At this point, all that we can assert with confidence is that even though it is true that explicit content can be manipulated in a way that is not available for implicit content, and even though it is also true that manipulating expressed beliefs in this way does create normative pressure to accept the conclusion of the deliberation, this does not mean that (a) gut feelings do not express our understanding of

---

[5] Huck intuitively believes that he has very good reasons to believe one thing and using his limited powers of creating coherence within the value system he grew up in, he finds it hard to find flaws with these reasons. He recognizes them as good reasons, at least in the sense that he knows his peers would be willing to accept them. But he also knows that what these good reasons recommend is not something that he feels is intuitively right.

the world, nor does it mean (b) that conscious deliberation plays a crucial role in action guidance.

6. Control by Effortful Reasoning?

The last argument raised in favour of the specialness of system two reasoning is that deliberation is about performing effortful syntactical operations on our explicit beliefs asserted in language. This effortful control exercised in deliberation is the only truly agentive form of cognition. As Levy writes: 'Only the latter [effortful reasoning] is an exercise of agency: something we do, rather than something that happens to us' (Levy 2014: 33).

Obviously, this brings us right back to the simple argument and the core topic of this book: what exactly is it that Levy might mean here, if, as discussed many times throughout the book, he can't mean that we have direct intentional control over acquiring new beliefs by means of rule-based processes?

The only alternative seems to be that explicit beliefs are special because they can be intentionally manipulated: but if Levy opts for this interpretation, then it becomes difficult to see what the difference between propositions that merely describe beliefs and propositions that express beliefs is supposed to be, as both of them can be manipulated in exactly the same way. We would be back to what Levy called 'the first pass', and which he rejected as insufficient.

In reply to this worry, Levy writes

> that implicit attitudes are not unconscious attitudes (that is attitudes with contents of which we are unaware of) [but that they] work in the same way as unconscious contents, activating semantically related representations in the same associative manner, whenever we lack the resources to inhibit or trump these processes. Being aware of their contents does not prevent them from exerting their influence associatively. (Levy 2014: 16)

In other words, we can manipulate the contents of described implicit attitudes in the same way as the contents of explicit beliefs, but only the latter attitudes are affected in a logical rather than an associative way by these manipulations.

However, it is not clear why explicit attitudes are affected in a logical way when the agent takes the conclusion of the logical operation to be justified.

The logical manipulation on the content takes place before the evaluative step that leads to accepting the conclusion. It is unclear why this later step is different in the two cases. One reason why explicit beliefs might sometimes seem more affected by manipulations than implicit attitudes is that the distinction between explicit and implicit attitudes nearly always assumes that the two have different contents. So, when we test explicit beliefs, what we really tend to test are situations where explicit and implicit beliefs are aligned, whereas when we test implicit beliefs, we test situations where they come apart.

The strictures of the simple argument make the special link between effortful reasoning and the rational acquisition of explicit beliefs appear unjustified. This is not to say, however, that there might not be something that is special for the unification of the moral agent in the intentional manipulation of explicit content. In a way, the arguments that Levy puts forward in his effort to justify the close link between effortful intentional manipulation of syntax and the rational acquisition of new beliefs can be used to give a new interpretation to Levy's first pass argument. While it might not be possible to distinguish between implicit and explicit attitudes with this argument, it is possible to show that explicit content can be used for unifying purposes, whether it is the expression of an attitude or not. Again, the mechanisms here are the mindshaping mechanisms described in Chapter 5.[6]

7. Intentional Mental Actions and the Moral Agent

Levy argued that effortful reasoning is important for moral agency because it helps to unify the moral agent. At the end of our discussion of Levy's text, we can agree that this is indeed the case, and we can also agree that it is the case because it is a crucial element required to ensure that agents are unified diachronically. We can even agree on some of the key elements of effortful reasoning that help to establish this constant diachronic profile of moral agents. In line with Levy and much of the philosophical literature on this issue (Bratman 1987; Velleman 1992; Gerrans and Kennett 2010), we can

---

[6] In this book we focus on agency, so in Chapter 5 the mindshaping mechanisms discussed are intentional ones. However, there is no claim here that it might not also be possible, indeed highly likely, that conscious content has automatic mindshaping functions (see e.g. Zawidski 2008).

agree that being able to form and pursue plans is one important ability for moral agency, and that this capacity is massively enhanced by effortful reasoning.

The only worry that has crystallized over the previous sections is that Levy's account seems to suggest a stronger connection between effortful reasoning and logic or rationality than is justified. Levy says that only effortful reasoning is agency, but as we already learned in Chapter 1, we have to be very careful about what agency actually means. Either we understand agency in the way that Hieronymi suggests we should read Frankfurt in Chapter 1, but then it is not the effortful intentional actions that make us agents in reasoning, or we understand agency as intentional agency but then we have to accept that intentional control is only indirectly connected to logic and rationality, i.e. it becomes mere tinkering.

This book is not called *The Tinkering Mind* for nothing. As we have seen in Chapter 5 and also in Chapters 6 and 7, tinkering is enormously powerful. But it is powerful in the ways that material symbols are powerful as we discussed in Chapter 5. Chapter 6 demonstrated another theme that runs through the whole book: if we ensure diachronic stability by means of intentional actions, then there are very good arguments not to differentiate between manipulations outside of the head and manipulations that are intracranial. Both types of actions contribute to diachronic stability in the same way.

Does this mean that it is clear that the moral agent is a tinkerer? Well, the book does provide a number of arguments that make that idea more plausible, but we can put forward the same caveat that we already encountered many times during the book. There is an alternative view here, and that is to argue that the fact that the control that an intentional agent can have over her mind is always in the same ballpark as changing one's socks is an excellent argument to simply accept that intentional control is overrated for moral agency. Even Strawson accepts that this is a possibility, as demonstrated in Chapter 1, where he admits that Kantian spontaneity might well be good enough for moral responsibility. Obviously, both attributionists like Hieroymi (2009), Smith (2005), Arpaly (2002), and defenders of traditional hierarchical accounts agree that having intentional control over a part of one's mind is not a necessary condition for being responsible for part of it. They only disagree about whether the metacognitive stances are about reasons and arguments (Frankfurt) or about the first order conclusion (Smith 2005).

Obviously, there are also reasons to be sceptical about this move. Very prominent amongst them will be the point that this really does not look agentive; there is also the worry raised in Chapter 4, that the ways by which we arrive at the relevant judgments are intransparent. In that respect, our account does put pressure on traditional accounts which seek to resist the attributionist move to accept that attitudes like hunches or biases might be part of the moral agent, because it becomes less clear exactly what is meant by the main criticism of these positions, i.e. that they allow that we are responsible for attitudes over which we have no control. Once we have made clear that when people speak of the specialness of effortful control they cannot mean that we have intentional control over our explicit attitudes, but that they are at best different evaluative judgments (perhaps simply about reasons according to Mercier and Sperber (2017)), then the claim that attributionist positions are unconvincing because control over attitudes is essential for moral responsibility becomes more difficult to maintain.

8. The Special Power of Aware Managerial Control

We established that intentional effortful control cannot be what distinguishes rational from intuitive decision making. This makes it more difficult to maintain that distinction, though obviously not impossible. In this section, we will now add that once we understand that the Frankfurtian idea cannot be about intentional control, but instead understand it the way Hieronymi suggested, we risk underestimating the importance of intentional control for moral agency. And this is not only because of all the shepherding that supports the evaluative, but because we need intentional mind-directed actions to provide a corrective to deliberation gone wrong.

In Chapter 5, we looked at Victoria McGeer's work on self-regulation and how the material symbols of language can be used to regulate our minds voluntarily. There, we discussed the key capacity of managerial actions to take into account the perspective of future person stages and to regulate present deliberation in the light of this. As we saw with the case of Parfit's young communist, this is a very powerful tool to ensure long-term diachronic stability.

McGeer is not alone in thinking that this ability to understand the perspective of future person stages is key for a diachronic moral agent. We can understand the discussion of Holton's account of willpower in this way. There is also fascinating work by Gerrant and Kennett (2010), who argue using a large corpus of empirical literature on the topic that the ability for mental time travel is what makes us diachronic moral agents rather than intuitions (as e.g. Haidt (2001) and Prinz (2006) argue or mere rational thought).

In all these examples, the managerial is used as an extra tool of the well-functioning deliberative agent. What I would like to pick up on here is how McGeer also uses the mindshaping machinery for a critique of the Hieronymi idea that mental agency as deliberation in the sense of rational evaluation is unproblematic. It is not that McGeer is unsympathetic to the importance of the deliberative stance; in fact, she is heavily influenced by it in her own work, but she thinks that Moran is too much of a deliberative purist. In her paper 'The Moral Development of First-Person Authority' (2007), McGeer explains why this purism is problematic. She uses two case studies from Middlemarch to make her point: one of them exemplifies the problem of Moran's position exceptionally well. This is the evil banker type Nicholas Bullstrode. Bullstrode is a master of what we would now call confirmation bias. He is very adept at finding new arguments that confirm the very high opinion that he has of himself and he is perfectly blind to all his very obvious deep character flaws, even when he points them out in others who act in precisely the same way that he does. The interesting thing about Bullstrode for McGeer's purposes is that he clearly is not a perfect moral agent, but he is very much constantly involved in deliberation, speaks with full first-person authority, and expresses his extremely one-sided reasoning with great gusto. In other words, we could say that he is a perfect specimen for Mercier and Sperber's (2017) account of reasoning. He does not use reasoning to find the truth, but to give arguments to the world about how he would like to be seen.

The second Middlemarch character drawn on by McGeer is the reverend Camden Farebrother, who, as McGeer writes: 'is not a poster boy for rational autonomy in the Kantian sense. Farebrother is too ready, as Moran might say, to adopt an "empirical stance"[7] towards himself as a psychological subject with a variety of inclinations, impulses, weaknesses and unsatisfied yearnings over which he seems unable to exercise much non-manipulative agential authority' (McGeer 2007: 93).

But while Farebrother cannot make his psychology be the way he would like it to be by means of deliberation, he is not powerless against it. He uses intentional self-regulation to make a truly heroic choice. Farebrother

---

[7] Moran calls this stance sometimes empirical and sometimes theoretical. In Chapter 3 we used the term theoretical stance when we discussed Moran.

believes that the marriage between two young friends of his would be best for both of them, but he is also aware that the girl is about to give up on the young man because he does not lead a responsible lifestyle. At the same time, Farebrother is also quite fond of the girl and secretly dreams about marrying her himself. Realizing that this is becoming much more realistic because of the behaviour of the young man and being aware that he might not have himself fully under control, he resorts to a brutal but effective manipulative trick. He tells the male friend of his affections for the girl and thereby jolts the boy out of his irresponsible lifestyle and towards better behaviour, and he himself is shamed into not pursuing his ambitions. Farebrother does not trust himself to behave according to what he thinks is the best thing to do and is worried that in the right (or rather, wrong) circumstances, he might be quite impressed by the powerful reasons that would speak against the marriage of the two young people and in favour of himself pursuing his ambition instead.

The situation Elliott describes here is very much an instance of the kind of managerial control discussed in Chapter 6. However, while in Chapter 6 our focus was on whether environment involving and purely intracranial manipulations can count in the same way as agential forms of self-control, here our question is how important managerial forms of self-control are in comparison to evaluative ones. As we have heard, Moran is very sceptical on this point, and it seems that Levy also thinks that these forms of self-control are just not good enough because they are not linked directly to the practical rational stance of the agent. In contrast, Mc Geer argues that these manipulative mechanisms might well be essential elements of diachronic moral agency. Sometimes the simple automatic falling into place of belief acquisition can be counterproductive.

What George Elliott's characters nicely illustrate is that it was obviously an idealization in Holton's willpower account and our discussion of it to assume that there is a time where the first order deliberation of the agent is completely unproblematic so that she only has to devise strategies of how to manage herself under temptation. Instead, using managerial techniques is a constant stabilizing feature of our mental life.

9. Is There a Middle Way?

At this point one could start to become suspicious. If managerial control is so closely connected with our evaluative machinery, does the distinction between managerial and evaluative really still make sense? Obviously, we have already agreed that there is a way in which the sharp distinction can be undermined if we are willing to accept that the intentional loops are a constitutive part of acquiring new doxastic states, but going this way requires also accepting extended cognition and many might feel that this is too high a cost.

In her book *Alien Experience* (2020), Maura Tumulty suggests an approach that could get us a form of control that is managerial but still does not treat beliefs like socks. Like McGeer, Tumulty argues that management is a key ingredient of the moral agent because 'our efforts at self-control are *efforts* extended in time' (Tumulty 2020: 121). But interestingly, Tumulty thinks that there is an important special kind of management that sits between the evaluative and the mere managerial.

What Tumulty does is distinguish between 'merely managerial control' and 'distinctively first-personal managerial control'. She makes out three distinctive features of the latter. Tumulty develops her concept of distinctively first personal managerial control from a discussion of the argument in Chapter 6 of this book (also Vierkant 2014a) according to which there is no deep difference between incapacitation techniques (tying to the mast strategies) and semantic techniques (reason rehearsals). Tumulty argues that this argument might not be correct, because semantic techniques have three distinct features which do justify a qualitative divide.

The first feature that Tumulty identifies is that some managerial control is distinctively first-personal, because the management will only work if the agent, to use Tumulty's phraseology, constantly keeps her mental hand on the mental tiller (Tumulty 2020: 111). This is clearly a valid point, but it does not seem to be a challenge to the issue that has occupied us in this book. Tumulty is thinking about cases where the agent for example has to control recalcitrant first order evaluations like unwanted and undeserved negative thoughts about a loved one. In order to control such thoughts, it might not be enough to rehearse an inner sentence that reminds the agent of a scenario that includes the loved one and is positively valenced. Instead, it will often be necessary to imagine this scenario in detail, which will require a number of managerial acts, all of which need to be endorsed by the evaluative system for this strategy to work.[8]

---

[8] In fact, this is very much an instance of mental time travel as discussed earlier in the chapter, because such time travel is really about any relevant counterfactual situation, rather than just about a potential future.

I would very much agree that absent futuristic sci fi neuroscientists or all-powerful gods this is not something that can be done by a third person. But I would also even go further and argue that the description of these many loops between managing actions and evaluative reappraisal are very much a feature of most acts of doxastic deliberation, but this does not mean that the evaluative part and the intentional part cannot be separated. Moreover, as we have discussed at length, the only way to argue that this undermines the thought that managerial actions are only indirectly connected to doxastic state acquisition requires accepting extended cognition.

According to Tumulty, the other two features of first personal managerial control are: 'that they can more easily announced to others and they have the potential to be seriously agency expressive' (Tumulty 2020: 112). Tumulty uses a wonderful example to illustrate her point. It seems to make a difference whether an agent announces that they managed to avoid infidelity because they reminded themselves of the reasons for their love of their spouse or whether they achieved the same aim by reminding themselves of the unpleasant consequences of being found out. The reason for the intuitive difference between these two techniques is that only the first one demonstrates that in using the managerial device the agent is aiming to make sure that she consistently is in touch with the reasons for her actions. This allows others to understand that the agent is engaging in the management not because of instrumental reasons but because the action is designed to help her to develop the evaluative agency that she feels expresses her real self.

Is this a case of a true middle way between managerial and evaluative agency? The answer to this question depends on what we mean by a middle way. It is certainly true that this is a distinct form of managerial agency, and it provides us with one clear reason why managerial agency is so crucial for the moral agent, but it does not show that there is a middle way between managerial and evaluative control, unless we use our much discussed looping argument which implies extended cognition. To see why, we have to look a bit closer at what exactly happens in these two cases.

Tumulty does not distinguish between different ways in which semantic strategies achieve their effect. It could be the case that in imagining the face of the loved one, what achieves the self-control effect is simply that the act of imagining achieves the aim, without the reasons themselves playing a role in the success of the management. Interestingly, in terms of the benefits for announcability and self-expression, this absence of reasons does not seem to make a big difference. The social benefit of the strategy does not seem to depend on the functional role that the reasons might play in bringing about the self-control effect.

However, as others (including even the agent herself) are unable to know what actually achieved the effect, they might well assume that the reasons did play a role even if they did not. Either way, the agent will reap all the social benefits, in spite of the fact that the reasons may have been causally inert. Tumulty presumably would want to insist that these managerial strategies do have a distinctive functional profile, because the reasons help to orient the agent and inform a particular course of action. But as soon as we assume this functional difference, it seems that the social argument collapses in the first argument about loops between the right kind of managerial actions and evaluative processes.

We have come to the end of this chapter. We have learned that it is essential for moral agents to be unified in order to stabilize their evaluative agency across time. We have also seen the crucial role that intentional mental agency plays in this regard. Finally, we have seen that despite the fact that managerial action can be used to correct failures of the deliberative stance, and the fact that managerial actions can be sensitive to reasons—and that this might have beneficial effects—that this still does not mean that there is a middle way between evaluative and managerial agency that does not use the looping argument. With this insight, we can now move to the final chapter to wrap up what we have achieved in our investigation.

9
At the Very End

1. Summing Up

Over the course of this book we have investigated exactly what the function of intentional mental action is. As we established in Chapter 1, it is surprisingly unclear what role intentional action plays in constituting human rational agency. It transpired that classic work in moral psychology is in the background in several important frameworks in the cognitive sciences. The investigation made clear that at the heart of the moral psychology literature, there is an unresolved debate about the nature of moral agents. We looked at Hieronymi's claim that the agency that constitutes the moral agent is not intentional action. In her apt phrase that gives this book its title, acquiring a belief through judgment does not require any intentional tinkering with the mind.

In order to better understand the consequences of this insight, we then focused in Chapters 2 and 3 on clarifying the relationship between intentional mental actions and the acquisition of doxastic states, and showed that the latter is either passive or a non-intentional form of agency. The book drew on two systems accounts, and in particular system two, to make this point, because two systems accounts invite misunderstandings: it is very easy to fall in the reflective control trap of thinking that system two processes can be both intentional and doxastic attitude acquisition processes at the same time. The book demonstrated that this can never be the case. Chapter 3 examined a number of interesting challenges to this sweeping claim, particularly with regard to unruly beliefs, acceptances, and doxastic deliberation and concluded that all of them are unsuccessful.

In Chapter 4, we began to work out exactly what the extension of intentional mental actions is, once it became clear that they are not actions that are directly responsible for the acquisition of new doxastic states. I argued that once we have made clear that intentional mental actions are never evaluative by themselves, it then becomes clear that there is no deep difference between intentional mental actions inside the head and intentional mental actions that are environment involving.

Following this, in Chapter 5 we investigated the relationship between metacognition and intentional mental actions. The agency problem is about understanding second order cognitive dynamics, with the agent taking a second order stance on their first order thought. However, it is surprisingly unclear exactly what that means. The different types of relationship between the cognitive and intentional actions that influence cognition do not get a lot of attention in the literature. Chapter 5 aims to rectify this problem and establish a new depth of clarity in the debate.

We saw that once we accept that intentional environment-involving actions can also be mental actions, it becomes urgently necessary to distinguish different forms of these actions. Because the skull boundary is less important than is usually assumed, we saw that what really matters are the different levels of metacognition and metarepresentation that guide intentional actions. Given permissive definitions, such as the one applied by Kirsh and Maglio, a vast amount of intentional actions can be understood as epistemic actions. According to them, epistemic actions are 'physical actions that make mental computation easier, faster, or more reliable' (Kirsh and Maglio 1994: 514f). Even if one does not want to be that permissive, there is still a very important difference between mental actions that have the explicit goal of managing or shepherding attitude formation and the much larger group of actions that is about the intentional manipulation of material symbols, without the explicit goal to do anything to attitudes. The former are very powerful in certain, especially moral contexts, but they are quite rare, whereas the latter are far more common and include, for example, all voluntary linguistic behaviour.

Once it became clear how important this second group of intentional actions is for human cognition, it became clear that it is absolutely possible to argue that it is this capacity of intentional self-regulation that is what is crucial about human mental agency. In fact, philosophers like Pettit and McGeer are explicitly pushing exactly the line that this is what distinguishes humans from other animals. A similar position, if slightly less explicit, can be constructed from the work by Bermudez and Clark on second order cognitive dynamics. In all these cases, it really does seem to be the ability to intentionally control the mind that makes the difference between human and other minds.

The interesting lesson for the book overall from Chapter 5 was that while tinkering might not be a part of direct belief acquisition, the regulation of the mind that the various metacognitive forms of tinkering allow might well be what gives us distinctive human rationality. Thus, in a strange way by the end of Chapter 5, we had found a way to justify the idea that intentional mindshaping actions might be what is special about human rationality. Hieronymi is right to point out that intentional actions are mere tinkerings, but then, as pointed out in this book, perhaps our minds are 'tinkering minds'.

With all these jigsaw pieces in place, we then returned to the focus of the very beginning of this investigation, i.e. the agency problem in moral psychology. In this context, we looked at Holton's accounts of willpower and choice. Both are two systems accounts of essential features of human agency, which is particularly fascinating because Holton's accounts are all about explaining the role of intentional mental action, while taking the agency problem into account. Holton's solutions in both cases are ingenious, but both invite important worries. Applying the lessons from the first half of the book allowed us to amend Holton's account in ways that can take care of these worries. Chapter 6 showed that willpower can be plausibly understood as a set of intentional self-control actions, but that this implies, in line with the argument in Chapter 4 that there are no deep differences between willpower and environment-involving, so-called 'tying to the mast' strategies.

Chapter 7 then showed us that choice also can be understood as a type of intentional self-regulation, but importantly, it also unearthed a further dimension of metacognition that was necessary in order to fully understand the phenomenon of choice. Holton understands choice as intentional actions that feel arbitrary to the agent, but which are modulated by what he refers to as 'hunches'. Holton did not give us a lot of information about exactly how we should approach his notion of hunches, but as their purpose is to allow the agent to deal with situations of uncertainty, we plugged in Joelle Proust's account of epistemic feelings as an explanation of how to think of them. This did the job nicely for a satisfying account of choice, but it also allowed us to obtain new clarity on two very different ways in which metacognition operates on intentional actions: on the one hand, metacognition provides hunches that trigger intentional actions (some of which will be explicitly attitude directed but others will not be); while on the other, it allows the regulation of the mind by making thoughts visible.

After this long journey, we then returned to the question with which this analysis began in Chapter 8, namely: what form of agency constitutes us as moral agents? We looked at the proposal by Neil Levy, one of the most empirically informed practical philosophers, who has presented a fascinating proposal on the role of conscious thought for moral agents in the literature. Levy has argued that explicit reasoning in system two is an essential feature of moral agents because it gives them a diachronic stability and practical identity that would be impossible to achieve for a system that only possessed system one type processing.

But as we saw, Levy's proposal does not make clear exactly what the role of intentional control is. Levy initially rejected what he described as a first pass argument against King and Carruthers, which was that conscious beliefs can be manipulated intentionally because we have them in linguistic form. Levy worried that this argument did not sufficiently differentiate between merely described states and ones that were expressed in linguistic form. But as we saw, his own argument did not make it absolutely clear whether he thinks that diachronicity-enabling features of explicit beliefs are about Frankfurtian meta-evaluations of one's mentality, or whether they are about the ability to intentionally inhibit and manipulate the mind. Wherever Levy himself would land on this question, the discussion of McGeer made the notion that diachronicity-enabling features might well to a significant degree be a feature of mindshaping mechanisms seem very plausible. Returning to Chapter 6, this might well also suggest that environment-involving intentional actions help to constitute the moral agent.

Obviously, it is absolutely acceptable to balk at this consequence and to opt instead for the evaluative one, but there is an interesting consequence here. In the literature on moral responsibility, so-called attributionists (e.g. Arpaly and Smith) have rejected the idea that an agent needs to be able to control having an attitude in order for it to be part of her practical stance. Levy, on the other hand, argues that control of the explicit mind is a crucial ingredient for the unification of the moral agent, especially across time. However, once we have clarified that this control cannot be intentional control—at least only if we don't want to buy the consequences—it becomes much more difficult to justify the claim that there is a deep difference between attributionists and classical hierarchical positions, because both positions have to accept that agents do not control their attitudes intentionally, and that the moral judgments that agents make are intuitive in Mercier and Sperber's sense. The argument of this book obviously does not set out to choose between the different positions in these debates, but to make the respective options, and their benefits and costs, clearer.

2. How the Tinkering Mind Became the Tinkering Mind

We have come to the end of this investigation. What have we learned at the end of this journey through the literature that deals with intentional mental actions?

Perhaps first a brief comment on the genesis of this book. While I had already done a lot of work on all the topics covered in this book over the last years, once I decided to write this monograph, the chapters were roughly written in the order that they are presented to the reader. I am happy to admit that writing the book had a quite profound impact on my own thinking, which some readers might well have detected.

When I started out on Chapter 1, making clear that the distinction between evaluative and intentional forms of mental agency did play a role in cognitive science contexts was my primary aim. I wanted it to be crystal clear that changing your beliefs is not like changing your socks. This is what led us at the end of Chapter 1 to the idea that intentional mental actions are tinkerings: they may be involved in changing beliefs, but their involvement is different from the kind of agency that many philosophers and scientists in the tradition have seen at the heart of rational moral agency. This other agency is evaluative agency, and it is non-voluntary. Some, like Galen Strawson, would even go so far as to deny that it is agency at all.

However, as we saw in the discussion of Holton's work in Chapters 6 and 7, it is so counterintuitive to think of this form of rational evaluation as agentive that this has led to the so-called agency problem of compatibilism. To use Wallace's (1999) apt phrase, the agency here appears 'hydraulic' and does not explain agentive phenomenology (Ginet 1990). There have obviously been many attempts to solve this problem, but not one of these solutions directly involves intentional action: this is no surprise, because intentional action requires an intentional agent with intentions, but if the intentions of that agent are formed intentionally, then we are on the way to a vicious regress and the homunculus.

The simple argument of this book showed that there cannot be any judgments[1] in system two, given that processing in system two is always intentionally controlled, and given that doxastic involuntarism is true. In other words, the simple argument asks us to clarify what we mean when we say that system two is concerned with effortful reasoning, or with inhibition, or with behaviour that is not ballistic and automatic to use Mandelbaum's (2015) very helpful phrase. All these terms seem to point to intentional (voluntary) control and most of the time, what dual systems are interested in is describable in one of these phrases, but if this is what system two is all about, then that is not the same as what Frankfurt and other philosophers, but also cognitive scientists like Stanovich, see at the heart of the rational agent.

---

[1] If judgments are direct belief acquisition processes.

I claimed at the beginning of this book that thinking about our problem can lead to better cognitive science. Now, at the end of the book, we can also ask ourselves whether we have achieved this aim. I think we can be satisfied on this score. I have perhaps not directly said anything that would illuminate classical experiments in the heuristics and biases literature in a new and different light, but the consequences of the choice forced on us by the simple argument are quite stark.

The simple argument asks us to decide how we should understand system two cognition, if we don't want to embrace the very radical move that there is no cognition in system two. One option is to deny that intentional in premise one really means the same as in premise two of the simple argument. Mark Sprevak[2] for example suggested to me that he could only understand the difference between system one and system two as the difference between propositional and associative processing, but he was happy to admit that this means throwing out all the talk about voluntariness and effort as a distinctive feature of system two.

This would represent a very big change from the standard understanding of how system two operates, but it would also make it very difficult to understand standard uses of the notions of cognitive control and executive function. To add one last recent example to all the literature discussed in Chapter 2 to emphasize how dramatic this step would be, let us look at what neuroscientist and philosopher Chandra Sripada has said in a recent paper on the link between self-control and cognitive control. Sripada (2021) writes:

> Our minds, however, are in addition equipped with a set of executive mechanisms linked to working memory. In situations where response pulses are inappropriate and conflict with one's overall goals, we can engage in cognitive control. In particular, based on EVC representations, as well as potentially other sources of information, we can make executive decisions to perform control actions, including inhibitional, attentional, and memory/thought actions. These control actions can prevent an initially activated response pulse from producing its associated response, and instead allow an alternative response to prevail.   (Sripada 2021: 9)

Sripada makes it very clear that he thinks of these actions as intentional and that they allow us to 'volitionally regulate' (6) the mind. He is also very

---

[2] Here used as an example for a number of people who have made similar suggestions.

confident that he is not alone in thinking that this is how executive mechanisms function. He continues:

> The preceding overall picture is what I take to be a fairly standard view among theorists working on cognitive control (for reviews, see Botvinick & Cohen, 2014; Cohen, 2017; Miller & Cohen, 2001). The picture enjoys convergent support from a very broad set of methods including: behavioral studies, computational models of accuracy and reaction times, computational simulation methods, neuroimaging including task-based fMRI and resting state fMRI, animal studies, lesion studies, methods involving manipulations (for example, working memory load, pharmacological challenge, sleep deprivation), and individual-difference methods.
> (Sripada 2021: 9)

Obviously, the consensus might be wrong, but if the result of this book were that talk of cognitive control needed to be purged of the language of voluntary control, then that would clearly not be a trivial result for a very large portion of the work done in the cognitive sciences. My suspicion is, therefore, that this will not be the most popular reaction to the simple argument, but rather, I suspect that many more people will prefer to choose option two.

Opting for this alternative is to shrug off the result of the simple argument. The reasoning for doing so also seems eminently plausible. Perhaps it is simply obvious that cognitive control is not about getting the right result: let us go one more time to Chandra Sripada, who in the same paper writes in a footnote:

> There is a need to clarify one feature of the atomic model that arises due to ambiguity in talking about cognitive control. If I exercise cognitive control to get the correct answer on a trial of the Stroop task, getting the correct answer is not the exercise of cognitive control. Rather it is what is enabled because I exercised cognitive control against the response pulse to read words. (footnote 20, 22)

This seems so obviously sensible that one might think it is surprising that it needs stating at all! It is also in line with Mandelbaum's idea that controlled actions are non-automatic and non-ballistic. But while the move might seem obvious (apart from people with Sprevak's disposition), it is not without consequence. As we have seen in Chapter 4, once we accept that intentional actions and evaluative agency cannot be separated inside the head, there is no non-arbitrary border between intentional cognitive control actions that happen inside the head and intentional cognitive control actions that involve the environment. In other words, not accepting the distinction seems to require accepting extended cognition.

Obviously, this might not be a bad thing. This book was written in Edinburgh, which can make a strong claim as being the home of extended cognition. In fact, once I had fully grasped the implications of the simple argument, while writing Chapter 4, I became a lot more sympathetic to this option, and the book truly became the tinkering mind. This became especially true by the time I had written Chapter 5 and worked through the many ways in which human cognition is shaped by intentional action, especially because of the links between language and intentional action. The move seems also very plausible when it is applied to moral psychology, as demonstrated in Chapters 6 to 8.

However, while I am sympathetic to this move, it is radical. This is not only because of the well-known fact that the idea of extended cognition is still considered a radical position in the philosophy of mind, but even more so because of the stark illustration of the general principle of extended cognition for deliberation.

The strictures of the simple argument mean that the only way to think of all the acceptances, rehearsals, and attention shifts as truly cognitive is to accept extended cognition. And once we accept that we could accept that, as Shepherd claimed in Chapter 3, deliberation is a skill. It would become in many ways quite literally like a physical skill such as mountain biking. On this model, deliberation is the fast looping between intentional managerial actions, which often are world involving, and some evaluative monitoring.

Obviously, one might think that the costs of going the other way are equally high, because on the alternative model, we now have to accept that all the many managerial parts of the deliberative process are just shepherdings and not strictly speaking part of the cognitive component of deliberation.

This book does not advocate one of these two options over the other. There will be research contexts where it is important to distinguish between the intentional and the evaluative contribution, and there will be others where it seems important to emphasize that the difference between intentional mental actions inside the head and environment-involving actions is far less important than one might have thought.

AT THE VERY END 179

Obviously, there is much more to do, but for now, my work in clearly separating rational and intentional control of attitudes is done. I will leave it to the reader to decide whether or not they think that it is a constitutive feature of the cognitive or moral agent that they can change their attitudes like socks.

Bibliography

Adams, F., and Aizawa, K. (2008). *The Bounds of Cognition*. Malden, MA and Oxford: Blackwell.
Adams, F., and Aizawa, K. (2009). Why the Mind Is Still in the Head. In P. Robbins and M. Aydede (eds.), *The Cambridge Handbook of Situated Cognition* (78–95). New York: Cambridge University Press.
Alston, W. (2005). *Beyond Justification: Dimensions of Epistemic Evaluation*. Ithaca, NY: Cornell University Press.
Apperly, I.A., and Butterfill, S.A. (2009). Do humans have two systems to track beliefs and belief-like states? *Psychological Review*, 116(4): 953–70.
Arpaly, N. (2002). *Unprincipled Virtue: An Inquiry into Moral Agency*. New York: Oxford University Press.
Barbey, A.K., and Sloman, S.A. (2007). Base-rate respect: From ecological validity to dual processes. *Behavioral and Brain Sciences*, 30: 241–97.
Bargh, J.A. (2005). Bypassing the will: Toward demystifying the nonconscious control of social behavior. In R.R. Hassin, J.S. Uleman and J.A. Bargh (eds.), *The New Unconscious* (37-60). Oxford University Press: New York.
Baumeister, R. Bratslavsky, E., Muraven, M. and Tice, D. (1998). Ego depletion: Is the active self a limited resource? *Journal of Personality and Social Psychology*, 74(5): 1252–65.
Baumeister, R. (2008). Free Will, Consciousness and Cultural Animals. In J. Baer (ed.), *Are We Free* (65–85). New York: Oxford University Press.
Baumeister, R.F., Tice, D.M., and Vohs, K.D. (2018). The strength model of self-regulation: Conclusions from the second decade of willpower research. *Perspectives on Psychological Science*, 13(2): 141–5.
Bayne, T. (2004). Phenomenology and the Feeling of Doing: Wegner on the Conscious Will. In S. Pockett, W.P. Banks, and S. Gallagher (eds.), *Does Consciousness Cause Behaviour? An Investigation into the Nature of Volition*. Cambridge, MA: MIT Press.
Bayne, T. (2013). Agency as a Marker of Consciousness. In A. Clark, J. Kiverstein, and T. Vierkant (eds.), *Decomposing the Will*. New York: Oxford University Press.
Bayne, T., and Pacherie, E. (2005). In defence of the doxastic conception of delusions. *Mind and Language* 20(2): 163–88.
Bermúdez, J.L. (2003). *Thinking Without Words*. Oxford: Oxford University Press.
Botvinick, M.M., and Cohen, J.D. (2014). The Computational and Neural Basis of Cognitive Control: Charted Territory and New Frontiers. *Cognitive Science*, 38: 1249–85.
Boyle, M. (2011). Making up Your Mind and the Activity of Reason. *Philosophers' Imprint*, 11(17): 1–24.

Bratman, M. (1987). *Intention, Plans, and Practical Reason* (Vol. 10). Cambridge, MA: Harvard University Press.

Bratman, M. (2003). A desire of one's own. *The Journal of Philosophy*, 100(5): 221–42.

Carruthers, P. (2007). The illusion of conscious will. *Synthese*, 159: 197–213.

Carruthers, P. (2008). Metacognition in animals: A skeptical look. *Mind and Language*, 23, 1: 58–89.

Carruthers, P. (2009). An architecture for dual reasoning. In J. Evans and K. Frankish (eds.), *In Two Minds: Dual Processes and Beyond* (109–27). Oxford: Oxford University Press.

Carruthers, P. (2011). *The Opacity of Mind*. New York: Oxford University Press.

Carruthers, P. (2015). *The Centered Mind: What the Science of Working Memory Shows Us About the Nature of Human Thought*. Oxford: Oxford University Press.

Chaiken, S., and Trope, Y. (eds.) (1999). *Dual-Process Theories in Social Psychology*. New York: Guilford Press.

Chalmers, D.J. (1996). *The Conscious Mind: In Search of a Fundamental Theory*. New York: Oxford University Press.

Chrisman, M. (2008). Ought to believe. *Journal of Philosophy*, 105(7): 346–70.

Chrisman, M. (2018). Epistemic normativity and cognitive agency. *Noûs*, 52(3): 508–29.

Christensen, W., Sutton, J., and McIlwain, D.J. (2016). Cognition in skilled action: Meshed control and the varieties of skill experience. *Mind and Language*, 31(1): 37–66.

Churchland, P.M. (1981). Eliminative materialism and the propositional attitudes. *Journal of Philosophy*, 78(2): 67–90.

Clark, A. (1998). Magic Words: How Language Augments Human Computation. In P. Carruthers and J. Boucher (eds.), *Language and Thought: Interdisciplinary Themes* (162–83). Cambridge: Cambridge University Press.

Clark, A. (2006). Material symbols. *Philosophical Psychology*, 19 (3): 1–17.

Clark, A. (2007). Curing cognitive hiccups: A defense of the extended mind. *Journal of Philosophy*, 106: 163–92.

Clark, A. (2009). Spreading the joy? Why the machinery of consciousness is (probably) still in the head. *Mind*, 118: 963–93.

Clark, A. (2014). *Mindware: An Introduction to the Philosophy of Cognitive Science*. Oxford and New York: Oxford University Press.

Clark, A., and Chalmers, D. (1998). The extended mind. *Analysis*, 58: 7–19.

Clark, A., Kiverstein, J., and Vierkant, T. (eds.) (2013). *Decomposing the Will*. Oxford and New York: Oxford University Press.

Coelho do Nascimento, R. (in preparation). Dual process theories of higher cognition. Disambiguating the debate.

Cohen, L.J. (1989). Belief and acceptance. *Mind*, 98(391): 367–89.

Cohen, J.D. (2017). Cognitive Control. In *The Wiley Handbook of Cognitive Control* (pp. 1–28). Chichester: Wiley-Blackwell.

Corballis, M.C. (2003). From hand to mouth: The gestural origins of language. In Morten Christiansen and Simon Kirby (eds.) *Language Evolution* Oxford: Oxford University Press.

Currie, G. (2000). Imagination, delusion and hallucinations. *Mind and Language*, 15(1): 168–83.
Dang J. (2018). An updated meta-analysis of the ego depletion effect. *Psychological Research*, 82(4): 645–51.
Davidson, D. (2001). *Essays on Actions and Events: Philosophical Essays Volume 1: Philosophical Essays* (Vol. 1). Oxford University Press on Demand.
De Neys, W., & Pennycook, G. (2019). Logic, fast and slow: Advances in dual-process theorizing. *Current Directions in Psychological Science*, 28(5): 503-509.
Dennett, D. (1987). True believers. In D. Dennett, *The Intentional Stance*. Cambridge, MA: MIT Press.
Dienes, Z., and Perner, J. (1999). A theory of implicit and explicit knowledge. *Behavioral and Brain Sciences*, 22: 735–808.
Dijksterhuis, A., and Van Olden, Z. (2006). On the benefits of thinking unconsciously: Unconscious thought can increase post-choice satisfaction. *Journal of Experimental Social Psychology*, 42(5): 627–31.
Do, A.H., Wang, P.T., King, C.E., Chun, S.N., and Nenadic, Z. (2013). Brain-computer interface controlled robotic gait orthosis. *Journal of Neuroengineering and Rehabilitation*, 10: 111.
Duckworth, A.L., Gendler, T.S., and Gross, J.J. (2016). Situational strategies for self-control. *Perspectives on Psychological Science*, 11(1): 35–55.
Epstein, S. (1994). Integration of the cognitive and the psychodynamic unconscious. *American Psychologist*, 49: 709–724.
Epstein, S., and Pacini, R. (1999). Some basic issues regarding dual-process theories from the perspective of cognitive-experiential theory. In S. Chaiken and Y. Trope (eds.), *Dual-Process Theories in Social Psychology*. New York: Guilford.
Evans, G. (1982). *The Varieties of Reference*. Oxford: Oxford University Press.
Evans, J. (1989). *Bias in Human Reasoning: Causes and Consequences*. Brighton: Erlbaum.
Evans, J. (2003). In two minds: Dual-process accounts of reasoning. *TRENDS in Cognitive Sciences*, 7(10): 454–59.
Evans, J.S.B. (2007). On the resolution of conflict in dual process theories of reasoning. *Thinking & Reasoning*, 13(4): 321–39.
Evans, J. (2008). Dual-processing accounts of reasoning, judgment, and social cognition. *Annual Review of Psychology*, 59: 255–78.
Evans, J.S.B. (2010). *Thinking Twice: Two Minds in One Brain*. Oxford: Oxford University Press.
Evans, J.S.B.T. (2013). Two minds rationality. *Thinking and Reasoning*, 20: 129–46.
Evans, J., and Stanovich, K. (2013). Dual-process theories of higher cognition: Advancing the debate. *Perspectives on Psychological Science*, 8(3): 223–41.
Evans, J. St. B.T., and Over, D.E. (1996). *Rationality and Reasoning*. Hove: Psychology Press.
Evans, T.A., and Beran, M.J. (2007). Chimpanzees use self-distraction to cope with impulsivity. *Biology Letters*, 3: 599–602.
Fairweather, A., and Montemayor, C. (2017). *Knowledge, Dexterity, and Attention: A Theory of Epistemic Agency*. Cambridge: Cambridge University Press.

Fernández-Castro, V., and Martínez-Manrique, F. (2020). Shaping your own mind: The self-mindshaping view on metacognition. *Phenomenology and the Cognitive Sciences*, 20(1): 139–67.

Ford, A. (2018). The Province of Human Agency. *Noûs*, 52(3): 697–720.

Frankfurt, H. (1971). Freedom of the will and the concept of a person. *Journal of Philosophy* 67(1): 5–20.

Frankish, K. (2007). Deciding to Believe Again. *Mind*, 116(463): 523–47.

Frankish, K. (2004). *Mind and Supermind*. Cambridge: Cambridge University Press.

Frankish, K. (2009). Systems and levels: Dual-system theories and the personal subpersonal distinction. *J. St. BT Evans and K. Frankish*, 89–107.

Frankish, K. (2012). Dual Systems and Dual Attitudes. *Mind and Society* 11(1): 41–51.

Frankish, K., and Evans, J. (eds.) (2009). *In Two Minds: Dual Processes and Beyond*. Oxford: Oxford University Press.

Fridland, E. (2014). They've lost control: Reflections on skill. *Synthese*, 191: 2729–50.

Fujita, K. (2011). On conceptualizing self-control as more than the effortful inhibition of impulses. *Personality and Social Psychology Review*, 15(4): 352–66.

Galan, F., Nuttin, M., Lew, E., Ferrez, P.W., Vanacker, G., Philips, J., et al. (2008). A brain-actuated wheelchair: Asynchronous and non-invasive brain-computer interfaces for continuous control of robots. *Clinical Neurophysiology*, 119(9): 2159–69.

Gerrans, P., and Kennett, J. (2010). Neurosentimentalism and moral agency. *Mind*, 119(475): 585–614.

Gertler, B. (2007). Overextending the Mind. In B.E. Gertler and L.E. Shapiro, *Arguing about the Mind*. New York: Routledge/Taylor and Francis Group.

Gigerenzer, G. (1996). On narrow norms and vague heuristics: A reply to Kahneman and Tversky. *Psychological Review*, 103: 592–6.

Gilbert, D., Krull, D., and Malone, M. (1990). Unbelieving the unbelievable: Some problems in the rejection of false information. *Journal of Personality and Social Psychology* 59(4): 601–13.

Gillebaart, M., Schneider, I.K., and De Ridder, D.T. (2016). Effects of trait self control on response conflict about healthy and unhealthy food. *Journal of Personality*, 84: 789–98.

Ginet, C. (1990). *On Action*. Cambridge: Cambridge University Press.

Gopnik, A. (1993). Theories and illusions. *Behavioral and Brain Sciences*, 16(01): 90–100.

Graimann, B., Allison, B., and Pfurtscheller, G. (2009). Brain–computer interfaces: A gentle introduction. In B. Graimann, G. Pfurtscheller, and B. Allison (eds.), *Brain-computer Interfaces*. Berlin and Heidelberg: Springer.

Greene, J.D. (2007). Why are VMPFC patients more utilitarian? A dual-process theory of moral judgment explains. *Trends in Cognitive Sciences*, 11(8): 322–3.

Grice, P. (1957). Meaning. In P. Grice (1989), *Studies In The Way Of Words* (213–23). London: Harvard University Press.

Haidt, J. (2001). The emotional dog and its rational tail: A social intuitionist approach to moral judgment. *Psychological Review*, 108(4): 814–34.

Heath, J., and Anderson, J. (2010). Procrastination and the extended will. In C. Andreou and M. White (eds.), *The Thief of Time: Philosophical Essays on Procrastination* (233–52). New York: Oxford University Press.

Hieronymi, P. (2006). Controlling attitudes. *Pacific Philosophical Quarterly*, 87(1): 45–74.

Hieronymi, P. (2009). Two kinds of mental agency. In L. O'Brien and M. Soteriou (eds.), *Mental Actions*. Oxford: Oxford University Press.

Hirstein, W. (2005). *Brain fiction: Self-deception and the riddle of confabulation*. Cambridge, MA: MIT Press.

Hofmann, W., and Kotabe, H. (2012). A general model of preventive and interventive self-control. *Social and Personality Psychology Compass*, 6(10): 707–22.

Hommel, B., Müsseler, J., Aschersleben, G., and Prinz, W. (2001). The theory of event coding (TEC): A framework for perception and action planning. *Behavioral and Brain Sciences*, 24(5): 849–78.

Holton, R. (2009a). *Willing, Wanting, Waiting*. Oxford and New York: Oxford University Press.

Holton, R. (2009b). Determinism, self-efficacy, and the phenomenology of free will. *Inquiry*, 52(4): 412–28.

Hutto, D.D. (2012). *Folk Psychological Narratives: The Sociocultural Basis of Understanding Reasons*. Cambridge, MA: MIT Press.

Jenkins, D. (2018). The role of judgment in doxastic agency. *Thought: A Journal of Philosophy*, 7(1): 12–19.

Kahneman, D. (2011). *Thinking, Fast and Slow*. New York: Penguin.

Kahneman, D., and Frederick, S. (2002). Representativeness revisited: Attribute substitution in intuitive judgement. In Gilovich, T., Griffin, D., and Kahneman, D. (eds.), *Heuristics and Biases: The Psychology of Intuitive Judgment* (49–81). Cambridge, MA: Cambridge University Press.

Keren, G., and Schul, Y. (2009). Two is not always better than one. A critical evaluation of two-system theories. *Perspectives on Psychological Science*, 4(6): 533–50.

King, M., and Carruthers, P. (2012). Moral responsibility and consciousness. *Journal of Moral Philosophy*, 9(2): 200–28.

Kirsh, D., and Maglio, P. (1994). On distinguishing epistemic from pragmatic action. *Cognitive Science*, 18(4): 513–49.

Kornblith, Hilary. (2017). In defense of a naturalized epistemology. *The Blackwell Guide to Epistemology*, 158–69. DOI: 10.1002/9781405164863

Krisst, L., Montemayor, C., & Morsella, E. (2015). Deconstructing Voluntary Action. In Haggard, Patrick, and Baruch Eitam, (eds). *The Sense of Agency*. Oxford: Oxford University Press.

Kruglanski, A.W., and Orehek, E. (2007). Partitioning the domain of social inference: Dual mode and system models and their alternatives. *Annual Review of Psychology*, 58: 291–316.

Kurzban, R., Duckworth, A., Kable, J. and Myers, J. (2013). An opportunity cost model of subjective effort and task performance. *Behavioral and Brain Sciences*, 36: 661–79.

Lavelle, J.S. (2018). *The Social Mind: A Philosophical Introduction*. Abingdon: Routledge.
Lavelle, J.S. (in press). When a crisis becomes an opportunity: The role of replications in making better theories. *British Journal for the Philosophy of Science*. https://doi.org/10.1086/714812
Le Pelley, M.E., Pearson, D., Griffiths, O. and Beesley, T. (2015). When goals conflict with values: Counterproductive attentional and oculomotor capture by reward-related stimuli. *Journal of Experimental Psychology: General*, 144, 158–71.
Levy, N. (2011). Resisting weakness of the will. *Philosophy and Phenomenological Research* 82(1): 134–55
Levy, N. (2014). Consciousness, implicit attitudes and moral responsibility. *Noûs*, 48(1): 21–40.
Levy, N. (2015). Neither fish nor fowl: Implicit attitudes as patchy endorsements. *Noûs*, 49(4): 800–23.
Levy, Y. (2019). What is 'mental action'? *Philosophical Psychology*, 32(6): 969-991.
Libet, B. (1985). Unconscious cerebral initiative and the role of conscious will in voluntary action. *The Behavioral and Brain Sciences*, 8: 529–66.
Lockie, R. (2018). *Free Will and Epistemology: A Defence of the Transcendental Argument for Freedom*. Bloomsbury Publishing.
Mandelbaum, E. (2014). Thinking is believing. *Inquiry*, 57(1): 55–96.
Mandelbaum, E. (2015). The automatic and the ballistic: Modularity beyond perceptual processes. *Philosophical Psychology* 28(8): 1147–56.
Mann, T., De Ridder, D., and Fujita, K. (2013). Self-regulation of health behavior: Social psychological approaches to goal setting and goal striving. *Health Psychology*, 32: 487–98.
Maoz, U., Yaffe, G., Koch, C., and Mudrik, L. (2019). Neural precursors of decisions that matter—an ERP study of deliberate and arbitrary choice. *eLife*, 8.
Masicampo, E.J., and Baumeister, R.F. (2008). Lemonade, willpower, and expensive rule-based analysis. *Psychological Science*, 19(3): 255–60.
McClelland, T. (2017). The mental affordance hypothesis. *Mind*, 129(514): 401–27.
McCormick, M.S. (2014). *Believing Against the Evidence: Agency and the Ethics of Belief*. New York: Routledge.
McGeer, V. (2007). The moral development of first-person authority. *European Journal of Philosophy* 16(1): 81–108.
McHugh, C. (2011). Judging as a non-voluntary action. *Philosophical Studies*, 152: 245–69.
Mechsner, F., Kerzel, D., Knoblich, G., and Prinz, W. (2001). Perceptual basis of bimanual coordination. *Nature*, 414(6859): 69–73.
Mele, A. (2007). Free Will: Action Theory meets Neuroscience. In C. Lumer (ed.), *Intentionality, Deliberation, and Autonomy: The Action-theoretic Basis of Practical Philosophy* (257–72). Abingdon: Routledge.
Mele, A. (2009). Mental actions a case study. In O'Brien, L. and Soteriou, M. (eds.) *Mental Actions* (17–37). Oxford: Oxford University Press.
Melnikoff, D.E., and Bargh, J.A. (2018). The mythical number two. *Trends in Cognitive Sciences*, 22(4): 280–93.

Mercier, H., & Sperber, D. (2017). *The Enigma of Reason*. Harvard: Harvard University Press.
Metzinger, T. (2017). The Problem of Mental Action—Predictive Control without Sensory Sheets. In T. Metzinger and W. Wiese (eds.), *Philosophy and Predictive Processing*: ch. 19. Frankfurt am Main: Mind Group.
Miller, E.K., and Cohen, J.D. (2001). An integrative theory of prefrontal cortex function. *Annual Review of Neuroscience*, 24: 167–202.
Mischel, W. (1996). From Good Intentions to Willpower. In Gollwitzer, P. and Bargh, J. (eds.), *The Psychology of Action* (197–218). New York: Guildford Press.
Miyake, A., Friedman, N.P., Emerson, M.J., Witzki, A.H., Howerter, A., and Wager, T.D. (2000). The unity and diversity of executive functions and their contributions to complex "frontal lobe" tasks: A latent variable analysis. *Cognitive Psychology*, 41(1): 49–100.
Moran, R. (2001). *Authority and Estrangement: An Essay on Self-knowledge*. Princeton, NJ: Princeton University Press.
Nahmias, E., Coates, D.J., and Kvaran, T. (2007). Free will, moral responsibility, and mechanism: Experiments on Folk Intuitions. *Midwest Stud. Philos.* 31: 214–42.
Newen, A., De Bruin, L., and Gallagher, S. (eds.). (2018). *The Oxford Handbook of 4E Cognition*. Oxford: Oxford University Press.
Nichols, S., and Knobe, J. (2007). Moral responsibility and determinism: The cognitive science of folk intuitions. *Nous*, 41: 663–85.
Nielsen, K.S., Gwozdz, W., and De Ridder, D. (2019). Unravelling the relationship between trait self-control and subjective well-being: The mediating role of four self-control strategies. *Frontiers in Psychology*, 10: 706.
O'Shaughnessy, B. (1980). *The Will*. Cambridge: Cambridge University Press.
Paglieri, F. (2012). Ulysses' will: Self control, external constraints, and games. In F. Paglieri (ed.), *Consciousness in Interaction: The Role of the Natural and Social Context in Shaping Consciousness* (179–206). Amsterdam: John Benjamins.
Parfit, D. (1984). *Reasons and persons*. Oxford: Oxford University Press.
Peacocke, C. (1998). Conscious attitudes, attention, and self-knowledge. In Wright, C., Smith, B. and MacDonald, C. (eds.), *Knowing Our Own Minds: Essays on Self-knowledge* (63–98). Oxford: Oxford University Press.
Peacocke, C. (2009). Mental action and self-awareness (II): Epistemology. In L. O'Brien and M. Soteriou (eds.), *Mental Actions*. Oxford: Oxford University Press.
Perdikis, S., Leeb, R., Williamson, J., Ramsay, A., Tavella, M., Desideri, L., et al. (2014). Clinical evaluation of BrainTree, a motor imagery hybrid BCI speller. *Journal of Neural Engineering*, 11(3): 036003.
Pettit, P., and McGeer, V. (2002). The self-regulating mind. *Language and Communication*, 22: 281–99.
Plantinga, A. (1993). *Warrant: The Current Debate*. New York: Oxford University Press.
Prinz, J. (2006). The emotional basis of moral judgments. *Philosophical Explorations*, 9: 29–44.
Prinz, J.J. (2004). *Gut Reactions: A Perceptual Theory of Emotion*. New York: Oxford University Press.

Prinz, W. (2008). Philosophie nervt. Eine Polemik. In *Zur Zukunft der Philosophie des Geistes* (237–48). Paderborn: Mentis.
Proust, J. (2013). *The Philosophy of Metacognition*. Oxford: Oxford University Press.
Reber, A.S. (1993). *Implicit Learning and Tacit Knowledge*. Oxford: Oxford University Press.
Rupert, R.D. (2004). Challenges to the hypothesis of extended cognition. *The Journal of Philosophy*, 101: 389–428.
Rydell, R.J., Van Loo, K.J., and Boucher, K.L. (2014). Stereotype threat and executive functions: Which functions mediate different threat-related outcomes? *Personality and Social Psychology Bulletin*, 40(3): 377–90.
Schwitzgebel, E. (2011). Knowing your own beliefs. *Canadian Journal of Philosophy*, 35 supplement, 41–62.
Scotus, J.D. (2003). *The Cambridge Companion to Duns Scotus*. Cambridge: Cambridge University Press.
Shah, N., and Velleman, D. (2005). Doxastic deliberation. *The Philosophical Review*, 114(4): 497–534.
Shepherd, J. (2015). Deciding as intentional action: control over decisions. *Australasian Journal of Philosophy*, 93(2): 335–51.
Shepherd, J. (2018). Intending, believing, and supposing at will. *Ratio*, 31(3): 321–30.
Sloman, S.A. (1996). The empirical case for two systems of reasoning. *Psychological Bulletin*, 119: 3–22.
Smith, B.C. (2019). *The Promise of Artificial Intelligence: Reckoning and Judgment*. Cambridge, MA: MIT Press.
Smith, E.R., and DeCoster, J. (2000). Dual-process models in social and cognitive psychology: Conceptual integration and links to underlying memory systems. *Personality and Social Psychology Review*, 4: 108–31.
Smith, M. (1994). *The Moral Problem*. Oxford: Blackwell
Smith, A. (2005). Responsibility for attitudes: Activity and passivity in mental life. *Ethics* 115: 236–71.
Smith, J., Shields, W. and Washburn, D. (2003). The comparative psychology of uncertainty monitoring and metacognition. *Behavioral and brain sciences* 26(03): 317–39.
Soteriou, M. (2009). Introduction. In O'Brien, L., and Soteriou, M. (eds.), *Mental Actions*. Oxford: Oxford University Press.
Sprevak, M. (2009). Extended cognition and functionalism. *The Journal of Philosophy*, 106(9): 503–27.
Sripada, C. (2017). Frankfurt's unwilling and willing addicts. *Mind*, 126(503): 781–815.
Sripada, C. (2021). The atoms of self-control. *Noûs*, 55(4): 800–24.
Stanovich, K.E. (1999). *Who Is Rational? Studies of Individual Differences in Reasoning*. Mahwah, NJ: Erlbaum.
Stanovich, K.E. (2005). *The Robot's Rebellion: Finding Meaning in the Age of Darwin*. Chicago, IL: University of Chicago Press.
Stanovich, K.E. (2011). *Rationality and the Reflective Mind*. New York: Oxford University Press.

Stanovich, K.E., and West, R.F. (2000). Individual differences in reasoning: Implications for the rationality debate. *Behavioral and Brain Sciences*, 23: 645–726.

Steinert, S., Bublitz, C., Jox, R., and Friedrich, O. (2018). Doing things with thoughts: Brain-computer interfaces and disembodied agency. *Philosophy and Technology*, 32(3): 457–82.

Stich, S. (1978). Beliefs and subdoxastic states. *Philosophy of Science* 45: 499–518.

Strawson, G. (2003). Mental ballistics or the involuntariness of spontaneity. *Meeting of the Aristotelian Society*, London.

Sun, R., Slusarz, P., and Terry, C. (2005). The interaction of the explicit and the implicit in skill learning: A dual-process approach. *Psychological Review*, 112: 159–92.

Toribio, J. (2011). What do we do when we judge. *Dialectica*, 65(3): 345–67.

Tumulty, M. (2020). *Alien Experience*. New York: Oxford University Press.

Ullmann-Margalit, E., and Morgenbesser, S. (1977). Picking and choosing. *Social Research*, 44(4): 757–85.

Velleman, D. (1992). What happens when someone acts? *Mind*, 101(403): 461–81.

Vierkant, T. (2011). Self-knowledge and knowing other minds: The implicit/explicit distinction as a tool in understanding theory of mind. *British Journal of Developmental Psychology*, 30(1): 141–55.

Vierkant, T. (2012). What Metarepresentation Is For. In M. Beran, J. Brandl, J. Perner, and J. Proust (eds.), *The Foundations of Metacognition*. Oxford: Oxford University Press.

Vierkant, T. (2013). Managerial Control and Free Mental Agency. In Vierkant, T., Clark, A., and Kiverstein, J. (eds.). *Decomposing the Will*. New York: Oxford University Press.

Vierkant, T. (2014a). Is Willpower Just Another Way of Tying Oneself to the Mast? *Review of Philosophy and Psychology*, 6(4): 779–90.

Vierkant, T. (2014b). Mental muscles and the extended will. *Topoi*, 33(1): 57–65.

Vierkant, T (2015). How do you know that you settled a question? *Philosophical Explorations*, 18(2): 199–211.

Vierkant, T. (2018). Choice in a two systems world: Picking and weighing or managing and metacognition. *Phenomenology and the Cognitive Sciences*, 17(1): 1–13.

Vierkant, T., Deutschländer, R., Sinnott-Armstrong, W., and Haynes, J.D. (2019). Responsibility without freedom? Folk judgements about deliberate actions. *Frontiers in Psychology*, 10.

Vierkant, T., and Hardt, R. (2015). explicit reasons, implicit stereotypes and the effortful control of the mind. *Ethical Theory and Moral Practice*, 18(2): 251–65 15 p.

Vierkant, T., and Paraskevaides, A. (2012). Mindshaping and the intentional control of the mind. *Consciousness in interaction: The role of the natural and social context in shaping consciousness*, 86: 107.

Vohs, K., Schmeichel, B., Lohmann, S., Gronau, Q.F., Finley, A.J., Wagenmakers, E.J., et al. (2021). A multi-site preregistered paradigmatic test of the ego depletion effect. *Psychological Science*, 32(10): 1566–81.

Wallace, R.J. (1999). Three conceptions of rational agency. *Ethical Theory and Moral Practice*, 2(3): 217–42.

Wason, P.C., and Evans, J. (1975). Dual processes in reasoning? *Cognition*, 3: 141–54.
Watson, G. (1975). Free agency. *The Journal of Philosophy*, 72(8): 205–20.
Wegner, D (2002). *The Illusion of Conscious Will*. MIT Press: Cambridge MA.
Weiskrantz, L. (1999). *Consciousness Lost and Found: A Neuropsychological Exploration*. Oxford: Oxford University Press.
Williams, B. (1973). Deciding to Believe. In *Problems Of The Self: Philosophical Papers 1956–1972*. Cambridge: Cambridge University Press.
Wu, W. (2013). Mental Action and the Threat of Automaticity. In A. Clark, J. Kiverstein, and T. Vierkant (eds.), *Decomposing the Will* (244–61). New York: Oxford University Press.
Zawidzki, T. (2008). The function of folk psychology: Mind reading or mind shaping? *Philosophical Explorations*, 11(3): 193–210.

Index

For the benefit of digital users, indexed terms that span two pages (e.g., 52-53) may, on occasion, appear on only one of those pages.

4E approaches 112-13

Acceptance 14, 60-3, 147
Action
   Arbitrary 137
   Bodily 68
   Cognitive 85-6, 92, 95
   Doxastic 42
   Effects (distal) 93
   Epistemic 83, 108-9
   Intentional 3-4, 6, 9-11, 16, 24-5, 38-42,
      45-6, 50, 52, 61, 67-71, 74-5, 84-7,
      92, 95, 107-8, 113, 117, 120-5, 127,
      130-2, 134-5, 137, 140, 143, 149,
      151-4, 171, 175, 178
   Guiding 161-2
   Managerial 40, 61, 84, 107, 110, 112-13,
      143, 146-8, 151, 170
   Mental 4, 8, 14, 27-9, 43, 67-8, 78, 81, 83,
      90-1, 139, 148, 151, 171, 173
   Mind directed 11
   Philosophy of 136
   Physical 81-2, 84, 108-9
   Shepherding 70, 140-1, 148
   Tying to the mast 120, 125
   Voluntary 25, 37, 67, 95-6, 107-9
Adams & Aizawa 11-12, 79, 81-2, 87
Agency
   Epistemic 9-11, 29-30, 110
   Doxastic 13-14, 18-19, 27-8, 43, 55-6,
      95-6
   Intentional 16, 23, 25, 55-6, 67, 101-2,
      117, 164
   Moral 16-17, 115, 154-5, 161, 163-7, 175
   Problem 16, 115-16, 136-8, 140, 172-3, 175
Akrasia 121
Alston, J. 32
Apperly and Butterfill 45
Arbitrary *see* (Arbitrary) Picking

Artificial intelligence 27-8
Assertibility 156-8
Attentional deployment 135
Attitude
   directed managerial action 42-3, 58, 88,
      112-13, 146-8, 173
   explicit 154-7, 162-5
   higher order 7
   implicit 155-7, 162-3
   propositional 7, 24, 101, 109-10,
      113-14, 154
APA Dictionary of Psychology *see*
   Psychology
Aquinas, Thomas 1
Arpaly 1, 159-60, 164, 174
Attributionists 164, 174
Automatic process (*see* process)
Autonomy 7, 19-24

Ballistic *see* Ballistic process
Barbey & Sloman 45
Baumeister 32, 45-6, 51, 115, 122-3,
   132-3
Baumeister, Bratslavsky, Muraven and
   Tice 46
Baumeister, Tice and Vohs 123-4
Bayne, Tim 18-19, 57-8, 107-8
Bayne and Pacherie 57-8
Belief
   Conscious 17, 54-5, 140, 174
   Dispositional 34-5, 61-2, 79-80
   Explicit 154-6, 160-3, 174
   False 100-1
   Formation 7-8, 54-5, 63-5, 72-4
   Updating 8
Bermudez, Jose 10, 100-5, 172
Blindsight 141-2
Bomb 59-60
Botvinick and Cohen 177

Bowling 81
Boyle 6, 34–5, 43–4
Braille 80–1, 84
Brain computer interfaces 91–2
Bratman, M. 137–9, 154, 163–4
Brentano 34
Bullstrode 166

Calculating on paper 5–6, 80–1, 83–5, 90–1
Cantwell Smith 27–8
Carruthers, Peter 44, 48, 50, 54–5, 74, 100, 149, 155–8, 161–2, 174
Cartesian accounts of belief acquisition 66
Chaiken and Trope 45
Chalmers, Dave 5, 10–11, 79–80, 83
Chrisman, Matthew 9, 13–14, 32, 35–8, 43–4, 86–7
Christensen, Sutton and Mc Ilwain 72
Churchland, Paul 103
Clark, Andy 5, 10–11, 79–83, 86–90, 100–6, 109, 112–13, 147, 172
Clark, A. 5, 10–11, 79–83, 86–90, 100–6, 109, 112–13, 147, 172
Coelho do Nascimento, R. 46–7, 53
Cognitive
 Bloat 79–80
 Impartiality 89
 Science 1, 11, 13–14, 17–18, 28–9, 76–7, 87–90, 100, 115, 175
Cohen, J. 60–1, 63, 177
Compatibilism 16, 116, 136, 146, 175
 Hierarchical 22
Conscious *see* conscious beliefs
Consciousness 25–6, 48–50, 140–2, 154–7
Constitutive 11–12, 30, 37–8, 76–9, 81–2, 86–8, 123–4, 167–8, 179
 Causal constitutive error 81
 Causal constitutive error error 82
Control
 aware managerial 165–7
 effortful 50–1, 115, 128, 165–7
 evaluative 7–12, 35, 37–8, 43–4, 55–6, 71, 75–6, 101, 151–2, 155, 162, 164–5, 169, 174, 179
 intentional 25–6, 28, 50–2, 61, 68, 72–6, 100–1, 107, 110, 116–17, 133, 145
 managerial 7, 9–10, 35, 37–8, 70, 76, 100–2, 106–7, 110, 112–14, 143–8, 153, 167–9
  distinctively first personal 168–9
 manipulative 38–9, 42, 72

rational 75
reflective 23–30, 44, 171
Self (*see* self control)
voluntary 35–6, 39–40, 51, 55, 61, 67, 95, 109, 175, 177
Corporealism 93–4

Dang 45–6
Darwinian 20–1
Davidson, D. 107
Deliberation 3–7, 11–14, 42–3, 58, 65–6
 Doxastic 39–41, 169, 171
 Effortful 133–4
 Rational 65–6, 132–3
 Reflective 1–2, 94
Delusions 38, 57–8
Demon 64–5
Descartes 32, 91
Determinism 116, 140
Diachronicity 154–7, 174
Dienes and Perner 45
Dijksterhuis and Van Olden 160
Distal (*see* distal action effects)
Distraction strategies 130–1
Doxastic
 Agency (*see* agency)
 Deliberation (*see* deliberation)
 environment 37–8
 involuntarism 30, 32, 35–9, 54–5, 62–3, 65, 67, 72, 75–7, 95–6, 175
 states 3–5, 29–30, 75, 93–4, 97, 101, 167–8, 171
 voluntarism 53, 95–6
Dual process (system) theories 13, 30, 44–50, 59–75, 97–9
Duckworth, Angela 16
Dun Scotus 1

Edinburgh 41–2, 82, 178
Effort 45–6, 51–2, 61–2, 75, 92, 106, 127–30, 138, 144, 146, 168, 176
Effortful 32, 51–2, 67, 122, 126, 132–3, 156
 Effortful control *see* control
 Effortful deliberation *see* deliberation
 Effortful reasoning *see* reasoning
Ego depletion 46, 51
Eliminativism 18, 20
Elliott 167
Environment 3, 5, 11–12, 16, 45, 76, 79–89, 100–2, 108–9, 117, 120, 126, 128–9

Environment involving 29–30, 112–14, 123–4, 133, 135, 147, 167, 171–4, 177–8
Epistemic feeling 16–17, 150–3, 173
Epstein and Pacini 31, 45
Evans, G. 57
Evans, J. 31–2, 44–53, 55, 57, 97, 130
Evidentialist 64–5
Evolution *see* language evolution 20
Executive function 11, 19, 29, 53, 55, 74–5
Extended
   Cognition 3, 5–6, 9–15, 29–30, 34, 44, 55–6, 78–82, 85–6, 89–90, 94, 167–9, 177–8
   Mental action 86–94
   Mind 5, 77–82, 87–9, 102, 113

Fairweather and Montemayor 13–14, 110
Farebrother 166–7
Feeling of knowing 142, 150
Fernandez-Castro and Martinez-Manrique 113, 149
Fireman 142
Folk psychology (psychological) *see* Psychology
Ford, John 91, 93–4
Frankfurt, Harry 1–2, 6–7, 9, 11, 13, 22–5, 98–9, 101, 114, 116–17, 164–5, 174–5
Frankish, Keith 41, 44, 50, 54–5, 61–5, 67, 95, 109,
Free Will 7, 12, 115–16, 136, 138, 152–3
Fridland, E. 72
Fujita, K. 134–5

Galan, Nuttin, Lew, Ferrez, Vanacker, Philips 91–2
Gerrans and Kennett 154, 163–4
Gertler, B 80, 89–90, 94–5
Gigerenzer, G. 46
Gilbert, Krull and Malone 66
Gillebaart, Schneider and De Ridder 134–5
Ginet, C. 175
Graimann, Allison and Pfurtscheller 91–2
Gray experiments 89
Grice, P. 100–1, 104–5
Gut feeling 145, 155–6, 159–62

Haidt, J. 165–6
Heath and Anderson 119–20

Hieronymi, Pamela 6–16, 24–5, 27–30, 32, 34–5, 37–8, 43, 58, 78, 85, 94–5, 101, 113–14, 116–17, 122, 143–4, 146–7, 151–2, 164–6, 171–3
Hirstein, W. 161
Hofmann and Kotabe 134–5
Holton, Richard 1, 16–17, 51, 68–9, 115–17, 120–53, 160, 165–7, 173, 175
Homunculus 19–22, 24, 28–9, 48–9, 136, 175
Huck Finn 159–61
Humean accounts 119
Hunch 16–17, 138–40, 142–4, 150–1, 153, 160, 173
Hydraulic 116–17

Implicit bias 155–6
Incompatibilists 115–16
Inferentially promiscuous 8, 38, 57
Inhibition 16, 33–4, 70, 74, 134–5, 175
Inner Speech 5–6, 39–40, 53, 61, 63, 68, 92, 144, 147, 153
Intention 27, 40, 42, 48–9, 68–9, 82–3, 85, 148
   Attitude-directed 112–13, 146
   Communicative
   Conscious
   Epistemic 42
   Formation 7, 27, 37–8, 54, 59, 61–2, 68–9, 71, 82–3, 85, 116, 120–1, 143, 148
   Managerial 61
   Unconscious 48
   Voluntary acquisition of 68–9
   World- directed 146
Intentionality 109–11
   Original 11–12

Judgment 24, 34–5, 40–1, 49, 69–71, 121, 129, 140, 144, 147, 159–60, 171
   All things considered 143–4
   Conscious 142
   Formation 5–6, 24, 69, 143–4, 153
   Practical 16–17, 143–4
   Intuitive 97
   Involuntary 147
   Metacognitive 60–1, 68, 145
   reflective
   shift 120–1
   suspending 60
   Unconscious 141–2, 153

Kahnemann, Daniel 32, 44–5, 51–2,
Kantian 27–8, 137, 164, 166
Keren and Schul 46
King and Carruthers 156–8, 174
Kirsh and Maglio 10–11, 83, 101–2, 108–9, 148, 172
Kruglanski and Orehek 45
Kurzban, Duckworth, Kable, and Myers 45–6, 102

Language evolution 108
Lavelle, S. 100–2
Levy, N. 1, 8, 19, 74, 124–5, 154–60, 162–4, 167, 173–4
Levy, Y. 5, 15, 17, 77–85
Libet, B. 138
Lockie, R. 13–14, 29–30, 52–3
Loops 5, 11–12, 79, 81–2, 84, 86–7, 167–70, 178

Mandelbaum, E. 66–7, 73, 95, 175, 177–8
Mandatory (*see* mandatory process)
Mann, De Ridder and Fujita 134–5
Masicampo and Baumeister 32, 51
Maoz, Yaffe, Koch, and Mudrik 138
Materialism 93–4
Material Symbols 10, 105–6, 109–13, 148
Mc Cleland, T. 84, 113
Mc Cormick, M. 35–6, 59, 62
Mc Geer, V. 14, 106, 109, 112–13, 147, 153, 165–6, 168, 172, 174
Mc Hugh, C. 43–4, 94–5
Mechsner, F. 93–4
Mele, A. 1, 18–19, 27, 37–8, 85, 94–5
Melnikoff and Bargh 46–7
Memes 20–1
Memory
    Biological 79, 87–8
    Experiment 66
    Working 34, 46–7, 52–5, 74, 88, 176–7
Mental time travel 165–6, 168
Mercier and Sperber 74, 96–9, 102–3, 105, 109–10, 151, 160–1, 165–6, 174
Metzinger, T. 83–4, 100–2, 109, 113
Metacognition 97–8, 140–1, 148–51, 153, 172–3
    Evaluativist (or procedural) 96–7, 150–1, 153
Metaphor mistake 18–20, 22–3

Metarepresentation 15, 102–14, 150–1, 172
Metzinger, T. 83–4, 109, 113
Mindreading 47, 54, 100–3, 105
Mindshaping 102–6, 109–10, 112–13, 147–8, 153, 157–8, 163, 166, 172–4
Miller and Cohen 177
Mischel, W 123–4, 130
Moore paradoxical 111
Moran, R. 6, 14, 43–4, 58, 64–6, 75–6, 94–5, 111, 113–14, 166–7
Moral psychology 1, 13–14, 18–19, 30, 87, 115, 136, 171, 173, 178
Motivated reasoning 14, 63–5

Nahmias, Coates and Kvaran 116
Nichols and Knobe 116
Nielsen, Gwozdz, de Ridder 16, 135
Noetic feelings *see* epistemic feelings
No Rewards Principle 35–7, 41–3, 59, 61–3, 68–72

Odysseus 119–20, 123–32
O'Shaughnessy, B 27, 43–4
Otto's notebook 79–80, 89–90

Paglieri, F. 119–20, 127
Parity principle 5–6, 79–80
    Inverse parity principle 82–6
    Negative parity principle 82–6
Parfit, D. 111–12
Pascal's wager 36–43, 59, 75, 113–14
Peacocke, C. 27, 34–5, 43–4
Perdikis, Leeb, Williamson, Ramsay, Tavella, Desideri 92
Personal level 52–3, 95–6
Pettit and Mc Geer 106, 109, 112–13, 172
Phenomenology 70
    Agentive (of struggle) 115–16, 122, 126, 128, 130–4
Philosophy 1–2, 11–14, 17–20, 22–3, 25, 29, 65, 76, 91, 115
    Experimental 152–3
    Of action 136
    Of cognitive science 115
    Of metacognition 109
    Of mind 3, 178
    Stanford encyclopedia of 57
Phobia 155–61
Picking 137–43, 145–6, 149–50, 152–3
Plantinga, A. 32

Predictive Coding 18, 83
Priming (conscious) 25–6
Prinz, J. 95, 165–6
Prinz, W. 17–20
Process
  Automatic 8, 73–4
  ballistic 73–4, 95
  doxastic attitude acquisition 33–4, 41–2, 52, 72–4, 171
  effortful 51–2, 73
  mandatory 73–4, 95
  Of learning 45
  rejection 67
  transparent 95–7
  transparaent (Moran sense) 111–12
Proust, J. 85, 96–7, 109, 148–53, 173
Psychology 16, 22–3, 58, 65–6, 80, 117, 131–2, 135, 140, 155–6, 159, 166–7
  APA dictionary of 3
  Developmental 122–3
  Folk 18–19, 23, 46–7, 103
  Moral 1, 13–14, 18–19, 30, 86–7, 115, 136, 171, 173, 178
  Social 122–3

Random 16–17, 138, 140–2, 152
Rationality 1–2, 13–14, 20–3, 28, 43, 75–7, 87, 125, 164, 172–3
  Human 20–3, 100–1, 112–14
  Practical 120–2, 132–3
  thick 22–3
Reappraisal 135, 169
Reasoning
  Effortful 154–5, 162–4
  Motivated 63–5
  Reflective 95
  Social 96–9
Reber, A.S 45
Rehearsal 33–4, 121–5, 129–32
Rejection *see* rejection process
Resolutions 116, 119–21
Rupert, R. 79, 87–8, 129, 132
Rydell, Van Loo and Boucher 53

Sartre, J. 136–8
Scaffolds 112–13
Schwitzgebel, E. 57
Self 105, 109–12
  Attribution of mental states 157–8
  Deception 64–5, 112

Directed mindshaping 110
Evaluation 22, 24, 109
Expression 169–70
control 11, 16, 20, 45–6, 51–2, 111–12, 117, 119–20, 122–3, 128, 134–5, 154, 167, 169–71, 173
Real 169
regulation 110, 112–13, 153, 158, 165–7, 172–3
Shah and Velleman 13–14, 39–40, 42–3
Sheba 104–5, 109
Shepherding 15, 29, 68–9, 71, 85, 94–5, 100, 106–12, 120, 140–1, 148, 165, 172
Shepherd, J. 13–14, 27, 32, 68–71, 144–5, 178
Sherlock Holmes 98
Simple Argument 14–15, 30–5, 44, 46, 49–51, 54–60, 62–7, 72–7, 94, 96–7, 115, 133–4, 151, 162–3, 175–8
Situation Selection 135
Skill 67–72, 81, 83–5, 178
Sloman, A. 45
Smith, A. 13–14, 164, 174
Smith, J. 149–50
Smith, M. 138
Sophie's choice 136–8
Soteriou, M. 4, 27, 43–4
Spinozean accounts of belief acquisition 66–7
Spontaneity 4, 25, 27–8, 73
Sprevak, M. 34, 79, 87, 176–8
Sripada, C 25, 130–1, 176–7
Stance
  deliberative (evaluative) 111–12, 166, 170
  theoretical (empirical) 111–13, 166
Stanovich, K. 13, 19–24, 44–55, 97, 100, 175
Stanovich and West 45
Steinert, Bublitz, Jox and Friedrich 91–2
Strawson, G. 4, 8–9, 25–30, 44, 73, 76, 85, 92, 94–5, 117, 137, 164, 175
Sun, Sluarz and Terry 45
System one 16–17, 31, 34, 44–51, 54, 62, 65–7, 74, 132–4, 155, 173–4, 176
System two 11–14, 19, 29, 31–4, 44–56, 61–3, 65–7, 72–5, 97, 100, 115, 132–4, 139–41, 152, 155–6, 160–2, 171, 173–6

Taylor, C. 22
Temptation 16, 120–30
Tetris 10–11, 83
Theory theory 102

Thinking about thinking 15, 98, 100–2, 105, 110, 114, 146–8
Tinkering 8, 10–16, 24, 28–30, 42–3, 58, 77, 97, 114, 164, 171–9
Toribio, J. 6, 43–4, 94–5
Tryings 90–1, 94, 126
Tumulty, M. 86–7, 168–70
Tying to the mast strategies 16, 117, 119–20, 125–34, 168, 173

Ullmann-Margalit and Morgenbesser 137
Uncertainty 96–7, 143–4, 147–52, 173

Velleman, D. *see also* Sha and Velleman 116–17, 136, 154, 163–4
Vohs, Schmeichel, Lohmann, Gronau, Finley, Wagenmakers 31–2

Volitions (second order) 22–3
Volitionism 91–4
Voluntary *see* voluntary action

Wallace, R.J. 116
Wanton 22
Wason and Evans 45
Watson, G. 23
Weakness of will 121
Wegner, D. 48–50, 161
Weiskrantz, L. 141
Williams, B. 32, 39–40
Willpower 11–12, 16, 115, 117, 119, 144, 147, 165–7, 173
Wu, W. 13–14, 67–9, 85, 94–5

Zawidski, T. 163